JANE M. HOGG was born in Madura, South India during the days of the British Raj. After India's independence she moved to England and Bedford High School. Jane graduated from the London School of Economics and Political Science before joining the Civil Service. While at LSE she represented London University as a sprinter. In October 1968 Jane was a speaker at the *Symposium on the Needs of the Fire Services* at the National Academy of Sciences, Washington, D C. Her research reports are listed in the Bibliography. Latterly Jane served as a Councillor for Adeyfield East in the Borough of Dacorum, Hertfordshire. With James Bell Hogg, she has a daughter, Sally-Ann, and a granddaughter, Yasmin. She now lives in Birmingham, United Kingdom.

BEWARE
THE
MANDARINS

JANE M. HOGG

This is a true story!

Immediately after taking early retirement I created a dossier of events over the period 1960 to 1982 – and found myself extremely grateful for the considerable amount of help and support I had received from numerous individuals. Under the Thirty Year Rule British Government records up to 1982 are now available for public scrutiny. Corruption in Britain still appears to be rampant with inadequate checks and balances in place to combat it. The Coalition Government has introduced tough spending controls to transform ways government departments spend money in order to tackle fraud, error and debt. However, a fundamental change in the structure of government is required.

It is recommended that the Department of Science and Industrial Research be resurrected, reporting to its own Secretary of State. This will keep the scientists and administrators separate so that the scientists will not be dominated by the administrators; and the scientists will be able to serve each administrative department as, and when, the need arises. The scientists should have control of their own budgets and be able to employ management consultants to augment their own expertise. In addition the creation of an openly independent body is required to deal fairly and expeditiously with the concerns of 'whistleblowers'.

This true account highlights weaknesses in the present organisational structure of British government. These need to be addressed if Britain is to be an honest open democratic state.

"All that needs to happen for evil to prevail is that good men do nothing."
Martin Luther King

Civil Service Ranks

Administrative

PUSS	Permanent Under Secretary of State	Head of Ministry
DUSS	Deputy Under Secretary of State	
AUSS	Assistant Under Secretary of State	Department Head
AS	Assistant Secretary	Division Head
Principal	Overseeing Executive and Clerical grades	

Scientific

CSO	Chief Scientific Officer	Chief Scientist
DCSO	Deputy Chief Scientific Officer	Director
SPSO	Senior Principal Scientific Officer	Deputy Director
PSO	Principal Scientific Officer	Section Head
SSO	Senior Scientific Officer	
HSO	Higher Scientific Officer	
SO	Scientific Officer	

Experimental

CEO	Chief Experimental Officer
SEO	Senior Experimental Officer
EO	Experimental Officer
AEO	Assistant Experimental Officer
Machine Operator	

Experimental Officers work in parallel with Scientific Officers and are overseen by them.

Organizations

DSIR	Department of Scientific and Industrial Research later Ministry of Technology
SAB	Scientific Adviser's Branch later Scientific Advisory Branch
PSDB	Police Scientific Development Branch
HORU	Home Office Research Unit
PRSU	Police Research Services Unit
LUCS	London University Computing Services
JADPU	Joint Automatic Data Processing Unit
HMSO	Her Majesty's Stationery Office
EIU	Economic Intelligence Unit
DOE	Department of the Environment
CUEP	Central Unit of Environmental Pollution
EEC	European Economic Community
DHSS	Department of Health and Social Security
ORS	Operational Research Section
ACPO	Association of Chief Police Officers
LGORU	Local Government Operational Research Unit
RMCS	Royal Military College of Science
LCD	Lord Chancellor's Department
IND	Immigration and Nationality Department
SRDB	Scientific Research and Development Branch
PRU	Planning and Research Unit
HMCI	Her Majesty's Chief Inspector

CHARACTERS

DSIR - FIRE RESEARCH STATION

CSO	Tristram Vane-Tempest
DCSO	Dennis Lawson
SPSO	Grey Silversides, Dr Bruce Rawlings
PSO	Jimmy Fry
SSO	Richard Lustig, Jane Hogg
SO	Jennifer Gaunt
AEO	Hyman Marks, Michael Firth

Machine Operator: Iris Day, Tom

Coder   Elaine

Home Office: Assistant Secretary David Lessing

Manchester Fire Brigade: CFO Noel Halford, DCFO McIntosh

Bristol Fire Brigade: CFO Bill Holland, ACFO Ponsonby

HOME OFFICE: SCIENTIFIC ADVISER'S BRANCH - FIRE

PUSS	Sir Philip Allen
AS	David Lessing
Principal	Gordon Renton
CSO	C J Stephens
DCSO	Eddie Benn
PSO	Alan Weston, John Miles
SSO	Jane Hogg
SO	Don Busby

JADPU: Mr Ramsbotham, Mrs Deignton

Glasgow Fire Brigade: Firemaster

Rand Corporation team

SCIENTIFIC ADVISORY BRANCH - FIRE

AUSS   Ralph Shuffrey
DCSO   John Culshaw, John Clayton
SPSO   Sid Butler
PSO   Jane Hogg, Dr Ronald Rutstein
SSO   Don Busby
SO   Diana Morrow, Bob Barnes, Mike Mytton
Administrative Officer: Brian Davenport
Huntingdon and Peterborough Fire Brigade: Chief Fire Officer
Northampton and Northamptonshire Fire Brigade: Chief Fire Officer
Greater Manchester Fire Brigade: Chief Fire Officer
LGORU: Frank Jenner

DOE's CENTRAL UNIT OF ENVIRONMENTAL POLLUTION

SPSO   Dr Penrose
Higher Executive Officer: Keith Jones
Project Officer: Stanley Hall
MARC Chelsea: Professor Stewart

DHSS's OPERATIONAL RESEARCH SECTION

DCSO   Dr MacDonald
PSO   Dr Ackroyd
Secretary
Cleaners

Police Scientific Development Branch – Systems III Group

DCSO	Nigel Lomax
SPSO	Roger Munn
PSO	Jane Hogg, Dr Alan Hardy
SSO	Max Perry, Elizabeth Neve
HSO	Penny Stevens
SO	Adam Tyler

PRSU: Chief Supt Albert Walton, Chief Supt Ron Davies, Supt Charles McKinnon, Supt Damien Grant, Supt Jeremy Bright, Supt Mike Vickers, Sergeant Mary Tierney

Humberside Police Force: Chief Constable Donald Purser, ACC Philip Hunt, Chief Supt David Lamport, Supt Leslie Rainer, Inspector Brian Nesbit, Inspector Robin Callaghan, Inspector Briant, Chief Supt Ralph Todd

Administrative Officer: Tony Murray

Police College: Supt Roland Baxter, Barry Hoare

LGORU: Frank Jenner

RMCS: Professor, Douglas Holden, Dr Milton Hubbard

HORU: Dr Ian Jamieson

P A Management Consultants: Gavin Fuller, Terence Ward

Scientific Advisory Branch – Civil Defence

DCSO	John Clayton
SPSO	Sid Butler
PSO	Alan Weston, Jane Hogg
SSO	George Carr-Hill

Administrative Officer: Brian Davenport

CO   Stuart
LGORU: Frank Jenner
LCD's SEO: Bruce Denby
Metropolitan Police Commander
Stalker: Timothy Devlin

F6 Division & Home Defence College

AS   Hugo Munro
Principal   Tom Elliott
Dr Delphine Somerville
Squadron Leader Jack Cornwell and wife Vera
LGORU: Bill Simpson, Martin Wooldridge
Assistant Commissioner Gerald Fenwick
Royal Holloway College: Professor McDowell

Establishment Department

AUSS   Charles Devereaux
Head of Welfare Section
Malcolm Brown of Security Branch
Brother: Pascal Ricketts
Solicitor: Harry Andrews
MP: Sir Nicholas Lyle

Note: Some names of the characters involved are not their real names, particularly in later chapters.

The Standards of Fire Cover

The Home Office Fire Service Department in 1947 drew up a set of recommended standards for the attendance of pumps to fires. These were confirmed with minor alterations by the Home Office Fire Department in 1958.

In 1955 a committee had been set up to undertake a comprehensive review of the Standards of Fire Cover. This committee concluded that in principle these Standards should vary according to the fire risk, such that the best cover is given to the area with the highest risk. A risk category classification thus forms the basis for the recommended standards.

There are five risk categories.

Category A includes only those congested urban areas where the concentration of buildings is so high as to present a serious risk of a major conflagration. Here it is recommended that three or four pumps should be sent on receipt of a fire call, and that the first pump should be on the scene within five minutes.

Category B refers to less congested urban areas.

Category C refers to residential areas within towns or suburbs.

Category D refers to small towns in country districts.

Risk Category E applies to the mainly rural areas with scattered villages and isolated homesteads, where the suggested Standard is a first attendance of one pump to arrive within the approximate time limit of twenty minutes.

While there may seem to be little point in sending a pump if it is going to take twenty minutes it is most important to have trained men on the scene, to ensure that the fire – in a haystack or a barn, say – is properly out. Besides, there is always a lot of clearing up and salvage work to be done afterwards, quite apart from the question of making damaged buildings weatherproof.

In addition to the above Risk Categories A to E, certain individual buildings, such as hospitals and chemical plants, are deemed to be a High Risk, and are given special treatment.

Contents

GIRL FROM THE BRITISH RAJ

I was born and brought up in South India. My birthplace was Madura, a city of temples dedicated to the all seeing Goddess, Meenakshi. My father, Charles Edward (Jack) Ricketts, loved the name and eventually, when I was 12 years old, persuaded my mother to have my name changed from Jane to Jane Meenakshi.

My mother, Emma, was a daughter of the Indian Civil Servant, Arthur Galletti di Cadilhac. The family was English, Italian and French.

My father, worked for the United Planters' Association of India but his real interest was gardening. He and my mother began their married life in Palamcottah. In the large grounds of their house my father would give me a new round bed of plants every time I had a birthday. By the time we left, when I was five years old, I had five round beds full of cornflowers, larkspurs, antirrhinums, nasturtiums, and many other lovely flowering plants. My father's favourites were cannas which he planted with military precision in long beds, each with a different colour; red, pink, orange and yellow.

Although I was an only child, (until my brother Pascal John arrived when I was three and a half), and had no other children to play with, I had a lovely time. My Ayah, unknown to my parents, used to walk me down the road to the junction where we would wait for her friend to come along in his bullock cart. We would hop in and be taken to the local bazaar where Ayah would buy me the most wonderful Indian sweetmeats, my favourite being halma. My Ayah would also take me to the servants' godowns (a barracks of little rooms at the bottom of the garden) where we would listen to the wonderful music the servants and their families made on their simple instruments. I can remember too the joy of having our potties replaced with water closets which flushed. There was also the excitement of going to the seaside for our holidays. I loved the sea and would rush into the water, leaving my poor Ayah waving anxiously at me by the water's edge.

At the onset of war in 1939 my father was called up for military service as he was a reserve army officer. To his disgust he was put in charge of a cordite factory in Aruvankadu in the Nilgiri Hills and we all moved there.

Again my father planted his cannas and I had my own little garden. There were lots of children to play with now but my mother loved to teach and was a strict disciplinarian. Pascal and I were taught our reading, writing and arithmetic at a very early age. As a result, when I was sent to a convent school in Ootycamund, I went up two classes in my one and only year there. Unfortunately I also spent a lot of time in the sick bay as my lungs did not like the cold air that high up in the ghats. After that Pascal and I attended a day school in Wellington where he was caned almost every day by the headmistress. We suffered a major tragedy when my father had to shoot our beloved dog, Puppy, because he was afraid she had picked up rabies from a rabid dog. Puppy was a long haired, white coated with brown spots, Labrador type mongrel that we had got as a puppy and to whom we were all devoted. However, as a precaution we still had to have our rabies injections all round our stomachs and, whoa, did they hurt! In December 1941 our brother Timothy Hugh arrived.

In 1942 my father was made a recruiting officer and was sent to Trichinopoly in the plains of South India. He decided we should remain in the hills so we moved to a house in Coonoor which had the most beautiful

Jacaranda tree in the front garden. I would often miss the bus to school and would have to run up the hill, through the park, and down again in order to get to school, just after the bus (which had had to go the long way round). Not long after we had moved to Coonoor and my father was still with us, having helped with the move, there was a plague scare. Both my mother and father refused to go for injections so I took Pascal by the hand and walked with him to the hospital to have our jabs. I even planned to get in touch with Uncle Tom if Mummy, Daddy and Tim all died which, a little to my chagrin, they did not. At Coonoor, my mother took in paying guests who all got on very well with Pascal, who was a charming and friendly little boy. I was less friendly which was probably due to being ill with bronchitis and spending one week out of every three in bed with a fever. When well, I would organise treks into the jungle with Pascal and our school friends, where we would build a camp fire, eat our picnic rations and hunt for wild guavas which were delicious to eat. For our holidays, Mummy, Pascal, Tim and I, went to Coimbatore. We had a magnificent suite of rooms at the luxurious hotel there, from which we could hear the waves crashing on the rocks below. We were allowed on the beautiful sandy beach with our surf boards only when accompanied by our mother. The waves were huge giving us the most enormous thrill as we surfed them.

When the War was over we moved to Trichinopoly to be with my father who was a civilian once more, employed as a tea planter. He recruited Tamil coolies who were shipped over to Ceylon to work on the tea plantations there. My mother got very frustrated because he never got promotion, preferring to work in his garden to going to the Club and socializing with the other Europeans. My mother loved the bridge, the tennis and the dancing at the Club, being excellent at all three. There was also swimming to be had at my father's boss' pool in the grounds of his magnificent house, at which the three of us, Pascal, Tim and I, became very proficient. My father had also been given a big house with a wide veranda all round it which made an excellent roller skating rink. The spacious grounds were excellent for our stilts and had many large climbable trees.

Pascal, Tim and I all loved climbing trees but it could be dangerous. One evening Pascal was at the top of a tree, I was half way up with Tim just behind me. Pascal looked into a bird's nest and discovered a snake in it. He came swinging down the tree, passing Tim and me in a flash, the snake slithering down after him. Tim and I nearly had heart attacks as we dropped to the ground as fast as we could go.

Pascal went about hunting for snakes to kill them after that, but I always gave them a wide berth having been made terrified of them by Ayah from my earliest memory. India was not a safe place for children and Ayah made sure we knew it. Scorpions were to be found under stones, mosquito nets were essential, the sun was deadly so that we always had to wear a hat and loose clothing; and we had to become immunised to Indian food from an early age.

Unfortunately, we had very little time to savour life in Trichinopoly as we were sent away to the Presentation Convent at Kodiakanal in the Nilgiri Hills for schooling, eleven months of the year; only coming home for Christmas and the New Year. As usual, I was very much the youngest in my class due to the excellent teaching by my mother and the cramming I had had from an Indian mathematics teacher, which did not make it easy for me to make friends. Fortunately I was very good at sports, particularly athletics which made me fairly popular. The nuns liked me because I was good at confessing my sins (when it was obvious I would be found out). They and the resident priests had the same attitude which I was to discover when it came to taking our entrance exams to the Bedford Schools our parents wished us to attend. Pascal and I took them together in the same room, where the Latin declensions had been left up on the walls, and I was able to help my brother with his maths and he provided me with a poem. The poem was *Daffodils* by William Wordsworth.

In 1947 India got its independence and Pascal and I had to go to school in England. The day we left the servants and their families all lined up to say "Goodbye". Ayah, who had been pensioned off, was there too. I had not realised how many servants we had but none of them would do each other's job, there being so much unemployment. The senior servants were the cook and the bearer. Then there were the matey boy, the peon, the sweeper, the cleaner, the dhobi wallah, the night watchman, the general dogsbody, the tailor, the chauffeur was an option my father chose not to have, the gardener and Ayah.

It took five days by train to reach Bombay, with monkeys hanging on the windows at stations which were patrolled by pedlars offering all kinds of goods. Tim had been left behind with our father. On board the P and O cruise ship 'Franconia' we lived like little gods. Our mother spent nearly all her time winning bridge tournaments leaving Pascal and I to roam the ship, playing all sorts of deck games. I was 13 years of age, when I could be either an adult or a child, whichever was the most convenient.

Liverpool and England were a shock. I wanted to turn around and go straight back home to India. The buildings were awful, the culture was foreign and the weather was appalling.

Bedford High School (the girls' school) was regimented. We boarders went everywhere in 'crocodiles'. The winter of 1947/8 was exceptionally cold and I spent virtually the whole of it in the sick bay as my coughing kept all the girls in our freezing dormitory awake. In spite of this I received a very good education and was in all the school teams (except the tennis and cricket teams). I asked to do athletics but was told it was not ladylike, and I had to play cricket. For the life of me I could not see how cricket could be ladylike and I was always out for a 'duck' and never caught the ball except when playing at silly mid-off, when I had no choice if I wanted to stay alive. In the school holidays Pascal and I stayed with Uncle Tom, Aunt Mollie and their two sons James and Robert. James was three years older than me and Robert was my age. They were not used to girls and treated me as a very inferior person, with the result I beat them at everything I possibly could. I beat them at chess, at making model gliders and boats, at photography, in shooting competitions down at their family home, Baggy Point at Croyde, North Devon, and at examinations. During one of the summer holidays at Croyde I had my school friend, Judy Slee, with me as she lived nearby in Barnstable. We decided to explore the caves on a point close to the house even though I knew Uncle Tom had banned this if he was not present. Needless to say, Uncle Tom was at the top of the cliff as Judy and I emerged. I was in very 'hot water' and my mother decided to come to England so that Pascal and I had somewhere to stay in the holidays. She took a job teaching French at a posh boarding school in Weybridge, but that came to a sticky end when Pascal burned a lot of sugar making sweets in the kitchen. After that, our mother rented a small bunga-low in the grounds of magnificent school buildings in Farnham where J M Barrie wrote Peter Pan. We were now neighbours to Aunt Rachel and her two children, David and Antoinette. Their father Arthur had been killed in the War, which was very sad for them.

Judy (Judith Anne Leithbridge Slee) and I passed out joint third in our School Certificates behind Mary Webb and Jocasta Innes. Judy was in the same boarding house as me. It was called Hilbre Grange and all of us sixth formers got caught up in the sorry saga of catching the attention of the boys at the nearby boarding house belonging to Bedford Modern School. I also got caught by my Headmistress, as she cycled by, walking in the street with a Bedford School boy! I was gated for a term and all us sixth formers were informed we were to be expelled from the boarding house at the end of the school year. My Headmistress asked that I should come and live with her so that I could pass my Higher School Certificate examinations in the following year. Unfortunately she had insisted I take Applied Mathematics when I wanted to take Economics. I did not like Ap-plied Mathematics, doubted I would pass the examination and so decided to leave Bedford High School altogether.

I was installed in a hostel for young women near Euston, together with Judy Slee. She went to Art School while I attended Regents Street Poly-technic. My mother returned to India leaving Pascal and Tim in the care of Uncle Tom. During the holidays I was left on my own, as Judy went home to Barnstable, so eventually I went to live with my Aunt Bella in Acton. Aunt Bella had divorced her first husband, William de Bruin, and was now married to Giacomo Titone. They both worked at the Italian Consulate and Aunt Bella's children, Elizabeth and Billy lived with them. Elizabeth was one month younger than me and Billy was two years younger. Elizabeth was very beautiful and was often in the newspapers as one of the ten most beautiful girls in London.

On passing my exams I expected to go on to take a B.Sc(Econ) degree, specializing in Statistics, at the London School of Economics. In spite of my mother's pleas my father refused to pay for me. With my agreement he enrolled me in St James' Secretarial College. I knew that when I was over 21 and had worked for two years I would qualify for a Major County Award. In the meantime I attended evening classes at the London School of Economics.

While my parents were on leave in England Aunt Bella discovered that her husband Giacomo was having an affair with their maid Maria. Worse still, Maria was expecting a baby. Pandemonium ensued. My mother immediately installed me in another YWCA (Young Women's Christian Association) hostel, this time in Netherall Gardens off the Finchley Road in Hampstead. Aunt Bella took off for Australia where her first husband, William de Bruin, was now living, in the vain hope of reconciliation. Elizabeth and Billy had a nomadic existence, moving from friend to friend. Eventually Elizabeth married Tony Furnival who was setting up a chain of restaurants each called 'The Soup Kitchen'; and Billy followed his mother to Australia.

Back in India my father committed suicide. His job in India was coming to an end and no job awaited him. His sons' education had still to be paid for. My mother returned to England and bought a house in Frensham, near Farnham, to be close to Aunt Rachel and her family. I got a job at the Senate House in the London University Entrance Department, staying there until I was able to attend the London School of Economics full time.

I finally got my B.Sc(Econ) honours degree in the summer of 1960. It had been a long five year struggle. Illness and the need for an operation on my sinuses had scuppered two sets of examinations; not helped by making the mistake of marrying a fellow student, Alan Wesley Mather, which I instantly regretted. I did, however, have one success. In my first year at the London School of Economics I took part in the London University athletics trials in the 100 yards, the 220 yards and the 440 yards. To my amazement I did not win any of them and was standing around, dejected, when June Paul's coach came up to me. (June Paul was an international sprinter at that time). Very little persuasion was needed for me to begin training. The following year I was representing London University in the 100 and 220 yards sprints as well as participating in other meetings which brought me up the rankings to be 18th in the United Kingdom in the 220 yards. How I wished I had been allowed to do athletics at Bedford High School!

When I was not at College I was on an athletics track. Health wise I could not have done better. The training cleared my lungs and virtually cured them of the bronchiectasis I contracted in the freezing dormitory at Bedford High School's boarding house, Hilbre Grange.

In my final year at the London School of Economics I met James Bell Hogg who was studying for his M.Sc in Transport under Professor Ponsonby. He was a Scot from Edinburgh. We became inseparable and he was kind enough to carry my starting blocks to all my athletic meetings.

CHAPTER ONE

THE FIRE RESEARCH STATION OPEN DAY

The telephone rang in the control room.

"Fire Service."

"Help us, help us …!"

"Your address, please."

But the telephone had been left dangling on its cord. Muffled screams, crackling sounds and stumbling about could be heard.

"Your address, please," the controller repeated, twice, her voice cracking slightly the second time. She signalled a colleague who got swiftly through to the exchange.

"Emergency! Please locate the address of the caller on line two."

While they waited, and the seconds seemed to be hours, the bumping, the stifled cries, the coughing of those who were so near, yet so far, continued. Then the female voice came on the line again begging for help, but again failed to respond to the request for her address.

The control room personnel knew from which district the call came. The controller had directed that the bells sound at the Salford wholetime station. There two pumping appliances were ready, engines running, with their crews aboard, eight men in all, the Leading Fireman standing by the telex machine waiting for the message giving the address.

A further delay, tense and protracted; at last the telex began to hammer.

"98 Bury Road."

The Leading Fireman leapt aboard the first pump. The appliances accelerated away, turning left onto the main road.

The journey seemed endless, but at last the pumps turned onto Bury Road. As they roared up to Number 98, sirens screaming, the roof vented with a bang; and flames shot upwards, to be followed by a pall of black smoke.

"Poor souls," the Leading Fireman said.

The fire statistics recorded five more deaths from carbon monoxide poisoning: a man, a woman and their three children, a boy of six, a girl of four and a baby.

The coroner brought in verdicts of accidental death, but the mother could have saved them if she had only given the address. The several minutes' delay was all that it took. There was also another factor. The fire station was situated at the other end of Salford.

On a dreary, wet autumn day in 1960, the Chief Fire Officer of Manchester, Noel Halford, sat in his office with his Deputy and other officers, in sombre mood. They were playing over the tape recordings, with their pitiful cries.

The CFO shuffled through photographs of the devastation as he listened. Almost certainly the fire had started in the downstairs front room. The greatest extent of charring was in a corner of the sofa, the floor beneath it and the ceiling above. The door of the sitting room had been left open so the fire had made its way out into the hall and up the stairs. More photographs showed the damage to the landing and then to the front bedroom and the back bedroom. There was a telephone by the double bed, the hand piece still dangling from the bedside table. The casement windows were tight shut, security locks having been fitted. The body of a man was slumped beneath the window. It was barely recognisable; the legs and bottom half of the torso merging into the burned ashes around it. The head rested sideways on the uplifted crossed arms, the nostrils showing the distinctive soot marks which indicated smoke inhalation and death from carbon monoxide poisoning before the flames found the body.

In the back bedroom were the bodies of the mother, her baby in her arms, her two other children huddled close. Only the outlines of the bodies were discernible, through the ashes of which they were now part. In this room, too, the windows were firmly secured. The hole in the ceiling above provided mute testimony to the explosive force that had been generated as the flammable gases expanded when a breach in the roof had brought the oxygen flowing in.

He sighed. "98 Bury Road is just a stone's throw from Priory Road, our proposed site for a new fire station."

"Those proposals have been before the Home Office for over two years now," his Deputy volunteered. "Each time I make a follow-up enquiry, I am told that the matter is under consideration."

Noel Halford turned to him. "Mr McIntosh, you will be sending your usual reports to Her Majesty's Chief Inspector of Fire Services, to the Fire Research Station and to County Hall. I should be grateful if you would append a confidential note to that to HMCI, pointing out that if the proposed station at Priory Road had been in operation this family would almost certainly have been saved."

Waking, hearing Maggie scratching at the door, I tumbled out of bed and fell sprawling on the floor; still forgetting the bed was on a raised plinth in the tiny bedroom at the end of my caravan. I got up, scrambled into my dressing gown and hurried through the living room into the small kitchen where Maggie was waiting, tail wagging, to be let out. Little Fuzza was queuing up behind her, jumping up and down on her four paws and turning circles.

I opened the door to the outside world and my two Pekinese shot out. I followed more sedately down the wooden steps on to the stone path. It was a wonderful autumn dawn with the first soft light awakening the birds, who chorused their joy. I always love the early morning with its promise of an exciting day ahead. Looking around as I breathed in the fresh cold air I could just see the neighbouring caravan through the tangle of trees and hedge beyond my small garden. I walked up the path beside my caravan towards the road fifty yards away.

There were only two caravans in my field; mine and the one on the other side of the mud track closer to the road and the squatting gypsies. In the adjacent field to my left there were only my neighbours who were served by a spur off our muddy driveway. The standpipe from which we got our water was in this neighbouring field close to the spur road and the tangled hedge.

I had joined the DSIR's Fire Research Station at Boreham Wood in Hertfordshire three weeks earlier, having just graduated from the London School of Economics. During my first lunch break I saw in a shop window in Shenley Road a caravan for sale in an unlicensed field for £120. The farmer who owned the field was to be paid a ground rent of ten shillings a week. The caravan was called Lyndoric and was painted blue. I fell in love with it at first sight.

I painted my caravan white to match my white Austin A40 car which I parked beside my tiny bedroom. After a good clean and the installation of a thick carpet my 22 foot caravan was ready for its occupants, Maggie, Fuzza and me It had a lovely slow combustion stove in the living room and calor gas lights throughout. It was really snug, warm and bright. In my little outdoor shed I had to ensure I had an ample supply of coal briquettes, calor gas cylinders and elsan for my miniscule toilet off the kitchen. When the toilet pan was full I had to dig a hole big enough to bury its contents somewhere in the field.

Fuzza was light brown with a black stripe on each of her small ears. She was the half sister of my mother's two Pekinese, Carmen and Picador. She was so small she could be held in the palm of my hand even though she was almost fully grown. The breeders at Farnham had given Fuzza to me because they were ashamed to sell her. So that Fuzza should have company I had bought Black Magic, otherwise known as Maggie, from local breeders. Even so I hated leaving my two little puppies alone all day in the caravan, although they did not seem to mind and always greeted me with great enthusiasm whenever I returned home.

Jim, my boyfriend, loved the Pekes. Jim, who I had met at the London School of Economics, was teaching economics at a school in Rickmansworth and was living in digs in Chorleywood run by two middle aged sisters, the Misses Angel, who were spoiling him with the most enormous meals so that he was putting on weight daily. Fortunately Jim was a tall man with wide shoulders so the extra weight hardly showed. I often wondered what he thought of my simple offerings, cooking not being my forte. At least eating my meals he would be unlikely to get fat.

I dressed in a black suit with a pinched in waist and velvet collar over a white silk blouse adding a necklace and matching earrings of blue eggshell beads and small pearls. Then breakfasting on coffee, cereals and mandarin oranges, I thought about the day ahead. It was Open Day at the Fire Research Station and I was to help man the 'statistics' stands.

"Maggie, Fuzza," I called, as I finished the washing-up.

Maggie came scampering along the path and up the steps. She bounded into her basket and lay looking up at me with big, round, dark brown eyes. Fuzza followed, daintily placing a paw on the bottom step. Then she hopped up slowly, one step after the other. I bent down, gathered her up, air-kissed her little nose and placed her in her basket next to Maggie.

Jumping into my car I drove up the muddy driveway to Theobald Street, the road which linked Boreham Wood to Radlett. Turning left I could see the sign announcing Boreham Wood 100 yards ahead. There were housing estates, schools and a sports ground on my left, single dwellings on my right as I drove down to Shenley Road and across it onto the dirt track which led to the back entrance of the Fire Research Station. The railway station was on my right and the film studios on my left. I drove slowly because of the pedestrians – mostly colleagues of mine at the Fire Research Station, heading in the same direction, towards the back gates: only visitors, it appeared, used the main entrance, opening onto Melrose Avenue.

I parked my car in the car park opposite the side of the main building and, getting out, savoured briefly the brightness of that autumn day. Then, at a steady pace, I passed along the front of the main building, through the door and into the hall.

The receptionist, who was also the telephonist, greeted me from her cubicle with a kindly, "Good morning", as I signed in. On I went, up the winding stairway to the second floor. On the right stood the door to the library; on the left, that to the corridor from which various offices branched out. First, was that of my overall boss, Jimmy Fry, a Principal Scientific Officer and Head of the Operational Research and Statistics Section. Next to Jimmy's office was that of Richard Lustig, his second in command. The third and fourth doors led into a big office which housed the coders. All these rooms on the front of the building were airy and pleasant, with windows giving on to the large lawn and the Hertfordshire fields stretching away beyond.

"Good morning everyone," I said, as I hung up my coat in the coders' office. "A lovely day it is too."

I stopped to chat with the coders. They were all ladies, supervised by a lady. Their job was to go through the fire report forms which were returned by fire brigades up and down the country, transferring the data from each onto a Hollerith card by punching the appropriate codes onto the 80 columns which made up the card. Iris Day, in her building opposite the canteen, then used her Hollerith machines to sort and tabulate the information contained on the cards to produce the Annual Fire Statistics and other tables we required for our research.

Elaine was just punching the details of the 98 Bury Road fire onto a Hollerith card as I arrived beside her. Looking over her shoulder I picked out the essentials: "… time from receipt of call to the arrival of FB, 11 minutes, … number of pumping appliances, 2, … risk category, B, … hazard or occupancy, residential dwelling, … number of non-fatal casualties, 0, … number of fatal casualties, 5, … number of rescues and escapes, 0… ."

"There is a tape and further details of the incident," Elaine told me, passing them over.

I listened to the tape and read the further details as the coders watched. "How distressing," I commented with tears threatening to flow.

Frowning, I made my way back along the corridor to the door opposite Jimmy Fry's, and went in. This was the dark side of the building, looking north towards the laboratories and the canteen block.

Hyman Marks and Michael Firth, the Assistant Experimental Officers, with whom I was to man the statistics display stands for the Open Days, were already there. The stands were set up in our own office, our desks and other bits and pieces having been moved out. Both Hyman and Michael were looking extremely smart in their best suits, shirts with stiff white collars and sober ties. Like mine, their black shoes were polished to a glossy shine.

Richard Lustig followed me into our office. He was a short and broad young man with a mass of curly dark brown hair above a high forehead. He was in a dark brown suit over a yellow shirt and his brown shoes did not compare well with ours.

"Good morning. Are you all ready for the fray?" he inquired with a grin.

"Yes," we chorused, a little shakily, taking our places beside our stands.

"Good! You will enjoy yourselves. Don't forget you know all about these statistics whereas your audience will know almost nothing."

Jimmy Fry appeared at the door. He was even shorter and broader than Richard with combed back greying hair above a patrician face with piercing blue eyes. His shoes were if anything even glossier than ours.

"Good morning, Jane. Good morning, Hyman. Good morning, Michael. Richard is right. You will have a captivated audience. Every one will have come eager to learn about fire statistics. It is your job to enlighten and inspire them." And he gave us a thumbs-up sign as he left the room.

Our first visitors began to drift in soon after, stopping to hear what Hyman, Michael and I had to say, and to put a question or two before moving on. Then the numbers swelled until there was quite a throng; and I was dazed. For the most part they were Fire Service officers in uniform, with their Chief Officers in mufti, but there were representatives, too, from other government offices, from the insurance world, from industry and commerce.

Amongst the crowd an imposing figure stood out. He was Noel Halford, the Chief Fire Officer of Manchester.

"Why is it," the CFO asked me, "that with all these statistics, you can't tell me how many fire stations and men I should have?"

I considered the problem.

"Do you know," he continued, "that Liverpool and Manchester cover roughly the same area, and have similar populations, exposed to similar risks, and yet Liverpool has twice as many stations and men as Manchester? Now then, which is right?"

I was thinking hard. Then I brightened. I had seen my way to a solution.

"If you would care to have a word with the Director," I replied, "he may be able to put such a project onto the Research Programme."

Noel Halford looked down at me from his great height. "Do you think that you would have the capability to sort it out?"

I flushed. "Yes," I replied, as I took up the challenge.

It was an idiosyncrasy of the Director's to require all incoming mail to be addressed to him, regardless of whoever would finally deal with it. He would arrive an hour early at the Station, and sit in his office clearing away any outstanding jobs, as well as going through the morning post, before the telephone started to ring or his staff needed him, when the day officially began at 9 am. Thus it was, on a cold frosty morning a week or two after the Station's Open Day, as he slit envelopes and skimmed their contents that he came upon the following letter:

"Dear Sir

It was my pleasure to attend one of your Open Days earlier this month, and I thank you for inviting me.

The demonstrations, exhibits and displays were well presented and were most instructive. The statistics displays impressed me particularly, as they made me realise, some-what forcibly, what a wealth of information is available on the fires attended by the local authority fire brigades. These statistics detail the demands which are placed on brigades, in terms of the requirements for pumping appliances and manpower; they show the attendance times and the extent of damage to property.

I am particularly interested to know if these statistics could be used to help me determine how many fire stations I should have covering Manchester, and where they should be sited. I should also like to know how many pumping appliances there should be in each station, and the best manpower arrangements; that is, whether the manning should be wholetime, day manned or retained.

I am sure that many of my fellow Chief Fire Officers would agree with me that a study along these lines would be very welcome. If you were to be able to extend your Research Programme to accommodate such a project,

I should be grateful if you would give me the opportunity to ask my Fire Committee for permission to propose Manchester as a suitable brigade to take part.
Yours faithfully
Noel Halford"

Dennis Lawson put the letter in the pile for filing with the instruction to place it in the Research Programme file. He proposed to introduce this project at the next Committee meeting. In the meantime he would ask Jimmy Fry to have his Section undertake some pilot studies on the effectiveness of fire cover using the present ad hoc methods.

Dennis Lawson was sitting at the top of the long table in the Conference Room next to his office, his Deputy, Grey Silversides, and the other Division Head, Dr Bruce Rawlings, flanking him. The Section Heads occupied their usual places further down the table.

Dennis worked through the research programme of each Section in turn. Finally he came to the Operational Research and Statistics Section. Jimmy read from his brief. "The coding of the fire reports is up to date. The coding of the supplementary reports returned by the fire brigades on fires caused by electrical appliances for the year 1959 has now been completed. Richard Lustig is about to begin the analyses. We shall start by tackling those fires in which the source of ignition was wire and cable, following that up with studies of those appliances which feature most frequently: television sets, electric blankets, electric fires, cooking appliances, kettles, toasters. The Section has also dealt with a couple of Parliamentary questions, one on explosions in back boilers and the other on the incidence of fires involving liquefied petroleum gas cylinders. The display stands at the Open Days drew a lot of visitors; and an informal request was received from the Chief Fire Officer of Manchester for a fire cover study in his brigade."

"Yes," said Dennis. "On that last point: Mr Halford has written to me with a formal request, subject to getting permission from his Fire Committee. Now, if I'm to put a proposal for a project on fire cover before the Research Committee, I shall need a case. Can we do any better than the present ad hoc methods? How are we to measure any possible improvement? Have you any ideas for a pilot study?"

Jimmy thought for a moment. "We could analyse the statistics to see how the present Standards of Fire Cover are operating on the ground. We could also examine in detail those brigades which have recently opened or closed or even resited a station, to discover what effect this has had on attendance times."

Dennis nodded. "Okay, see if you can fit that in – not forgetting of course that we have a deadline for the electrical survey results. A symposium has been fixed for July 1963. In the meantime, as you probably know, the Royal College of Architects has been pressing the Fire Research Station for an Index of Fire Hazardousness by Standard Industrial Classification. Perhaps your new SO, Jane Mather, could produce one as a matter of urgency. Also, that question on LPG cylinders reminds me that the Research Committee wants a report on the subject. Who answered the PQ?"

"Jane Mather," replied Jimmy.

"Please ask her to produce a report on that too."

It was 12.15 pm, and Dennis brought the meeting to a conclusion somewhat abruptly. The assembled scientists rose and trooped down to the canteen for lunch.

CHAPTER TWO

CFO MANCHESTER WANTS A STATION SITING STUDY

It was the summer of 1962.

Richard Lustig poked his head around the door of the big office I shared with Hyman and Michael. "Jane," he said, "Jimmy would like to discuss our note on the Standards of Fire Cover. Would you come into his office, please?"

When we had settled ourselves around Jimmy's conference table, Jimmy opened the discussion. "Well, you've started something interesting here, if I read you correctly. Are you telling me that certain urban areas in the UK fall short of the Standards recommended by the Home Office?"

"Yes," replied Richard, "the B risk areas we have analyzed appear to have insufficient fire stations covering them. Jenny and I have used two different approaches and both appear to be giving the same result."

"Right, let's have a review of those results, and then we'll go through the conclusions in detail."

Richard leant back in his chair and closed his eyes. It was always difficult to describe results painstakingly achieved in a few words. After a moment he said:

"In Middlesex and Lancashire, comparatively fewer fires are attended within the first three minutes in the urban areas, than in the residential areas within towns and suburbs."

"What you're saying is, the mainly commercial and industrial areas are less well served than the mainly residential ones are?"

Richard nodded.

"Yes," he confirmed, "the urban, B Risk, areas we have analysed appear to have insufficient fire stations covering them. Jane and I have used two different approaches and both appear to be giving the same result." And Richard summarized his analysis ending with the conclusion, "In the two county brigades we investigated, Lancashire and Middlesex, the attendance times to B Risk Category areas are considerably inferior to those for C Risk Category areas."

Jimmy turned to me.

I summarised my study with the conclusion, "Fires in dwellings are spreading beyond the room of origin more frequently in the urban areas than in the suburbs. This is what would be expected if it is taking the Fire Service longer to get to these B Risk areas than to the C Risk areas."

"Well, maybe," said Jimmy, "but why should it be taking longer? By rights, the reverse should be the case. The Home Office fire cover regulations were designed to ensure that the higher risk areas received the greatest cover. This is present policy. Let us review it."

Richard took over again: this was something of a pet subject with him. "The Home Office fire cover regulations," he pontificated, "consist of a set of recommended standards for the attendance of pumps to fires. These were originally drawn up by the Fire Department in 1947. In 1955 a committee was set up to undertake a comprehensive review of these standards. This committee concluded that in principle standards of fire cover should vary according to the fire risk, such that the best cover is given to the area with the highest risk. A risk category classification thus forms the basis for the recommended standards."

Richard paused for breath and Jimmy looked at me.

"And those categories are …?"

I responded. "There are five in all. Category A includes only those congested urban areas where the concentration of buildings is so high as to present a serious risk of a major conflagration. Here it is recommended that three or four pumps should be sent on receipt of a fire call, and that the first should be on the scene within five minutes."

"Hold it," interrupted Jimmy. "Let's first concentrate on defining the risk categories."

I could feel myself blushing. "Sorry, sir. Er, well, that's category A. Category B refers to less congested urban areas, category C to residential areas within towns or suburbs, category D to small towns in country districts, while risk category E applies to the mainly rural areas with scattered villages and isolated homesteads – where the suggested standard is a first attendance of one pump to arrive within the approximate time limit of twenty minutes. I looked up at Jimmy. "I must say, sir," I added, "there hardly seems any point sending a pump if it's going to take twenty minutes."

"I don't agree," he replied. "It's most important to have trained men on the scene, to ensure that the fire – in a haystack or a barn, say – is properly out. Besides, there's always a lot of clearing up and salvage work to be done afterwards, quite apart from the question of making damaged buildings weather-proof. But we're straying from the point. Is there anything else about risk?"

"Yes," I continued. "Certain individual buildings, such as hospitals and chemical plants, are deemed to be a high risk, and are given special treatment."

"Okay, so that covers the risks. And we know that the recommendations are, that the higher the category of the area in which the fire occurs, the more pumps that should be sent to it, and the quicker they should arrive. How can that be achieved? Jane?"

"It would be achieved by siting a greater density of fire stations in the areas of higher risk."

"Quite. And your note appears to show that this is not happening – Richard?"

"No, indeed," agreed Richard. "In the two county brigades we investigated, Lancashire and Middlesex, the attendance times to B risk category areas are considerably inferior to those for C risk category areas."

"Any guesses why that should be?"

"Presumably because more fire stations are being sited in C risk category areas than would be expected under the recommended standards."

"To the detriment of the urban areas," mused Jimmy. "So for some reason the B risk category areas appear to be underprovided." He fell silent; his head was bent down on his chest, his eyes were downcast, and his fingers drummed the table. For a minute or two, nothing was heard in the room except for the sound of Jimmy's fingers.

Then abruptly, he straightened up. "Clearly, this requires further investigation. It's the B Risk areas we're concerned about and we need to limit our geographical scope. That means County Boroughs. Jane, please ask Hyman to find out which County Boroughs have made changes in their station sites between 1957 and the present. Then I want you to do a before and after study using average attendance times as your measure."

I nodded; and the meeting broke up.

In the corridor outside I turned to Richard. "Why didn't Jimmy give you the responsibility for the follow-up study?"

"Because I'm leaving," he replied. "I've got another job, with better pay and prospects."

"Oh, congratulations! Well, I wish you every success. When do you go?"

"At the end of the month."

Jimmy, meanwhile, left alone, thought for a moment, then summoned his secretary and began to dictate a confidential memo to the Director:

"FIRE COVER

At the last meeting of the Research Committee, the Home Office again vetoed our proposed project on Fire Cover, optimising the siting of fire stations.

The evidence is very strong that siting policy favours residential areas to the detriment of commercial and industrial areas.

I am now investigating whether fire stations are being moved from the latter to the former.

A cynical view is that soaring land prices in urban areas are making fire station sites valuable prey for the property tycoons."

I took an extended Christmas and New Year period of leave from the Fire Research Station in order to marry Jim. We motored up to Edinburgh in my car with my dogs, Maggie and Fuzza. I stayed with his parents, Robert Bell Hogg and Catherine Matheson Hogg, while Jim, Maggie and Fuzza stayed with Duncan, an old friend of his from his Edinburgh University days. Duncan was now a pharmaceutical representative who visited general practitioners to show them his samples. Duncan's wife had recently left him so Duncan was glad of the company on his first Christmas and New Year without his wife. We were glad of his invitation to stay as he lived in a house and garden which was suitable for the dogs.

Jim's parents were the kindest of folk. His father was a grocer who, for years, had had his own business in another part of Edinburgh to which he would travel by bus. He was so kind and generous that the business barely made enough for him to support his family. Anyone who came in to the shop who was clearly having difficulty paying would not be charged the going rate for the goods they bought. Eventually Robert Hogg had to sell his business and get employment as the manager of someone else's shop. Robert Hogg was also an unpaid Deacon at the Cathedral where he spent a lot of his free time. For generations the Hogg family tree had just one male child whose name would alternatively be Robert, James, Robert,

James...... A famous James Hogg was the poet, the Ettrick Shepherd. Jim's father, the last Robert, had married Catherine Matheson who came from a large family which had made Robert feel very much at home. Jim's mother, Catherine, had spent her whole married life as a housewife, and by the time I met her, was badly afflicted by arthritis.

Jim, Duncan and I had a grand time enjoying the sights of Edinburgh and mixing with their University friends. On Hogmanay, red-headed Duncan first footed the Hogg household, bringing bottles of beer. Everyone sobered up for our wedding, which was held in Edinburgh's Registry Office, after which there was another feast at a nearby hotel. Then, we drove back South with our little dogs, to our caravan home close to Boreham Wood.

Dour, broad Hyman and an even dourer, large Michael both grinned broadly as I entered our office on my first day back at work. They made a cursory attempt at hoping my holiday had gone well before Michael's excitement got the better of him.

"A Mrs J Hogg is arriving today. She is to have Richard's office."

"I'm not sure I can put up with a woman boss," grumbled Hyman, almost in unison with Michael.

Jimmy Fry put his head round the door. "Come and see me in my office when you are ready, Jane." And he disappeared, seemingly leaving a Cheshire cat smile behind him.

Feeling somewhat giddy, I placed my handbag and brief case on my desk "Boy, what a surprise! I must go and see what Jimmy wants."

Jimmy was waiting for me. "Come and see your new office," he smiled as he led me down the corridor to the office next to his, which had been Richard Lustig's office.

Obviously I had been in this office many times, and it was a lovely bright room with windows all along the south facing wall from waist level upwards. Now it contained two desks facing each other with a filing cabinet and a mirror for each occupant; and Richard's carpet was still on the floor. (The Civil Service was very strict about office furniture.)

"That's your desk," said Jimmy pointing to the one furthest from the door and backing onto the party wall with his own office. "Jennifer Gaunt is having the other desk. She will be joining us later this morning. She is just going through her introduction ceremonies with Dennis Lawson and Grey Silversides."

"Oh, by the way, you have been promoted. Congratulations." And Jimmy held out his hand to shake mine. "I'll call the others in now."

I had to laugh at the expressions on Hyman's and Michael's faces when the two of them arrived in my new office.

"I didn't really mean it, about a woman boss," Hyman spluttered.

"I suppose I'll have to stand on ceremony now," grumbled Michael.

Iris Day arrived. "I didn't know you were getting married." Iris was a motherly lady who looked after the sorting and tabulating of all the statistical tables required for the Annual Tables and for our various research projects. Iris also took care of the Station's white cat, Snowy, and found homes for all the kittens Snowy had in her yearly litters.

Before I could reply, Jennifer was ushered in by Jimmy. She was a blue eyed blond with short straight hair and a sunny smile. At this moment she was trying very hard not to look nervous.

"How convenient! Only the coding ladies missing. Let me introduce you to Jennifer Gaunt, newly recruited to the Operational Research and Statistics Section." There were handshakes all round in the now rather crowded office

"Jane, I'll leave Jennifer with you to look after," and Jimmy departed.

I introduced Jenny to the coders in the adjacent large office and, of course, had to explain my new name. Further down the corridor were the members of the Physics and Mathematics Section so I took Jenny to see them as well. The staff of the Testing Laboratories, Sprinkler Laboratories and Chemical Laboratories, I felt could wait for another day. We both had a lot of settling in to do, but first we had to go down to Iris' domain opposite the canteen.

Iris proudly showed Jenny round. She had one very large room which held the sorters and tabulators and a small room off which was her store-room, and held her paper, spare cards and the cards from the coders wait-ing to be processed. In this storeroom was Snowy, curled up in her basket.

"Snowy is pregnant again." And Iris looked at me with a broad smile. "You must have one of her kittens as a wedding present."

"I would love that," I responded politely.

"In that case," continued Iris, arms akimbo, "you shall have one and your husband another."

It was always difficult for Iris to find homes for Snowy's kittens so I accepted with as much pleasure as I could muster. Jenny hurriedly shook her head, explaining she was living in digs where no cats were allowed.

The agenda of the Fire Research Committee was a lengthy one as always. All the top brass were there, and the programme for each Sec-tion had to be gone over painstakingly: Structural Engineering, Chemical Engineering, Theoretical Physics, …. Operational Research and Statistics, too, when its turn came.

Grey Silversides reported on the Fire Cover pilot studies. He reminded the Committee of the strong evidence that existed of a bias in cover towards residential areas to the detriment of commercial and industrial ones. Siting policy in County Boroughs in the past was now being examined.

David Lessing, an Assistant Secretary in the Home Office Fire Depart-ment, spoke. "The Home Office's concern is the risk to life from fire. The Government is not responsible for losses to property."

"The position is being monitored in relation to the Home Office's own recommended Standards of Fire Cover," Grey assured him. "Presumably the loss of life was taken into account in the construction of these stand-ards."

David Lessing changed tack. "Who's the project officer?" he wanted to know. "Is he well qualified? What experience does he have?"

Grey laughed. "He's a she – Mrs Jane Hogg. She's highly qualified, and has been with the Station since 1960."

"That's only three years," murmured Lessing. "Isn't that rather light on experience?"

Dennis Lawson interposed crisply. "Jimmy Fry is an excellent Section Head. He's providing all the support and guidance that is required."

The point was conceded; and they passed on to other business.

Directly the meeting was over, Lessing, together with the Chief Inspector for Fire Services (HMCI), returned to London, and went to see the Assistant Under Secretary of State (AUSS) in charge of the Fire Department.

David Lessing looked troubled as he made his report. "It won't be long before the Fire Research Station has sufficient evidence to persuade the Committee to give the go-ahead to the fire station siting in Manchester project," he finished.

The AUSS turned a cold eye to HMCI, who nodded his assent.

"So what do your propose?" asked the AUSS of David Lessing.

David Lessing told him.

CHAPTER THREE

CARBON MONOXIDE POISONING

I was sitting alone at a table for four, tucking into a plate of roast beef, carrots, green beans, mashed potatoes and a small helping of parsnips. The parsnips had been given to me as a present and were the cook's speciality. I usually hate parsnips but our cook certainly knew how to make them really delicious.

"May we join you?" Grey Silversides was standing beside my table, holding his lunch tray and Jimmy Fry was with him.

"Please do," I replied, moving my sweet of apple crumble to give them more room.

They placed their plates of food, cutlery and serviettes on the table, and Jimmy took away their trays while Grey settled his long lean body comfortably into his chair. Grey always wore a smart grey suit, starched white shirt and beautiful grey tie. Today, Jimmy was in grey flannels and heather coloured sports jacket but sporting his usual blue check shirt, open at the neck.

"Thank you for promoting me," I said politely.

"It was your paper on the ranking of industries by fire hazard which clinched it. The Architects loved it. They can now make sensible judgements based on your findings. As you know, previously they were using measures such as the number of employees to predict the incidence of fire, which was useless in cases such as the water industry where there are virtually no people on site." And Grey took a mouthful of his cottage pie as he considered my paper's findings.

"Yes, it was constructing the component which reflected the size of the industry which was the key," continued Jimmy as Grey nodded his assent.

"However," growled Grey, and I knew something was bothering him, "I am much more interested in the Director's proposed research project on the siting of fire stations. *That* will certainly be extremely useful."

"How is that progressing?" I asked with considerable interest, not liking to bring the subject up myself and very glad that Grey had done so.

"The Home Office people are being extremely negative. Their representative on the Research Committee, David Lessing, is continually finding reasons why the project should not go ahead. Instead, David Lessing is proposing that a project looking at the climatic effects on fire incidence and spread be put on the Station's Research Programme," and he gave another growl in disgust.

Jimmy laughed, knowing how much Grey scorned projects when the results appeared to have no useful application. "Perhaps improvements in long range weather forecasting could be used to predict periods when the risk of fires starting, and spreading, would be high."

"And the dangers of fire could then be publicised at a time when the publicity would invoke the maximum benefit," I added in order to cheer Grey up.

"Okay," responded Grey, "you can have the project, Jane, as you are so keen on it. For my part, I am set on the Station getting the siting of fire stations project." He paused as he took another mouthful before turning to me. "You scored a hit with the Chief Fire Officer of Manchester. He wants you to do a station siting study for him. I believe he has his hands full with the competition from the garage and hotel interests."

"Interests which are vying for the same sites," commented Jimmy dryly.

Grey paused, waiting for Jimmy to explain himself. When he did not Grey prompted, "What interests?"

"They are Freemason bad apples who call themselves 'The System'. They are business men who have their tentacles in all walks of life but especially in the Civil Service, local government and the police. Here we are talking about magnificent buildings being erected using public funds only later to be found surplus to requirements and sold off at a loss to 'The System'."

Grey looked dumbfounded but he was a great fighter and he fervently believed in the value of research. The Station did a lot of work on fire protection, fire prevention and fire publicity but the Home Office regarded work on fire cover as part of their own empire. However, the work was not being done which left a vacuum Grey was determined the Fire Research Station would fill.

"Well, let us hope we can continue with our research without hindrance from 'The System'," exclaimed Grey, appearing both unbelieving and combative.

Jimmy nodded worriedly. Jimmy had a considerable amount of political nous which was why he had become Head of the Statistics Section and although he was very positive about the value of research into fire cover, he was fearful of the political consequences. I was full of youthful enthusiasm and although I was at one with Jimmy's concerns, was desperate to start work on the siting of fire stations project.

Grey turned back to me. "Have you thought what criteria you would use to decide whether an extra fire station was needed?"

I replied promptly as I had indeed been mulling over that very question. "I would want to minimize the total cost of fire to the nation. I would argue that each additional station should more than pay for itself from the resultant savings in fire losses. Loss of life, principally, and the direct damage to property: but also the consequential losses due to lost production, trade and jobs."

I raised my eyes to Grey's and registered his look of surprise. Jimmy was laughing. He had got used to me.

Suddenly, I was embarrassed. "Would you excuse me, please?" I asked Grey. "I have some shopping to do."

"Of course," he replied.

Still red, I practically ran down to the shops. Besides, I did not have much time before I had to be back in my office.

❧

Jim was home when I entered the caravan to be greeted by a bouncing Maggie and a turning-round-in-circles Fuzza. I had driven Jim to Rickmansworth Grammar School that morning and he had taken buses back. We had a hug and a kiss before getting down to the important business of feeding ourselves, Jim having already fed the dogs.

We were half way through our pasta and salad, with the dogs sitting beside the table waiting for every crumb which fell, when I mentioned our new arrivals.

"Iris is giving us two of Snowy's kittens."

"I didn't know Snowy had any."

"They are on their way."

I got up to take our empty plates to the sink in the little kitchen and to get some fruit, cheese and biscuits.

"Oh, look! There are no lights on in Boreham Wood."

Jim rose and bent to peer out of the window facing the town where there were usually a myriad of twinkling starry lights. "Yes, indeed, the lights are out. There are certainly some advantages in living in a caravan."

❧

My beautiful mother visited us. She had curly raven hair, bright blue eyes, high cheek bones and a strong chin with a mouth which was a little too wide. She had made a long journey, all the way from Farnham in Surrey. She did not have a car, cycling everywhere, often with her Pekinese dogs, Carmen and Picador, sitting in the wicker basket hung on the handle bars. So my mother arrived by train and we met her at the station.

My mother made a valiant attempt at admiring the caravan and its small but beautiful garden.

"The air is so fresh," I told her, "and the caravan is so warm and cosy."

"What do you do about the toilet?" my mother asked.

"Oh, we use elsan and when the toilet is full Jim digs a hole in the field and buries it."

"In the dead of night," added Jim with a smile at my mother.

"It is not so different to the time in Palamcottah before we had flushing water closets, and the Indian servants had to empty all the toilet pans," I reminded my mother.

"No indeed. Fancy you remembering that!" (I had been born and brought up in South India).

We had a pleasant meal of rump steak, chips and salad followed by fruit and cheese. Having three round the table made the caravan seem a bit crowded as we really only had enough furniture for two, along with the cupboard for clothes, in the main room. The dogs' baskets also took up a lot of space.

The meal over, my mother insisted on doing the washing up, with me drying and Jim putting away. Unaware that she was doing it, my mother ran us completely out of hot water and some emergency refilling of the hot water tank had to be done by Jim.

"You cannot possibly have a baby in this caravan," insisted my mother, as we sat sipping our coffee. "You must buy a house. I will give you £2,000 towards the cost."

I nearly choked on my coffee at this sudden offer of a present of £2,000. I had to put down my cup, pull out a handkerchief and have a good cough. Jim, who had not been affected at all, gave me a nod. We had been discussing the price of houses and how they were likely to rise. My mother's present would be the deposit we needed.

"Thank you very much," I spluttered, giving my mother a hug.

"Bye the way," my mother continued, "I am selling Chrysanthea and returning to Le Casacce. I am giving Carmen and Picador back to the breeders." (The Casacce is my Italian mother's home).

"Ma, you can't do that!" I cried in horror. "We will have Carmen and Pica. Won't we, Jim?"

"Yes, indeed! We will have Carmen and Pica," echoed Jim, who loved dogs.

❧

Iris was waiting for me as I arrived to collect Smouja and Rupert. We went together into her small room where there were now only two white kittens. Rupert came bounding up to me with Smouja following more slowly. They seemed to know they were leaving the only place they had ever known. Snowy was nowhere to be seen.

"Thank you for looking after them for me, Iris. I am sorry to have left them with you for so long."

"That's my pleasure. I did not mind a bit," responded Iris, getting out a cardboard box in which to put the kittens. "So, you are going to your new house tomorrow. What is happening to your caravan?" Iris liked to know what everyone at the Fire Research Station was doing, especially her colleagues in the Statistics Section.

"It is coming here, to the Fire Research Station, to be used for testing. Dennis Lawson is very happy to have it. In many ways I shall be sorry to leave Lyndoric. It has grown on me, like a faithful friend." I was much more upset than I let on. I loved living the caravan life and Jim enjoyed it as much as I did.

Iris put some paper into the cardboard box. I picked up Smouja and Rupert and put them into it. The car was waiting for them outside and they were soon settled into the back. I waved to Iris as we set off. She looked a little sad.

Four little Pekinese dogs were waiting for me at the gate into our small garden as I carried the cardboard box with the kittens from the car. Jim opened the gate, looking at the newcomers with interest. Rupert yawned at him, his whiskers coming forward. Smouja nestled down amongst the paper.

We entered the caravan with four dogs trailing behind. Once their cardboard box was on the floor Rupert jumped out to be sniffed by Carmen and Picador. I picked up Smouja and placed her on the floor where she was licked by Maggie. Fuzza was sitting in the middle of the room, wagging her tail, looking delighted she was no longer the smallest.

We left our pets to get to know each other while we got our evening meal. As soon as we sat down to eat it, Carmen, Pica and Fuzza were sitting beside us waiting for the crumbs which invariably fell from the table. Black Maggie was curled up in her basket with white Smouja nestling in the middle of the curl. Rupert had taken over Fuzza's basket and was fast asleep.

Early the next morning we packed our few belongings. They and our pets went into the car, while Bill, the gypsy, and Jim loaded our few bits of furniture onto Bill's lorry.

Soon we were at our new home. It was an immaculately kept three bedroom detached house in Leverstock Green, Hemel Hempstead. It was the first house in a cul-de-sac called The Wayside and it overlooked a green, beyond which were the back gardens of houses on the Laing's estate. We were all delighted with our new home. Even Bill, the gypsy, looked impressed.

As the house was a corner house, the garden curved from the front, round the side, and into the back. It looked enormous to us in comparison to our little patch of ground in front of Lyndoric. After making sure the gate has shut, we put the dogs into the garden to explore it as we unpacked. We kept the kittens in, making sure they knew their box was in the kitchen.

The door bell rang. Our next-door neighbours were standing on the step.

"Welcome home," they said together. "Would you like to come round for a cup of tea and meet Buster, our little Scottie dog?"

I sat at my desk in the living room from where I could look out of the front bay window and out of the little side window. Picador and Carmen were in the garden romping about. Pica's long coat was white overlaid with dark brown patches and he rolled as he walked. Carmen was white and gold. These Pekinese dogs were full brother and sister. Fuzza was their younger half-sister.

Our property was surrounded by a waist high wall at the front and the side beside the pavement. On the pavement side there was a fence on top of the wall to give privacy to the side and back gardens. A man came round the corner walking his big dog. Pica immediately jumped on top of the front wall and dived down onto the offending dog. The big dog ran off onto the green. Pica saw to it that no dog ever stepped onto the pavement in front of our house. All dogs gave it a large berth, using the green instead. Fortunately, their owners seemed to find the situation very funny.

We felt very fortunate. Everything was going so well. My mother had given us quite a lot of furniture which had belonged to my father's mother and we had bought the rest fairly cheaply. The bedroom suite had been bought from the previous owners of the house, the Blenkinsops, as had the carpets. Instead of curtains, we had covered the house in blinds. We would wait until we were richer to indulge ourselves in really good furniture.

Mr Blenkinsop had worked at the Building Research Station in Garston as a cement expert. He and his wife came from the North of England. They had been homesick so Mr Blenkinsop had found a suitable job which took them back to their roots.

It was a Friday evening. Jim was already home when I arrived back from the Fire Research Station. He was marking children's essays.

The dogs and cats had to be fed first. A very nice man came round selling horsemeat and fortunately our pets loved it. Another very nice man came round selling vegetables fresh from his allotment. These, together, with some fish would make us a lovely supper. As I was cooking I began to feel giddy and faint. I opened the kitchen window as wide as possible and also opened the back door. Somehow I got our meal together as Jim laid the table.

A lovely hot pot of tea helped me to revive slightly but I just could not face the washing up. I felt sick.

"I'm sorry, Jim, I really do not feel very well. I am going to bed. My apologies for leaving you all the washing up."

I staggered off, not even clearing the plates from the table in spite of Jim's grumbles. I opened the window in the hall, then the window at the top of the stairs. Dressed and ready for bed, I opened the window in the bedroom, popped into bed and fell straight into a deep sleep.

In the middle of the night I woke. There had been a loud crashing sound. I put out my hand to feel for Jim. He was not there. I got up and staggered out to the landing. I could see Jim's long legs protruding from the toilet. He had obviously been relieving himself, with the door open fortunately, when he had collapsed. (The toilet and separate bathroom were immediately above the kitchen). Jim was a big, tall man and quite heavy. Somehow I got him to his feet and almost carried him back to bed using a fireman's lift. He lay there groaning while I went back to sleep. I will call the doctor in the morning, I thought hazily as I passed out.

Morning came and Jim was still groaning. I went downstairs and opened the kitchen door. The dogs were all splayed out on the floor, the cats on the counter. It occurred to me that something was very wrong. Quickly I carried our pets outside into the fresh morning air, except for Rupert who padded up the stairs, along the landing into our bedroom. He jumped onto Jim's bed which was nearest the door. He curled up beside Jim with several plaintive, "meows", which said, "I've got a splitting headache. I've got a splitting headache."

I dressed hurriedly and rushed round to get the next-door neighbour. He opened up the outside hatch door of the chimney to the slow combustion stove in the kitchen. The chimney was completely choked with fallen cement which had coated the chimney. We had all been overcome by carbon monoxide fumes and were extremely lucky to be alive. My lungs' sensitivity to air pollution, which caused me to throw open the windows, had saved us.

It took some time before the dogs and Smouja were walking about again and they were subdued for the rest of the day. Jim remained in bed even after Rupert got up. As usual, when Jim felt ill he refused to eat anything. I decided not to get the doctor as we knew what was wrong. I remembered that the previous owner had been a cement expert and wondered what he would have made of the blocked chimney.

"We had better start thinking about putting in a central heating system," decided Jim as we were having breakfast the following morning. He had now fully recovered from his ordeal.

"I agree; and I should like to have the wall between the living room and dining room taken down to give us one big light triple aspect room. Also, it would be nice to have a sunroom. It would give us a better room than the kitchen in which to keep the dogs and cats during the night." I put some butter and marmalade on a piece of toast wondering if my dreams were carrying me away.

"We might as well do everything at once," Jim responded after drinking a mouthful of coffee. "We will have to increase our mortgage anyway."

"In that case," I continued in delight, "what about us having a paved sunken garden with a pond in it and steps up to the sunroom?"

Jim, the kindest of men, agreed with all my ideas. I just had to make sure I did not get carried away and land us with a huge mortgage we could not afford.

CHAPTER FOUR

THE STATION SITING
PROJECT GETS UNDERWAY

Jenny and I were in Hyman and Michael's big office. We were sitting round a large table working on the electrical survey. There were fires involving space heaters, hot plates, ovens, kettles, toasters, electric blankets. In every instance these appliances were the source of ignition. The aim was to help manufacturers make their appliances safer. Each of us had to choose which appliance fires to study in depth. I picked fires in electric ovens leaving the others to make their own choices.

"Jenny, you should take electric blanket fires," said Jimmy Fry who had just arrived without anybody noticing. "They are a high priority because of the number of casualties involved."

Hyman took space heater fires, while Michael volunteered to work on hot plate fires. Later on they would work on fires involving kettles and toasters.

Jimmy, who had been standing, turned a chair round and sat down, legs astride so that he could lean forward on the chair's back. It was a favourite habit of his when he wanted everybody's attention.

"Dennis Lawson has finally got the fire station siting project onto the Station's Research Programme," Jimmy announced with a crooked smile.

"David Lessing of the Home Office agreed to it at the last meeting of the Research Committee on condition it is a pilot study. Bill Holland, the Chief Fire Officer of Bristol, has volunteered his brigade for the project."

"That is wonderful news. When can we start?" I asked, looking around at the others hoping they were as excited as I was.

"Not for some time," Jimmy replied. "At least the project is finally in the queue of work to be done. Now I have some more news for you, Jane," Jimmy continued. "Dennis Lawson wants you to give a presentation on statistical testing to the Station's scientific staff."

"He wants a presentation on the theory behind the derivation of the chi-squared test, the t test and the F test?" I asked in amazement leaning back in my chair.

"Yes. He thinks statistical tests are simple and easily understood," Jimmy explained.

"But they are not!" I objected.

"I know, but that is what Dennis Lawson wants."

"This is worse than when he had you singing that duet at the last Charity party," Michael teased. "It is going to be awful. No one will understand a word you say."

"I am sure you will do very well, Jane," said Jimmy, giving me moral support as he got up from his chair and smoothed his sports jacket. "I am sure Jenny, Hyman and Michael here will understand everything you say, as will all of the Mathematics Section."

I discovered I was having a baby and decided to stay at work until the last moment. I assured Jimmy Fry and the rest of the Operational Research and Statistical Section I would certainly be returning to work as soon as possible after the baby arrived. Grey Silversides nodded his approval at lunch in the canteen while Dennis Lawson called me into his office so that I could convince him I intended to continue with my career.

"I shall only be away a month," I assured him. "Some employees take as much as that in sick leaves in a year."

"There are several projects lined up for your attention and I need to be sure of your availability," Dennis Lawson stressed, looking very stern as he sat behind his handsome desk in his large and very attractive office with its conference table, comfortable chairs and lovely pictures on the walls. It was obvious Dennis Lawson was the Director from all the accoutrements surrounding him.

I left Dennis Lawson's office hoping I had put his mind firmly at rest, giving his secretary a smile as I passed through her office into the main corridor on the floor above ours.

Time seemed to pass very quickly during my pregnancy. The builders were in our house knocking down the wall between the two main downstairs rooms, adding on the sunroom which had been designed by one of the Fire Research Station's architects, and installing the central heating. An elegant bookcase filled the aperture where the door between the dining room and hall had been. All the fireplaces were removed and the walls emulsioned in white so that the house felt airy and bright. Outside the paved sunken garden with its pond and steps leading to the sunroom was constructed. We were ready for the arrival of our baby in very good time.

At the Fire Research Station the tension began to mount as the time for my baby's arrival got nearer. The sick room was got ready in case the baby arrived while I was still at work.

Two gentlemen from one of the electric oven manufacturers came to see me. They were ushered into my office by one of the messengers and did their best not to show their surprise at how pregnant I was. (Jenny had taken herself off to Hyman and Michael's office). The two gentlemen were very worried about my findings that electric ovens were a much greater fire risk than gas ovens. Why was that they wanted to know.

"Almost certainly because they catch fire more readily when the oven has not been cleaned," I told them.

"We had better make them self-cleaning," they concluded. "Would you yourself buy one then rather than a gas oven?"

"I use an electric cooker rather than a gas cooker," I assured them, "in spite of the higher fire risk. *And* I make sure it is spotlessly clean."

"But in your report you are so adamant that gas ovens are superior to electric ovens," they complained.

"Where fire risk is concerned gas ovens are much safer than electric ovens. It is my job to make sure the public are aware of this," I stressed, struggling to my feet to indicate the meeting was over. I was feeling very uncomfortable and the baby was due in a week.

After the two gentlemen had left I went to see Jimmy Fry.

"I think I had better start my maternity leave now," I told him.

Jimmy jumped to his feet in agitation. "Are you sure you are able to drive yourself home?"

"Yes. Don't worry about me. But I think I had better go now."

Jimmy had no choice but to let me go, but from the look on his face he did not like doing so one little bit.

"The best of luck," he called after me as I left his office. "Do come and show us your baby."

❧

Jim was besotted with his baby daughter, Sally-Ann. I did not feed Sally-Ann myself because I took prescribed antihistamine pills for my hay fever and I did not want anything foreign getting into Sally-Ann's system. During the night I would be the one to wake, hearing my baby cry. Feeling overcome by wooziness I had just sufficient energy to shake Jim awake before falling back into a blissful slumber. Jim would get up, go downstairs, prepare a bottle of milk, come upstairs and feed Sally-Ann in her little bedroom at the front of the house. He would then put her on his shoulder and pat her back to dislodge her wind. Finally he would change her nappy before putting her back in her cot, a contented, happy baby.

The days passed blissfully. All I had to do was clean the house, cook the meals and look after my baby. Jim did the shopping so that our very small baby was not put at risk from any nasty virus from the outside world.

The dogs adored Sally-Ann. Pica would stand guard. Maggie would nestle up to her at every opportunity. Carmen would look on majestically from afar, and Fuzza would turn circles to show her pleasure. Rupert and Smouja would either be slumbering where they could find some sun or exploring their domain.

As promised, I took Sally-Ann to be admired by everyone at the Fire Research Station when she was three weeks old and I was due to return to work the next week. I was only taking a month's maternity leave. A month was paid for on full salary and I was entitled to have another month's maternity leave but would be paid nothing. We could not really afford the loss of a month of my salary so we had found a nanny to look after Sally-Ann. The nanny, Carol, had parents who lived near-by and she had come home to visit them while she was between jobs. Carol normally worked for rich Arab Sheiks or American multimillionaires, so she was doing us a tremendous favour looking after Sally-Ann. We hoped she would not be found another real job by her Agency for a long time.

"Hello, Jane," said Jenny rising from her chair as I came into our office on my first day back at work. "I wasn't sure you would be returning so soon, ... or even at all, to be truthful."

"It is nice to be back although, to be honest, I did wonder whether I would be able to cope," I replied, hanging up my coat, beret and scarf on one of four hooks supplied on the wall. Jenny's anorak was already in place. "After all, I am a little later than usual, having to learn a new routine."

Jimmy, who had heard me arrive, came in, took hold of a chair, turned it round and leaned on it. "How are you? Are you sure you haven't returned too early?"

"I am fine. Although it is wonderful being a mother, the need for an intellectual challenge is overwhelming. I am delighted to be back," I replied making myself comfortable behind my spotless and empty desk. Jenny's desk opposite was crowded with the papers she was working on. One of the Station's rules was that all papers had to be put away at the end of the day so that the offices could be cleaned properly.

Grey Silversides' lanky grey-suited figure appeared at the door. "Welcome back, Jane. I am delighted to see you. How is the baby?"

"Sally-Ann is very well, thank you. She is with a wonderful nanny who adores her."

"I am glad to hear it. We are very pleased to have you back with us. There is so much to do. Now, Jimmy, Jenny and Jane, I'll leave you to your conference," and Grey disappeared.

"What's on your agenda, Jane?" asked Jimmy, stroking his moustache and tilting his chair.

"I have to finish work on my study of the climatic effects on fire. I have looked at the effects on fire incidence in buildings and now I have to work on the effects on fire spread."

"Remind me what data you used," prompted Jimmy.

"Fires in buildings in England and Wales over the period 1951 to 1961," I replied.

"And the weather variables?" continued Jimmy.

"We were limited to the climatological data which were readily available or obtainable." And I listed them, counting them on my fingers. "However only variations in the amount of sunshine, rainfall and vapour pressure were found to affect the number of occasions the fire brigades were called to a fire."

"I shall now act as the Devil's Advocate," smiled Jimmy, tilting his chair even further so that I wondered whether he was going to fall off it. "What is the point of all this work at taxpayers' expense? After all Jenny has already written a report on the causes of fires in dwellings in London, Birmingham and Manchester and their relationship with climatic conditions," and Jimmy looked at Jenny for confirmation. Jenny nodded. She was still rather shy.

"With the achievement of long range weather forecasting it should be possible to use the results to predict periods of high fire incidence. The dangers of fire could then be publicised at a time when the publicity would invoke the maximum benefit," I pontificated, remembering Dennis Lawson's words in support of the project to the Fire Research Committee. Although the project had been the brain child of David Lessing, the Assistant Secretary at the Fire Department of the Home Office, our Director had given it his support. He would wish to remain on good terms with the Home Office.

"Well, all this grand research adds to the extent of human knowledge. Particularly so, when it is published," concluded Jimmy as he stood up, put his chair back in its place and got ready to leave. "Please finish it as quickly as you can, Jane. Dennis Lawson wants you to start work on the siting of fire stations project. That is a project which will certainly have plenty of applications!"

"You must be pleased about that," remarked Jenny, looking at me across our desks after Jimmy had left our office. She was very attractive with her blond hair, bright blue eyes, blue skirt and blue jumper.

"I am more than pleased. I am euphoric!"

After the trolley came round, Jenny and I took our coffee and bun into the large office where Michael and Hyman worked. A month was a long time to be away; so much had happened in the interim and I needed to catch up. Also it was a pleasure to see Michael and Hyman once more, even if Michael was disturbingly inquisitive and Hyman rather ingrained in his ways.

Later on that morning, Dennis Lawson summoned me to his office for a friendly chat and an informal discussion on how the siting of fire stations project might be tackled.

CHAPTER FIVE

SULPHUR
DIOXIDE POISONING

Hyman Marks came bustling into my office with his hands full of graphs.

"Glad to see you back," he said happily. "I have some results for you."

Hyman had spent the morning at the dentist but the experience did not seem to have dampened his enthusiasm in any way.

Then he remembered something. "Oh!" he exclaimed. "How's the baby?"

"Fine, thank you," I replied, knowing that he was not really interested.

He spread out his graphs on my desk.

"Do you remember the 'changes in station sites' job – the one where I had to find County Boroughs which had had a change in a station site between 1957 and 1962? Well, I've plotted the average attendance time for each month for three years before the change, and, where possible, for the three years after. This vertical dotted line shows when the resiting took place."

I examined the sixteen graphs one by one.

"Good," I said. "Now we'll have to fit 'before' and 'after' trend lines to each of these, and then test for significant differences between them."

"It looks as though the trend in attendance times is upwards in quite a few of the brigades," remarked Hyman. "Worsening traffic conditions, I should imagine."

I nodded, and then tapped a graph that had caught my eye. "That's an odd one," I said. "The trend was virtually static there until about ten months after the resiting, when it appears to have improved dramatically."

"Ah yes, that's Huddersfield: I looked into that," responded Hyman. "It seems a ring road had been brought into use at around that time."

The door opened and Jimmy Fry joined us.

"You've done a good job with these, Hyman," he said after a bit. "Sixteen brigades, though: that makes the analyses very repetitive. Just the thing for a computer," he added with a twinkle in his eye.

"Computer?" I looked at Jimmy in surprise.

"Well, yes," he replied, definitely smiling now. "I've arranged for you to go on a three day computer course starting this Wednesday."

"Where?" I was thinking about Sally-Ann.

"Don't worry." Jimmy guessed at my concern. "Just down the road at Elliott Automation. They hire time on an 803 and on a 503. I imagine this job can be done on the 803; but you'll probably need to use the 503 for your station siting project."

"Has that come through then?" I asked eagerly.

"Not yet, but most of the members of the Research Committee are in favour; and the results from this latest study will probably get the rest of them to give us the go-ahead."

"Oh good!" I exclaimed. Suddenly everything seemed to be coming right.

The computer turned out to be surprisingly easy to use. I took to it at once, appreciating the immense saving of time that it would represent. I romped ahead, and in less than two weeks the results for Hyman's sixteen brigades were ready for inspection.

I went into the large office so that we could go through them together.

In three brigades the effects of resiting could not be determined because the trend in the average attendance time had changed significantly at some point in the period of study. In a further seven, where a single station had been resited, some improvement was discernible; as it was in two more, where the changes had been more complex; while another two brigades appeared to be unaffected. At Preston and Tynemouth, however, the resiting of a single station had led to a clear deterioration in the average attendance time.

I asked Hyman if he could account for this.

"I think so," he replied. "Jimmy saw the graphs while you were away and wrote to the Chief Fire Officers asking them for their views. The Chief Fire Officer of Preston sent us a map of his area (it is in the file) which showed that the station in the centre of the town had been replaced by one on a peripheral ring-road. The map also had plotted on it the fires attended in the year after the resiting. Most of these occurred around the town centre. The new station is therefore further away from the majority of fires than the station it replaced. The same story applied to Tynemouth."

I ruffled my hair as I tried to think of mitigating factors.

"I suppose that the pattern of fire incidence in any brigade area would be very similar from one year to the next," I remarked eventually.

"I should imagine so," agreed Hyman. "Every year the number of fires increases but the pattern remains the same."

"Would you mind checking that, please?"

I returned to the office I shared with Jenny, pondering the results of Preston and Tynemouth. The sites in both town centres would be very attractive to property developers. I wondered if they had been sold off at their true value or at the value placed on them as fire station sites.

Then my brain went numb. How tired I feel, I thought. I do hope I can buck up after Christmas.

I awoke in the middle of the night, hardly able to breathe. I struggled onto my knees and put my head down which helped my breathing, but I was wheezing badly. The situation was awful. I struggled for breath. Ten minutes went by and there was no improvement. Jim began to panic and rushed downstairs to call the doctor.

Our young doctor came. "Your wife has got asthma," he told Jim.

"But I've never had asthma before," I wheezed, from my hunch-backed kneeling position on the bed.

"Well, you have asthma now at this moment." And I could tell from the tone of the doctor's voice that he did not believe me. "Your bronchial tubes are in spasm. I will give you some medication to open them."

Within minutes of taking the medication I was feeling much better and the doctor left, to return to his bed and his much needed sleep.

Night after night, almost every night, I would have another asthma attack. Jim would call the doctor. The doctor would come and I would be medicated. Eventually our young doctor got fed up and refused to have us on his list. We had to find another doctor, and quickly.

We went to Dr John Jamieson at 4 Leys Road in Bennetts End, Hemel Hempstead. Dr Jamieson was a dour Scot who had a reputation as an excellent doctor. He was a member of the British Medical Council and his mother had also been a doctor back in Scotland. Dr Jamieson's surgery was actually nearer than our previous one at Everest Way, Adeyfield.

Dr Jamieson came round to have a look at our home. "What is new?" he asked when he had completed his inspection and was sitting in a chair in our living room, facing us on the sofa. Sally-Ann was in her cot upstairs. The dogs were gathered around us and the cats were eyeing us from their vantage point on a window ledge.

"The central heating," we replied.

"Turn it off at once!" Dr Jamieson almost shouted. "You are being affected by sulphur dioxide fumes. Have the flue examined immediately."

We sat together on the sofa, stunned.

Dr Jamieson continued with his diagnosis. "Mrs Hogg, you have been made allergic to everything in the house. First, you have to get rid of all gas appliances, especially the boiler. You will, also, have to get rid of all natural fibres, which means these woollen carpets," and Dr Jamieson pointed to the carpets on the living room floor, "also your cotton sheets, woollen blankets and feather pillows."

"What do we replace them with?" I asked stupidly.

"Carpets and bedding made of synthetic fibres," replied Dr Jamieson as he looked round at our dogs and cats. "Also, I am afraid you will have to find new homes for all your pets."

"Oh, no!" I cried.

"That's out of the question," protested Jim.

"I am afraid you have no choice if you want your wife to recover from this catastrophe," Dr Jameson insisted firmly, leaning forwards with a hard look at Jim. "*And*," he stressed, "you need to consider what effects the sulphur dioxide fumes have had on your baby. Sally-Ann's lungs may also have been affected and they need to be given every chance to recover."

Jim nodded, close to tears. There was clearly no choice but to find new homes for all our pets.

⌘

We went to our vet for help in finding new homes for our pets. A lady had just had to have her dog put to sleep and she agreed to have one of ours. However when she had to choose between Maggie and Carmen, she found it impossible, so she had them both. Rupert was wanted by another family. A friendly lady was delighted to have Fuzza; but nobody came for Picador and Smouja. I telephoned a dogs' home and was told they would easily find a new home for Picador and that Smouja would be welcomed as the home's cat. Jim was, by this time, so upset, he had taken to his bed. So I drove Picador and Smouja to the dogs' home.

A young man welcomed me as I arrived with Pica in one basket and Smouja in another. Safely inside the reception area, the young man took Pica and Smouja out of their baskets, examined them and pronounced them in excellent health.

"Would an elderly lady be the right owner for Picador?" asked the young man.

"Oh, no! Certainly not. Picador is a man's dog." I was adamant that Pica would be an ideal companion for a man, who would take him for long walks, brush him and romp around with him.

"And what about Smouja?" I asked.

"She will be the perfect companion to all the dogs we get in here," the young man assured me, putting a comforting hand on my shoulder.

I had no choice but to accept his assurances.

As I drove home I could hardly see, my eyes were so full of tears.

A week later I telephoned the dogs' home. The young man answered.

"How are Smouja and Picador?" I asked.

"Smouja is a great friend of all the dogs; while a young man came for Picador and took him home," he answered and a weight seemed to fall off my shoulders. All our pets would be happy.

The kopex lining in the flue to the central heating boiler was found to have been put in crooked. An outside boiler house had to be built to house the boiler as I was now allergic to gas. The building of the boiler house had to wait until the weather was suitable. In the meantime we managed with electric space heaters. There were no carpets on the floors and there were synthetic sheets and blankets on our beds.

Above all, there was no brave Picador, dignified Carmen, black Maggie, little Fuzza, bolshie Rupert or shy Smouja.

The house was empty.

Except for Sally-Ann.

A scientist from the Chemical Section was sitting with me in my office. Jenny was down in Iris' domain preparing a computer program.

The scientist wanted help with the design of one of his experiments. I was quite unable to help him. My head was woozy and I had a stabbing pain in my left lung.

"I am so sorry," I apologized, "I am afraid I am not feeling well. I have got to go home."

Sally-Ann was now at a nursery in Boreham Wood's Shenley Road. She loved it there with all the children to play with, and the ladies who ran the nursery loved her. I picked her up, explaining I felt ill, and we went home.

Jim returned from Rickmansworth to find me in bed and Sally-Ann in her cot in her little bedroom. He cleaned her up, fed her and left her in her playpen.

"What would you like for supper?" Jim asked, bending over me and looking concerned.

"Just a little clear soup," I replied, really feverish now.

The following morning, Jim felt he had to go to work. There was a really important event on at Rickmansworth Grammar School which required his attendance. Also neither of us realised how seriously ill I was.

Jim telephoned the doctor's surgery saying I was ill and would the doctor please visit. Then he put Sally-Ann in her cot at the end of my bed and rushed off, running late.

I succeeded in remaining conscious until Dr Jamieson arrived and I had let him in. I remembered nothing more until I woke up in hospital.

I found myself in an airy two bed ward facing large windows which looked out onto a grassy area with Japanese cherry trees. There was another person in the ward with me. She looked to be in her late twenties, had short dark curly hair and light brown eyes. She was very pretty with a pale round face. She was now a terminal patient in the hospital where she had been a nurse. "I hope I see the Spring blossom on the trees," she told me during my stay with her in the terminal ward.

Apparently I had contracted double pneumonia and pleurisy but somehow I had pulled through. Now I was to be given a bronchiogram so that the surgeons could assess the state of my lungs. The bronchiogram would also have the effect of clearing my lungs of most of the bronchial casts with which they were clogged. The terminally ill nurse in the ward with me insisted in helping with the procedure. It was terrifying as they cut my throat and inserted the tube. Having the nurse there holding my head helped me enormously. She was so brave and I was determined to be just as brave.

When the procedure was over I was placed in another ward to recover and never saw the terminally ill nurse again. Over the next weeks and months I was continually coughing up huge bronchial casts with the intervals between coughs fortunately getting longer and longer.

As soon as was possible I returned home to convalesce. It had been a long way for Jim and Sally-Ann to come to visit me. Dr Jamieson had organised a home help and the house had been kept lovely and clean. I was wondering what we would do after the home help left when a near neighbour, Mrs Barbara Watts, visited us and offered to be our cleaning lady. We accepted gladly, with considerable relief.

It was a wonderful time to convalesce. I spent as much time as possible lying in a chaise longue in the garden; with Sally-Ann on a rug in her playpen beside me. The roses we had planted in the autumn were all blossoming. There were Iceberg standards alongside the drive interspersed with golden floribunda roses. There were pink Queen Elizabeth giant floribundas beside the front wall. On the other side of the paved sunken garden on top of the rockery, there were pink standard roses under five arches. Beside the waterfall flowing into the pond in the sunken garden we had placed a weeping standard which had white flowers. Also in the sunken garden there was a bamboo, *Arundinaria viridistriata*, with its erect, slender, purplish-green canes and dark green leaves with rich yellow stripes. A beautiful red, *Danse de Feu*, climbing rose grew up a trellis on the front of the house between the front porch and the bay window. Along the back fence the splendid thornless climber, *Zephirine Drouhin*, looked wonderful covered in pinkie purple roses. Along the side fence, opposite the sun room, was a winter flowering viburnum alongside a trio of lilacs with scented flowers in white, purple and blue. Following on was a magnificent golden weeping willow, whose long graceful branches were reflected in the small pond which lay in front of it. Other trees included a *Prunus x amygdalo-persica 'Pollardii'*, with its abundant pink flowers in the spring, growing beside the gate and the front lawn, a *Prunus serrula* with its glossy, red-brown, mahogany-like bark and small white flowers in the back garden and a *Betula pendula*. This latter tree grew between the *Zephirine Drouhin* climber and the small paved garden planted with tea roses. To complete the picture, a swathe of green lawn flowed around the side and back of the house to a garden shed covered with honeysuckle; with three rhododendrons in their large tubs standing beside it.

It was heaven, so peaceful and serene. Inside, the house shone with Mrs Watts' ministrations. We celebrated by carpeting it, in acrilan, from wall to wall with different colours, (blue, gold and red), in every room except the kitchen, bathroom and toilet. These were given top of the range light coloured linoleum.

It was early in May 1965. Spring was in the air. The day was warm and sunny. The magnolias, prunus and malus blossoms were vying with the lilacs, berberis and ribes as to which made the best show. My convalescence was almost complete but I was still very weak. I telephoned Jimmy to let him know that I expected to be back at work the following week.

"Please take care of yourself, and be sure not to return too soon," said Jimmy, but he sounded distinctly relieved.

At the Fire Research Station, Grey Silversides was called in to see the Director.

"Ah, Grey, have a seat," Dennis greeted him, offering him a chair at his conference table and taking one himself. "I want to talk to you about the Fire Cover project – the siting of fire stations."

Grey nodded that he was all attention.

"You know the position, I think: after four years and more of procrastination, the Research Committee finally agreed in February that we could go ahead with a pilot study. Now it's we who seem to be holding things up. Is there any movement to report? The next meeting of the Research Committee is in a fortnight's time and we shall have to say something about the project."

Grey looked at Dennis with his very blue eyes. He liked the older man a lot. They had always worked very well together.

"The fact is," he said, "we are very short staffed. With Jane Hogg on the sick list for three months already, we have had to resurrect that post in Jimmy's section which we transferred elsewhere when Richard Lustig left."

"I can't see that should prevent us getting started, at least," said Dennis somewhat severely. "Jane had already outlined the method to be used in one of her papers."

"Michael Firth and Hyman Marks have been fully committed to the production of the Annual Tables – the UK Fire Statistics for 1963," responded Grey. "We have to give this top priority, and we're late as it is."

"Yes. True." Dennis frowned. "I'm being bombarded with letters and telephone calls from the press, MPs, local authorities, industry, commerce, insurers, Uncle Tom Cobbley and all – all wanting the most up-to-date statistics, which means the last twelve months if possible. If that is not available they want their last financial year which is often April to March, but they will make do with the last calendar year. When I tell them that the best they can have is the previous year they are horrified."

"There are three possible solutions," said Grey. "First, we persuade the Home Office to give us money for more coding staff; second, we could code an even smaller sample of fires than we do at present; third, we could cut down on the amount of information we code."

"Risky that," replied Dennis. "If we meddle with the status quo, we'll have the Home Office taking over the statistics altogether. There have already been hints in that direction; after all, the fire brigades are their responsibility already, and they could well claim that the production of the statistics from the fire reports provided by the brigades should also come under their control."

"Well, unless something is done," commented Grey drily, "the Home Office could take over anyway on the grounds of inefficiency."

"Possibly," said Dennis, "but I had not intended to discuss the fire statistics today. The problem which concerns me at the moment is the project on the siting of fire stations. The Home Office administrators are arguing strongly that this too comes under their province. However, having mooted the project, we can hang on to it, at least for the time being. It was annoying that the Research Committee gave way to Home Office pressure on the brigade to be used for the study. I pressed hard for Manchester, but Bristol got it on the grounds that a pilot study should deal with a smaller area, with less data to collect, so that the results would be available quicker. Now three months have gone by and we have not even started."

"I'll ask Jimmy to begin work on it himself," Grey assured him.

CHAPTER SIX

THE FIRE STATION SITING RESULTS FOR BRISTOL FB

Jimmy Fry was waiting anxiously for me on my return to the Fire Research Station. He arrived at the door of my office as I put my brief case on my desk.

"How are you, Jane?" he asked trying to remain still. "You look a little pale."

"I am fine," I replied, wishing I had had time to comb my hair. "I am ready for anything."

"Good, good. Please come into my office. I need to discuss the siting of fire stations project with you." Jimmy turned and on his way back to his office he put his head around the door of the large office and called to Hyman to join us.

Jimmy seated himself behind his desk. Hyman and I sat down in front of him.

"Well, let's start with coffee to get you settled in," he smiled at me as he rang through to his secretary. "Unfortunately the Research Committee chose Bristol rather than Manchester as the brigade to be studied," he added.

"What a pity! Noel Halford will be upset. It was really his project after all. But it's nice to know that it's finally got through the Research Committee. How many years did it take?"

"A little over four," Jimmy told me. "That could be a record. Now, of course, they want the results yesterday."

The coffee came and I sipped it gratefully. Hyman was all attention,

"I have arranged for you both to visit Bristol Fire Brigade," explained Jimmy. "The Chief Fire Officer, Bill Holland, has asked for a list of data requirements so that they may be ready in time for your visit. Assistant Chief Fire Officer Ponsonby is the officer in charge of liaising with you. Now let's talk through these data requirements before I write to Bill Holland." And Jimmy looked piercingly at me with his sharp blue eyes.

"First, we need to know the locations of available sites for fire stations and the number of pumping appliances in each," I responded as Jimmy wrote. "Then we need the National Grid Reference for each fire incident for the seven years 1958 to 1964 inclusive, and also for special service calls in those years."

"But special service calls are not recorded at the Fire Research Station," objected Jimmy."

"Why do we need them?" Hyman supported Jimmy. "Special service calls include rescuing cats up trees and pumping out flooded premises. The journey times to these incidents are not critically important; not like those to fires which are spreading with each minute's delay."

Jimmy put down his pen and looked solemnly at Hyman. "But special service calls also include freeing victims of road accidents trapped in their vehicles, rescuing children and animals from dangerous situations, people stuck in lifts ...," he paused, stapling his fingers as he considered the matter. "Although the brigade's attendance times to these incidents are not as critical as they are to fires I think the victims' stress needs to be minimized."

"That's true," I pressed on impatiently, "and the brigade records these incidents. We need to include them in our study as they affect the availability of appliances to attend fires. If a station is empty when a fire call comes in because its appliances are attending a special service call the next nearest station will need to attend. The journey time to the fire will then be longer," I explained watching Jimmy's pen move once more.

When Jimmy's pen stopped moving I continued. "We will need a large map of the area to be covered, showing the major road network with its junctions and the links between junctions. The brigade needs to supply us with their appliance journey times along each of these links so that we are able to calculate the attendance times along the quickest route according to which station sites are assumed to be in use."

"Will these journey times alter according to the time of day?" asked Hyman.

"That's a good point," and Jimmy added it to his list.

"Also," continued Hyman pulling at his tie as he continued with his train of thought, "are all the stations manned whole time? If any of them are to be manned by retained crews the turn-out time will be two or three minutes longer than that of a whole time crew."

"All stations are manned by whole time crews. The attendance time will therefore be a one minute turn-out plus the journey time to the fire," confirmed Jimmy. He turned back to me. "Please continue, Jane."

"We should explain to Bill Holland," I stressed, leaning forward to be more emphatic, "that we should have liked to know the financial loss from each fire and the cost of each fire station. Then we would have been able to determine the optimum number of stations to cover the brigade area. We would have calculated the losses from fires as we increased the number of fire stations from one to two, to three and so on until the costs of the additional station would be greater than the savings in fire losses."

Jimmy continued to write rapidly.

"Instead," I sighed, "we will calculate the total attendance time to fires for every pumping appliance. For each number of stations to cover the brigade area we will choose that set which minimises the total attendance time. As the number of stations increases from one to two, to three and so on, the total attendance time will decrease and we will have to decide how many stations should cover the brigade area. At the moment I believe Bristol Fire Brigade has six stations covering its area. We will need to look at how much attendance times are reduced if we add a seventh station or indeed an eighth station. It will also be interesting to see where these additional stations should be sited."

Our discussions continued until the tea trolley arrived. By that time we were satisfied we had covered most, if not all, our data requirements in detail. Hyman and I returned to work, very excited by the prospect of working closely with Bristol Fire Brigade; and having an important application as part of the Fire Research Station's current Research Programme.

As soon as I came through the door, and heard the way Iris was thumping the cards as she got them ready for the sorter, I knew she was in a bad mood.

"Good morning, Iris," I greeted her. "What's the trouble?" With Iris it was always a good idea to come straight to the point.

Iris continued with her work crossly. "It's that new-fangled machine in there," she replied, pointing in the direction of the next room where a computer terminal was being installed. "It'll take over my work."

"Well, yes, in a way," I admitted. "But it's these machines that will be made redundant, not you."

"That's not what I mean," bemoaned Iris. "With the Holleriths I have a real part to play. I know the coding scheme, I've a detailed knowledge of fire reports; it's up to me to weed out any anomalies in the cards. Once that computer comes into operation, any responsibility I may have had will have gone. You, Michael or Hyman will program it to throw out the inconsistent data."

"That's true," I agreed. "I'm sorry, Iris; progress, I'm afraid. Look, why not apply for a Clerical Officer post?"

Iris looked glum. "I was that when I first joined the Service," she said, "but then I was assigned to Hollerith machines. After a while the new grade of Machine Operator was introduced, and then after a time Machine Operator pay slipped in relation to a CO; and now I'm too old to be promoted to CO."

"Oh dear." I felt very sympathetic. "That sounds like the problem the Scientific grades have in relation to the Administrative grades. Anyway, let's go and have a look at this computer terminal."

Iris stopped the machines and together we went into the next room. Snowy, the cat, was there too, tail waving, not sure that she liked the change either.

The installation was just about complete. There was a printer, a paper tape reader and a card reader attached by modems to the telephone system. Alongside were two flexiwriters which produced paper tape.

"So what happens here?" asked Iris.

"Well," I explained, "first of all you need to write your computer program, which you then turn into little holes on paper tape via one of these flexiwriters. Data can also be punched onto the paper tape the same way; or it can be punched onto cards as we do now. If there's a lot of it, it's best to transfer it from cards to magnetic tape held at the computer centre."

"And how's that done?"

"The computer's own software copies the imprint of the card straight onto the tape. Feeding the cards through the card reader would be rather laborious, so probably they'll be sent over by van to the computer centre."

It was obvious from Iris' expression that she realised that she had lost her cards as well as her machines.

I continued hurriedly. "When you have your program and data ready, the next stage is to phone up the computer operator, so that she can activate the computer to receive it. You then start feeding your material through the reader. When you've done, you alert the operator and replace the phone. When the output is ready, she rings you back, and tells you to prepare your printer to receive it. Then the printer gets to work and, once you've confirmed there's no more to come, you ring off. The speed of the whole process is quite amazing. It'll make such a difference to what I'll be able to do." I could not hide my enthusiasm for this new and powerful aid.

Iris was slightly mollified. "And who is the other end, and what computer is it?" she asked.

"Oh yes," I exclaimed. "It's the London University Computer Services in Tavistock Square; and the computer is the Atlas."

"Why aren't we using the Elliott computers?"

"Ah! Well, Dennis Lawson had one of the mathematicians do a cost-effectiveness study of the services available, and this was the one chosen," I explained.

Hyman and I travelled down to Bristol by train. The Fire Brigade's Headquarters was just a short walk from the railway station. Assistant Chief Fire Officer Ponsonby was waiting for us and showed us into a lecture room which contained an easel and board on which was pinned a large map showing the area covered by the brigade. We were introduced to a couple of officers who had been collating the data for our study. All the officers were very smartly dressed in their uniforms. Fortunately we were in our best suits. Most scientists at the Fire Research Station dressed informally. Hyman never did and I also liked to dress smartly.

After we had been supplied with coffee and biscuits (badly needed after our long journey) Mr Ponsonby led us to the map of the brigade area.

"The brigade covers the whole of Bristol County Borough and some surrounding areas of Gloucestershire and Somerset," said Mr Ponsonby waving his long stick around. "The population is relatively stable and traffic problems are not acute. Your recommendations should therefore apply for many years to come."

"I see you have marked out the major road network," I commented. "Have you managed to obtain the journey times along each link?"

"Yes, we have them all for you," responded Mr Ponsonby with a smile.

"Were these journey times affected by the time of day?" asked Hyman voicing one of his pet hobby horses.

"Indeed they were, especially in the town centre," responded Mr Ponsonby, "and, as requested by Mr Fry, we have averaged them by weighting them by the number of appliance journeys made during those periods." Mr Ponsonby paused and with a broad smile added. "We would not like this to be widely known, but in the course of doing this study we found several quicker routes from our existing stations to various locations than those we had been using."

"That *is* nice to know." Hyman was delighted.

"I see you have marked 15 road junctions on the map with a circle," I continued quickly. "How many feasible station sites are there and where are they?"

Mr Ponsonby took hold of his stick and pointed. "There are 19 feasible sites altogether which the CFO has been assured are available. They are each marked with a star with a number in each star, giving the site number. We have chosen the routes from each of these 19 sites to each of the 15 road junctions and obtained the journey time in each instance."

"Excellent," said I, realising we would not need to use our quickest route computer program after all. The brigade had done the job for us. "Now all we have to do is determine the frequency of fires and special service calls in each square kilometre," I continued, aware the officers had enjoyed themselves working on the project.

"We are providing you with those too!" Mr Ponsonby almost chortled, standing up straight and proud. His officers had broad grins on their faces.

As we continued our discussions Hyman and I were quite overwhelmed by the keenness of the Bristol Fire Brigade officers. All the data Jimmy Fry had requested had been provided and the Fire Brigade team had even taken the initiative in producing the tabulations we had expected to have to work on ourselves. Everyone was very happy as we were taken into the Officers' Mess for drinks before partaking of an excellent lunch. The Chief Fire Officer, Bill Holland, resplendent in uniform, joined us in the Mess and proposed a toast to the success of our joint project. Everyone joined in with enthusiasm.

⚜

Hyman and I set to work coding the Bristol Fire Brigade data and writing computer programs.

Early one morning he burst into my office with the results. Fortunately Jennifer was on holiday.

"10,740 journeys were made to 6,813 fires, not including the fires confined to chimneys, railway embankments, grassland and heathland," he announced. "This was over a seven year period in an area covered by six fire stations."

I made some rapid calculations. "On the face of it, Bristol Fire Brigade does not appear to be very busy," I remarked. "That's 1,138 fires a year per station, or just over three a week."

"Yes, it doesn't sound bad when you consider the size of the brigade area," agreed Hyman, "but in fact, except for a patch around the Avonmouth docks, the fires are concentrated in the heart of the brigade area – in the city centre. Look at these figures here, showing the fire frequencies in each square kilometre." And he plonked a paper down on my desk in front of me.

"Well," I said, "it seems obvious from that that the city centre should be covered by at least one station. I shall be interested to get the results. Now let's construct the sub-areas and check whether there has been any change in the pattern of fire incidence."

Together we worked on Mr Ponsonby's huge map which was hanging on my office wall. Then Hyman rushed off to put the fire data for each sub-area through the computer, using a program which checked for differences in the pattern of fire incidence.

Within half an hour he was back. "There has been no significant change in the pattern of fire incidence in the seven year period," he announced.

"Good," I said, "that makes our lives easier; as we can now assume that our results will be valid for a considerable period ahead. No major redevelopment is planned for Bristol, according to Mr Ponsonby."

So Hyman and I settled to our task with enthusiasm. By lunch time we had succeeded in preparing all the data and were ready for the computer run.

After lunch, we stayed on in the computer room while Iris fed the station siting program through the terminal. I had written this one myself and validated it against test data, but this was the first time it was being used in earnest. My heart pounded as I waited for the results. Even at this late stage the program could fail. There was always the possibility that some small part of it had slipped through unchecked.

The tension was very real. I looked out of the window; Iris got the printer ready; Hyman inspected the geraniums on the window sills one by one. The Atlas was a time sharing computer and would not produce any results until the run was complete – then, they would arrive all in one batch. The three of us began to fidget as we waited. Normally we would have got on with other tasks, but this particular run was special. And we all knew it.

The waiting seemed an age, although it was only minutes.

"The County Borough of Bristol covers 111 square kilometres, but the area served by Bristol Fire Brigade is approximately 200 square kilometres," I explained nervously to Iris. "We do not know how many stations should be chosen to cover this area from the 19 sites available to us. We are looking at how much the total attendance time to fires decreases as the number of stations increases."

The phone rang at last. It was the operator, wanting to know if we were ready.

"Yes," replied Iris.

Then the printer began to move.

Hyman and I stood over it as it banged out the findings, a line at a time. There was the result for just one station covering the brigade area – site 1.

"That's the new central site CFO Holland wants," I remarked.

The result for two stations covering the area followed – site 1 and site 12.

"Twelve is the best site to cover the whole of the north of the brigade area," said Hyman.

I was following the print-out avidly. "The third site is 16; that covers the east," I said, "and with four stations we have had a swap! Site 1 is replaced by sites 7 and 5."

"Isn't site 7 the brigade's present central station?" asked Hyman.

"Yes, it is," I agreed, "and 5 covers the south."

The printer stopped; all the results were through but Hyman and I had not been able to keep up.

Iris detached the paper and handed it over.

"Thanks a lot, Iris," I said. "Hyman and I had better go and study these. I've a feeling that Bill Holland is not going to be all that pleased."

Back in my office, Hyman and I found the result for five stations.

"Another swap," I remarked. "Site 12 is replaced by sites 2 and 3."

Hyman looked at the map. "Site 2 is their present northern station just slightly east of site 12; and site 3 is their present station covering Avonmouth docks in the north west," he told me.

I could hardly bear to look at the computer print-out. The moment of truth had arrived.

"Now we come to the six stations result," I said at last. "That's how many they have at present – and which Mr Ponsonby has numbered 2, 3, 4, 5, 6 and 7. But the computer says … 2, 3, 5, 7, 16 and 17."

Hyman checked these on the map. "Well, 16 is not very far east of 6 … and 17 is another central site, about two kilometres north west of 7!"

We continued methodically to work through the whole list; but we had both come to the same conclusion.

Hyman voiced it first. "It looks as though the city centre is not being properly covered at present."

"My feeling exactly," I agreed. "Even though many of the possible sites are very close substitutes for existing ones, the need for another station in the town centre is coming over loud and clear."

"But I thought you said," queried Hyman, "that all nodes on the major road network were to be considered as possible sites?"

"It doesn't fit in with their plans, I fear," I told him. "Though in any future study that's what I'll try to achieve."

"So why not rerun the Bristol study with a new set of sites?"

"I'd love to, Hyman, but then the fat really would be in the fire. After all, Bill Holland hasn't got the result he wanted as it is. This need for a new central station is pretty radical."

Hyman thought about this for a moment and then remarked. "Strange that CFO Holland should have overlooked that, in a way. But then, I suppose, we all make mistakes; even the man on the ground."

I nodded. "Let's hope he's not too committed to his own findings," I said. "After all, he did volunteer his brigade for the study."

∞✳∞

Jimmy Fry had restrained his curiosity as long as he could. He had heard our excited voices through the wall, and hoped that I would bring the results to him; but when I did not, he popped in to see me the following morning.

"Good morning, Jane," he said. "How's the Bristol study going?"

He turned a chair round and took a seat in his usual manner.

"Good morning, sir," I responded – I could never bring myself to call him by his Christian name. "The results came through yesterday."

"And what are the main conclusions?"

I suspected that he already had a good idea as to that; presumably he wanted to hear it from the horse's mouth.

"It would appear," I told him, as neutrally as I could, "that six stations covering the brigade area is about right, but that at present there is insufficient cover in the town centre. A second central station is required."

He nodded sagely. "I understand that CFO Holland has plans to replace his existing central station with a larger one nearby." This was a prompt for me.

"Unfortunately, that would be a bad move. The existing central station is included in the solution whereas the planned station is not." I paused before continuing. "But I rather think that CFO Holland might be committed to moving his central station regardless."

"Really!" Jimmy was not pleased. He got off his chair and went over to the map for a closer inspection. "This may be a pilot study," he muttered, "but I would have thought that the results provided us with some useful pointers which even Chief Fire Officers might care to note."

He stood for some time before the map, but his attention was no longer concentrated on it. At length he turned, came over to my desk, and leaned on it.

"Jane," he said slowly, "I want your first report to be aimed at Chief Fire Officers. The technical report can follow later, and be submitted for publication to the Operational Research Quarterly."

"Very well, sir," I said.

I had never seen him look so cross. He tried to smile as he left the room.

CHAPTER SEVEN

'SECRET' LETTER FROM THE HOME OFFICE

It was the week before Easter 1966. *The Siting of Fire Stations in Bristol* draft report had been sent to CFO Holland for his comments. When they came they were very bland.

"That's okay then," said Jimmy to me. "You can go ahead with the reproduction; would you bring me the distribution list, please?"

I went and got it.

"Good," he said as he signed the distribution list. "It's nice to see all the Chief Fire Officers down for circulation." He handed the list back to me with a broad smile on his face and a twinkle in his eye. "By the way, Jane, I shall be taking leave all next week. I'm having a long Easter break."

The trolley arrived in the corridor outside our offices. Jenny and I collected a cup of coffee and a bun each and headed for Hyman and Michael's large office. It was good for the team's morale to compare notes regularly and we had got into the habit of having our coffee together.

Hyman was on his own reading a report and drinking his coffee. He looked up with a happy smile as we came in. We were closely followed by Michael who was in a state of agitation. He held up a letter with a finger to his lips, warning us not to speak. I took the letter from Michael as he rushed off to get his coffee and bun before the trolley disappeared.

I waited for Michael to return before looking at the letter. Hyman and Jenny gathered around me to get a sight of the letter's contents. On Michael's return I unfolded the letter and laid it on the table in front of us beside the windows.

The word 'SECRET' leapt out at us. It was stamped on the top and bottom of the letter, in big, bold, red capitals. I could feel adrenalin flowing through me. The letter was from David Lessing, the Assistant Secretary in the Fire Department at the Home Office.

We all stooped in a huddle to read the contents of the letter. Certain words and phrases stood out. "… Fire Cover … responsibility … Secretary of State … Home Office …. Siting of fire stations in Bristol … pilot study …. Standards of fire cover …. His wish … report shelved."

Jenny, Hyman and I looked at each other in horror as Michael picked the letter up and fled with it out of the door.

"What did you do with the letter?" I whispered to Michael on his return.

"I took it back to Registry and returned it to its file." Michael held his head down and his whisper could only just be heard by the three of us gathered as close as possible around him. "The file is marked 'SECRET' and only the Director and his secretary are allowed access to it."

"Dennis Lawson must have already seen the letter," I concluded also in a whisper. "He opens all the post himself, first thing in the morning. He must have sent the letter to Registry for filing. … By the way, how did you come to see it?"

"Oh, I was just mooching around, in my usual fashion, having a chat with the chaps in Registry," responded Michael airily.

"Dennis must have already seen the letter," I said aloud to no one in particular. I was alone in my office. "He opens all the mail himself, first thing in the morning. And he sent a 'SECRET' letter to Registry for filing! … What is it that he wants me to do?"

I decided to do some investigating. I went down to reception, and asked to see a copy of the Easter leave list.

"As I thought." My eyes gleamed as I perused the list. "The Director *and* Grey Silversides are both out, *as well as* Jimmy. That gives me the responsibility over the Easter week – or rather Monday to Thursday morning."

I mounted the stairs back to my office. There sat the report *The Siting of Fire Stations in Bristol*, beautifully typed and ready for reproduction in my in-tray. I added the signed distribution list to it and slid it into a folder. Then I made my way along the corridor to the back exit, down the stairs, out of the building, and across to the hut which housed the Reproduction Unit. I very rarely went there; few members of staff, other than the messengers, did.

Tom was sitting down on a high chair having his coffee break. He was surprised to see me. "Good morning, Mrs Hogg. What can I do for you?"

Tom ran the Reproduction Unit all on his own. There was a queue of reports on a long slatted bench awaiting his attention. On a long table bundles of completed copies were stacked up ready to be distributed.

"Tom, would you please do this report for me?" I asked holding out the folder to him.

"Certainly," Tom answered flourishing an arm. "Just put the title and author into the book."

I looked at the book which was open on the table. There were lists of titles in it, most with ticks against them. I noted that the last dozen or so titles had no ticks.

"How long will it take you to do all these?" I asked, indicating the list without ticks.

"Well, Easter is next week; so, sometime the week after."

That will never do, I thought. Then I saw a familiar title: *Computations for Series I of Tests carried out under the CIB Programme on Fires in Compartments*. It was almost at the top of the list and was an internal note, which I myself had recently completed.

"What about this one?" I asked Tom, pointing at the long title of my internal note.

"Let's see: if it goes through the photocopier, Friday afternoon, then it'll need collating and stapling … . Early Monday, I should think," he concluded.

"May I exchange it for this report *please*?" I begged. "It is *very* urgent!"

"Please yourself," said Tom who couldn't have cared less.

So I crossed out the long title of my internal note in the book, and wrote in *The Siting of Fire Stations in Bristol* instead. My internal note was removed to the end of the queue, and my report put in the empty place.

"Thank you, Tom," I said as I left his hut.

I almost danced with excitement as I made my way back to the office I shared with Jenny. Iris passed me as I went. We gave each other cheery waves.

❧

Jim was reading the newspaper, his long legs stretched out on our new long curvy sofa in brown-gold acrilan. I was sitting in a matching chair watching Sally-Ann playing with her toys on the carpeted floor. We had just had our supper and were relaxing over coffee.

I was considering the course of action I proposed to take with *The Siting of Fire Stations in Bristol* report.

"Jim, there is something I want to tell you," I began as Jim grunted, reluctant to put down the newspaper.

"The Home Office administrators want my report *The Siting of Fire Stations in Bristol* to be shelved," I continued relentlessly. Jim put the newspaper down and turned his full attention on what I was saying.

"Surely the study was approved by the Research Committee," he remarked as he sat up straight in the middle of the sofa.

"A letter marked 'SECRET' has arrived from the Home Office. It was quite clear the report is not to see the light of day."

Jim picked up his coffee cup from the table in front of him, took a sip, cogitated for a while, put the cup back on its saucer and turned to me with a quizzical look.

"So, what are you proposing to do about it?" he asked. He obviously knew me well.

"I am proposing to send the report out before I know anything, officially, about the ban."

"Good gracious! How will you get by Jimmy Fry, Grey Silversides and Dennis Lawson?" Jim had really woken up now.

"They are all on annual leave over the Easter week. I shall send the report out then. It will go to all the Chief Fire Officers."

We sat in silence for a few moments. My career was obviously at a crossroads. If I supinely did nothing, and allowed the report to be shelved, I would feel that my professional integrity had been compromised. If I sent it out, untold consequences might follow.

"I'm virtually certain," I said, after a while, "that if the report is distributed, the Station's work on fire cover will be taken over by the Home Office."

Jim sat back on the sofa and closed his eyes while he considered the implications.

"And the coders' jobs might be at risk," I continued.

Jim opened his eyes. "Why's that?"

"Because the Home Office will probably also take over the responsibility for the production of the annual fire statistics; and its Statistical Department is based at Tolworth Tower in Surbiton."

I was beginning to get upset; it was amazing how talking about a situation clarified it.

"Are you sure you're not over-reacting?" asked Jim.

"Perhaps I am," I conceded, "but not only are there inter-departmental rivalries in the Civil Service, there are also interclass rivalries. The fire cover work would give the scientists the ability to produce objective proposals on brigade establishments, organization, etcetera. This might cause problems for the administrators."

"Why?"

"Because adminisrators go through a consultative process before submitting proposals to the Minister."

"They would surely consult the scientists," Jim pointed out.

"Being presented with options based on objective criteria may cause difficulties," I explained. "The administrators' task is to reconcile conflicting interests. They may be more concerned with perceived political repercussions than with financial costs and benefits. To have the latter stated clearly may inhibit the choice of a solution which is satisfactory in their terms."

Jim frowned. "Jane," he said sternly, "your job as a scientist is to ensure that your findings are published. Freedom of speech is the font of democracy. That must take precedence."

"Those are very noble sentiments," I protested. "But if I do publish, the work will go to the Home Office and can be silenced there."

"Not if you go too."

I gasped in dismay. "But Jim, I don't want to commute! And how would I be able to look after Sally-Ann?"

"Sally-Ann's nursery is not a problem," Jim assured me. "I can manage that. If you use the Underground from Edgware I can drop you off first and pick you up last."

"You sound as if you're actually advocating it, Jim!"

"The fire cover work is important to you, you know that," he pointed out gently. "How would you feel if it were to be shelved?"

The image of Noel Halford at my first Open Day rose before my eyes. "You're right," I agreed. "I'd feel responsible for more fire deaths, for more gutted properties."

Jim pressed on. "If the work really is of value, then it's your duty to ensure its continuation."

"At whatever cost to us?" I asked.

"What do you think?" he replied.

"At whatever cost to us," I agreed.

Jim returned to his paper. It was up to me now.

That Sunday night I tossed and turned in my sleep. A premonition came to me in my dream. Bruce Rawlings will try and stop me ... Bruce Rawlings ... Bruce ... .

I woke with a start at 5.30 am. It was as if an alarm clock had gone off. What time did Sally-Ann's nursery open? 8.00 am. I had better aim for that; and I was up in a flash. I got myself and Sally-Ann dressed. We both had breakfast. I cleared up and we were on our way out of the house just as Jim was stirring.

"Have a good day," I called up to him as I left.

"Good luck," his voice followed me out.

Sally-Ann and I arrived at her nursery at 7.55 am. We sat waiting in the car until the two ladies in charge arrived. As they opened the nursery door I got Sally-Ann out of the car. She ran legs akimbo, arms spread wide, to greet them. One of the ladies took her hand. My little daughter turned and waved to me. Then they were gone, through the nursery door. As I drove away several other mothers were arriving, some in cars but mostly pushing prams and push chairs.

The Fire Research Station car park was virtually empty when I arrived. I forced myself to walk at a natural pace to the Reproduction Unit's hut. Tom was already in occupation.

"Good morning, Mrs Hogg," he greeted me as if it was the most natural thing in the world for me to turn up almost an hour before the Fire Research Station officially opened. "I'm just binding your reports. Ready in about ten minutes."

"Do you mind if I wait?"

"Not at all," and he continued with the binding while I tried to read my newspaper.

Tom's ten minutes stretched to almost twenty. Finally the reports were ready: two hundred of them in their neat green covers. One hundred and forty seven were destined for the Chief Fire Officers; the rest for those on the usual distribution list, the file, and some spares.

My profuse thanks were mingled with Tom's concern as to whether I could manage such a load on my own, as I made my way out of the door of the Reproduction Unit.

Needless to say, by the time I had crossed the open space to the main building, climbed the stairs, tottered along the corridor and practically fallen into my office, my arms were aching as though they were about to fall off. I dumped the reports on my desk and stretched my arms to relieve the cramp. *The Siting of Fire Stations in Bristol* by Jane M Hogg; I looked at the inscription with some pleasure, although I would have preferred the study to have been *The Siting of Fire Stations in Manchester*. I checked my watch. Almost 8.20 am already! Fortunately Bruce Rawlings did not come in early.

I had the franked envelopes, already addressed, waiting in my cupboard. Out they came and in the reports went, with a compliments slip attached. What a time it seemed to take, especially the sealing of the envelopes!

Before I had completed my task I had to rush down to reception and sign myself in before the 9.00 am deadline.

It was almost 9.10 am when I put the large pile of brown envelopes into the boot of my car. Driving slowly towards the back exit and Shenley Road, I waved to the latecomers. At the post office I gratefully handed the whole consignment over to the girl behind the counter. Once in the possession of the Royal Mail they were beyond recall, even by me, I thought.

Back at the Fire Research Station I decided to visit Iris. After all, I had to have an explanation for not being in my office.

"Hullo, Iris," I greeted her. "How are you today?"

Iris looked at me with her head on one side. "I saw you leave the Station just after ten past nine," she said accusingly.

Iris liked to know what was happening, and she could sense that something unusual was. I decided to oblige her.

"I was posting the reports on the siting of fire stations in Bristol," I answered.

Iris raised a questioning eyebrow.

"I was afraid that Bruce Rawlings might stop them going out," I explained.

Just at that moment the telephone rang.

I looked at Iris. "If that is Bruce Rawlings, please tell him I've just gone."

Iris picked up the telephone, and nodded at me as she heard the voice at the other end. On my way out I heard Iris saying, "Yes, Mrs Hogg was here, but she left a few moments ago."

Bruce Rawlings must have had appointments to keep because it was not until the next day that he came to tackle me in my office. By that time several Chief Fire Officers had been in touch, praising the study, and hoping for something similar in their own brigades.

"When did the report go out?" Bruce asked me.

"Yesterday," I told him.

His expression was less than happy as he left my office.

Chapter Eight

Death in the lift at the Home Office

Michael kept us well informed. Numerous Chief Fire Officers were writing to the Director requesting a siting of fire stations study in their brigade area and some were telephoning.

After the Easter holiday Dennis Lawson invited Jimmy Fry and me to an informal conference in his office. Grey Silversides was there too, and we all sat round the Director's conference table.

"The report *The Siting of Fire Stations in Bristol* has been very well received," Dennis Lawson told us sombrely. "We have had any number of requests from Chief Fire Officers for a similar study to be done in their brigade area."

We sat up straight as Dennis Lawson put on his reading spectacles and picked up a letter on the table in front of him.

"Unfortunately," Dennis Lawson continued, "the Home Office are insisting that fire cover is their provenance. Their Chief Scientist, C J Stephens, is setting up a Fire Section within his Scientific Adviser's Branch and all fire cover work will be done there."

Dennis Lawson looked round at his horrified audience.

Jimmy had a question to ask. "What is likely to happen to the production of the Annual Fire Statistics? The Home Office have always claimed ownership of the fire reports."

"The Home Office propose to put one of their Statisticians in charge," Dennis Lawson replied. "I have agreed that he be based here, at the Fire Research Station."

"This is all very unsatisfactory," grumbled Grey. Jimmy and I nodded our heads in agreement.

"However, that is the position," replied Dennis Lawson sadly. He turned to me. "Jane, the Chief Scientist wishes to see you at the Ministry of Technology's headquarters in London. Please see my secretary and arrange a suitable date."

Dennis Lawson rose indicating the meeting was over. We gathered the papers we had brought with us so hopefully, thinking we would be planning our next phase of our fire cover studies. On the way out I stopped in the Director's secretary's office and arranged a date for my meeting with the Ministry of Technology's Chief Scientist.

Jimmy was waiting for me as I emerged into the corridor, his hands in his pockets. "Have you any idea what the Chief Scientist wants to discuss with you?" he asked.

"Maybe he is going to castigate me for sending out the report on *The Siting of Fire Stations in Bristol* to all the Chief Fire Officers," I suggested. "Look at what has happened as a result."

"You must not blame yourself." Jimmy, as usual, was very supportive. "We are all responsible for the situation, from the Director downwards."

I arrived for my meeting with the Chief Scientist, Tristram Vane-Tempest, in a state of considerable trepidation and waited for some time in his secretary's office before being shown into the inner sanctum. The Chief Scientist's office was spacious and luxurious.

Tristram Vane-Tempest came from behind his large desk and shook my hand. He showed me to one of two comfortable chairs beside a coffee table.

"Would you like tea or coffee?" He asked me.

"I should like coffee, please."

He nodded to his secretary who had followed me into his office. She turned and left. We had hardly settled ourselves in our chairs and exchanged a few pleasantries before she returned with a silver salver on which stood two dainty china cups and two small china plates alongside a silver set containing coffee, milk, sugar and biscuits.

Tristram Vane-Tempest poured, handed me my cup of coffee and told me to help myself to milk, sugar and biscuits.

After a few sips of delicious coffee and bites of succulent biscuit I began to feel quite relaxed and able to join in more than adequately with the continued exchange of pleasantries.

Finally we discussed the issue of fire cover.

"You were responsible for sending out the report on *The Siting of Fire Stations in Bristol* to all the Chief Fire Officers," Tristram Vane-Tempest stated, after we were well into our discussion.

"Yes, I was," I agreed, expecting the full weight of the Chief Scientist's disapproval.

He turned towards me and looked straight into my eyes. "You will go a long way," he said.

"I hope so," I replied, trying not to show my surprise.

Back at the Fire Research Station, Jimmy Fry's Operational Research and Statistics Section was being emasculated; but he took it stoically, bearing no malice. He asked me to produce a technical report on *The Siting of Fire Stations* for the Operational Research Quarterly. Then I was to start work on two new projects, *The Feasibility of Assessing the Economic Value of Roof Ventilators in Fires* and *A Model of Fire Spread*.

I received a call from the Director's secretary asking me to come and see him in his office. There I was shown to the chair facing him across his desk.

After the usual pleasantries, Dennis Lawson leaned forward. "There is room for two Principal Scientific Officers in Jimmy's Section," he informed me, "and I would like you to accept the second post."

"Thank you very much for the offer," I replied. "May I think about it, please?"

⚜

I attended an interview with Eddie Benn, the Director at the Scientific Adviser's Branch at the Home Office. He offered me a post as a Senior Scientific Officer in the newly formed Fire Section subject to a security vetting. It would not be a promotion as I was already a Senior Scientific Officer. However I could see no long term future for me at the Fire Research Station and I badly wanted to continue with my work on fire cover.

I probably made the greatest mistake of my life when I decided to join the Scientific Adviser's Branch at the Home Office.

⚜

Jimmy Fry called me into his office. We sat down together at his conference table.

"Are you sure you would be wise to go to the Home Office?" asked Jimmy with a very worried expression on his face.

"No," I replied, "but I think it is what I ought to do. The siting of fire stations and other fire cover projects are, in my opinion, vitally important. At present, I am the only person with the experience and expertise to take them forward successfully." I paused and looked at Jimmy. He was obviously very upset and worried. "Believe me," I continued, "I don't want to go to the Home Office. I am dreading the commuting and the possible effect on Sally-Ann."

"Why then, for heaven's sake? Surely you realise the Home Office is a very negative Department?"

"Yes, but I should like to try and change that," I responded with all the naivety of youth.

"What about your work here – on fire protection and fire spread?" Jimmy was almost pleading with me now.

"I suspect that those will be done at the Home Office in any case." I was very depressed about the prospects for the Fire Research Station.

Jimmy had one final point to make. "Have you really thought this through, Jane? You know what is going on at the Home Office. You will be up against 'The System', with their garage and hotel interests… and goodness knows what else."

"Don't worry," I assured Jimmy, "I'll put a stop to it."

"That may be easier said than done," he warned, but I would not listen. I had made up my mind, trusting that good would overcome evil.

The security vetting was not coming through. Jimmy tried to find work for me as we waited for the date on which I was to join the Home Office. Finally, in desperation, I telephoned Eddie Benn. "Start on the first of April," Eddie told me. "I will ask my Administrative Officer to send you an official note confirming this."

There was a fantastic farewell party for me in the canteen at the Fire Research Station. Numerous gifts appeared. Iris and the coders gave me a lovely tea set in the very best china. I would always treasure it. Speeches were made. Grey Silversides was at his most flattering. I said how sorry I was to go, and I hoped I would return.

It was 1ˢᵗ April 1967; April's Fool Day.

It was also the day I started work at the Home Office. The irony did not escape me. It marked the commencement of the commuting which I found so ghastly; of poor Jim being tumbled out of bed long before he would choose, to get me to the station. Sally-Ann, too, must be washed and dressed, so she could start at the nursery at 8.00 am, there to remain until 6.00 at night. And Sally-Ann was just two years and seven months old.

A variety of warning and accusing voices were ready to assail my mind if I would admit them. The burden of their complaint was always the same: was I being wise?

At Edgware Station, the terminus of the Northern Line, I got out of the car and waved a goodbye kiss to Jim and to Sally-Ann.

"See you at 6.15," shouted Jim as I headed off.

I nodded dumbly; my travelling days had begun.

A train to the West End was standing at the platform, and within two minutes the doors closed and we were off. For several stops the line stayed above ground, at rooftop level sometimes, and the train rattled along, taking on crowds of passengers. Soon the seats on either side of me were filled, and I had to keep my elbows well in as I read my folded newspaper. In no time at all the aisles were filled to capacity by standing commuters. I thought of Jim, now working as a lecturer at the Watford Technical College. What a blessing that he was a teacher: when Sally-Ann started school, he would be at home with her during the holidays.

At Golders Green the train plunged into the tunnel system, and my companions read their newspapers by the cabin's electric lighting. Many were standing in the aisles now.

At Camden Town more commuters struggled to get on, squeezing the already squashed into smaller and smaller spaces. Packed like sardines, was my thought. Then gradually, as we continued southwards, the coach began to empty as the travellers reached their respective destinations.

I left the train at the Strand, where a crowded lift carried me up to street level. I found the exit and breathed in the relatively fresh air with relief. A short walk along the Strand itself brought me by way of Trafalgar Square into Whitehall. There I caught a bus which carried me down Millbank to Lambeth Bridge; where I got off.

Horseferry House was the second block on the left in Horseferry Road. A stand full of pornographic magazines was on the steps just before the entrance. That struck a jarring note as I went through the door into one of the Home Office buildings – to be stopped by a security guard.

"Your pass, please."

I got Mr Benn's Administrator Officer's note out of my handbag and showed it to the security guard. He checked with a lady sitting in a glass cubicle; she consulted a list in front of her, asked my name, and issued me with a temporary pass. A messenger in a navy blue coat arrived to escort me to the lift.

We stepped out at the fifth floor, onto a hallway with, on the left, stairs coming up towards us and then away from us to the floor above. On the right was a set of double doors, and in the opposite wall another lift shaft. The exact centre of the hall was occupied by a square cubicle in which sat an angelic-looking old man with a shock of white hair. He stepped from the cubicle, keys in hand. St Peter guarding the gates of Heaven, I thought irreverently. Taking my temporary pass from the messenger, he unlocked the door, let me and himself through, locked up again, and then led the way along a succession of corridors, interrupted at intervals by swing doors. Finally we reached a suite of offices on the right, and I was ushered into a room.

This was the secretaries' office, where sat two elderly ladies. They introduced themselves: Miss Storey, a dear old soul with kind brown eyes, worked for the Director of the Scientific Adviser's Branch; and Miss Darnley for the Chief Scientist – their desks met in the middle of the room.

The man who reminded me of St Peter gave my temporary pass to the former, and took his departure with a little bow in my direction.

"Have a seat, dear." Miss Storey beckoned me to a chair. "I'll let Mr Benn know you are here."

Miss Darnley gave me a gracious smile. "Welcome to SAB," she said. "I hope you will be happy here."

"Thank you," I replied with a weak smile.

Miss Storey reappeared. "Mr Benn will see you now. Do you take coffee or tea?"

"Coffee, please," I told her gratefully, as I stepped into an office of imposing dimensions.

Eddie Benn rose to greet me. He was a lean, dapper man with curly dark blond hair which was beginning to go grey at the sides. He was most distinguished looking and very charming. He shook hands with me before offering me a leather chair.

"Did you have a good journey?"

"Not too bad, thank you."

He laughed at my wry look. "You'll get used to it," he said. "I'm lucky. I live locally, in Vincent Square."

The coffee arrived. I helped myself to sugar and milk, and with my first sip began to feel human again.

"I'm so glad you decided to join us," Eddie went on. "We need to get our new Fire Section off to a flying start. You'll be working to Alan Weston. He's a good man; a first class mathematician. You'll be meeting him shortly, but perhaps I'd better begin by giving you the history of SAB."

Then Eddie recounted how the Branch had been set up after World War II to advise on the scientific aspects of civil defence; and to train the Civil Defence Corps on the effects of a nuclear attack and how best to combat it. In 1964, following the recommendation of a Royal Commission, the Branch had expanded into police work; but this side had grown so much that recently the staff had been split off to form the Police Scientific Research Branch. PSDB also reported to the Chief Scientist and occupied the fourth floor.

Horseferry House, Eddie continued, contained both the Administrative and Scientific staff working on Civil Defence, Police and Fire matters. It also housed the Police and Fire Inspectorates. The main Home Office building was in Whitehall; the Establishment Department was situated there. However, the Branch had an Administrative Officer who acted as the liaison officer between the Establishment Department and SAB. He would provide me with my pass, conditions of service, and so on. He was also responsible for the Registry and the Branch's accounts.

"Well, that's enough for the moment, I think, to give you a sketch of what's what," Eddie finished. He picked up his telephone and spoke to his secretary. "Please ask Alan Weston to come for Mrs Hogg; and then I will see Mr Busby."

Alan arrived and was introduced. He was a lean stooping man with a ring of short dark grey hair around a bald pate. He wore grey flannels, tweed sports jacket, and round gold-rimmed glasses. He peered short-sightedly at me as he put out a large hand. The typical absent-minded scientist, I thought, as I shook hands.

"Alan will introduce you to the rest of the staff and show you to your office," said Eddie, as he showed us out.

On our way through the secretaries' office, I saw the waiting Mr Busby, who was looking a little uncertain and anxious. I smiled at him, and he managed a small smile in return.

"Horseferry House is shaped like a figure of eight," Alan told me as he led me back along the corridor. "This is a secure area, as you will have noticed: that's because much of the civil defence work is top secret. It stretches from the Chief Scientist's office to the office you are sharing with me. A key is kept in Registry which you will have to sign for if you want to use it. Otherwise Mr Groves at the main door will let you out."

He took me to see the Administrative Officer first. He gave me my pass, leave chit, and conditions of service.

Then I had a quick tour of the offices with their inmates.

We went into the Registry. It was a large office stocked with files. The male and female staff there were cheery and full of smiles.

Another large room held the Scientific Assistants, also male and female. One young lad was very much in charge.

A series of offices followed, most of them with a single occupant, a Scientific Adviser with the rank of PSO. Just one of them held two people of lesser rank. They were all male.

During the tour, I gathered that Alan was not at all pleased about his transfer to head the new Fire Section. He was very dedicated to Civil Defence and did a lot of voluntary work as a Scientific Adviser to his local Civil Defence Corps.

The final office we reached was the one I was to share with Alan. It overlooked Dean Ryle Street and Westminster Hospital and was the last belonging to the Branch in that corridor. The corridor, indeed, continued; but a locked door prevented further access. A key hung from a nail beside it; in a small, round, glass-fronted cupboard, which was also locked.

"H M Chief Inspector of Constabulary has the suite of offices beyond," explained Alan. "The protuberance in our office is his fitted wardrobe."

I looked around. It was a standard civil service office for SSOs. Alan was a PSO.

"Eddie will be coming to the end of his chat with Don Busby so I'll take myself off," said Alan. "You'll find some reading material in your in-tray."

I was left alone. I looked out of the window at the hospital. Then I took a seat at the empty desk beside the back of HMCIC's wardrobe. It was nearer to the door. I picked up a journal from the in-tray and started to read.

Moments later the door opened. A big man came in noiselessly, his hair shining with brylcream. He gave a good imitation of Denis Compton, the cricketer.

Sitting down on the hard chair beside my desk, he said ominously, "I am the Head of Security at the Home Office. You arrived without clearance from me. Don't ever do so again."

I looked at him trying not to let my amazement show.

"I'll never do it again," I promised solemnly.

The big man, appearing satisfied with my contrite demeanour, arose, a cold expression on his face, and left as quietly as he had entered. I put my hand to my mouth to hide a smile. After all, I thought, however can I do it again?

I tried to settle to my reading. Another navy blue coated messenger came in with some more journals which she added to the heap in my in-tray. She looked upset.

"Is something wrong?" I asked sympathetically.

"Oh dear, what a thing to happen on your first day!" the messenger burst out. "Poor Mr Lessing collapsed and died in the lift on his way up to his office this morning."

I recognised the name. "Is that David Lessing – he's an Assistant Secretary in the Fire Department?" I asked.

The messenger nodded her assent.

I felt my heart sink. I did not know why.

CHAPTER NINE

GLASGOW AND SIR PHILIP ALLEN'S PARTY

The newly arrived young man called Don Busby was given an office opposite us on the other side of the corridor where our flexiwriters were set up. We had a modem to London University's Atlas computer in a near by room manned by a lady Machine Operator.

Alan called a conference of his staff. John Miles, another PSO, and Don Busby joined us in our office. John had a long face with aquiline features. He was medium built and dressed conservatively in a dark blue pin striped suit with matching waistcoat. Don was short with an honest looking face and winning smile. He wore a dark brown suit, a very white shirt with starched collar, and a dark tie; all of which went well with his dark brown eyes and hair.

Alan leaned on his elbows; he was obviously a little ill at ease.

"Eddie would like us to formulate a programme of research," he began, "and he is insistent that the key-stone of the work should be a model of fire spread."

He paused, looking at us all in turn. We nodded our agreement.

I felt sorry for Alan. It must be difficult for him, I thought, taking charge of a subject about which he knows little, while a member of his staff is the acknowledged expert in the field. I wondered how I could help him in his dilemma.

"I hear that the Fire Department has set up a committee under Sir Ronald Holroyd to undertake a wide-ranging review," I commented, trying to discover where the Home Office interest in the research programme might lie.

"That is so," agreed Alan, "but that has no bearing on our research programme."

I was taken aback.

Don interceded. "Won't we be asked to produce results for Holroyd?" he asked.

Alan laughed: it sounded cynical. "The Administrators at the Home Office are very naughty," he told us. "If they get a result from us they don't like, they've not seen or heard of it."

"They don't wish to be confused by the facts," suggested Don.

"Something like that," agreed Alan.

"What are the Scientists here for then?" I asked.

"To give them the results they do want to hear," Alan told me. "We have to proceed in the way we think best, and produce what we hope will be acceptable to them."

He bent over his notes while Don and I exchanged glances. To this philosophy we could only attempt to acclimatize ourselves, for it could not be condoned. John Miles leaned back in his chair with his hands behind his head, a small smile on his face.

"Our immediate task," continued Alan "is to undertake a station siting study for the city of Glasgow. It will be on a rather larger scale than your Bristol study, Jane, and our major problem is that the city is undergoing a radical re-development."

"Oh, wonderful!" I felt my eyes shining with excitement. "But what about Manchester? Have you heard from the Chief Fire Officer or the Chief Executive?"

John Miles spoke up with his cynical look. "I don't think you understand the Home Office yet, Jane. The request to study Glasgow came from the Scottish Home and Health Department. Anything similar emanating from an English or Welsh brigade would have to go to the Fire Department."

"And they would take their time considering it," Don was becoming cynical too.

"Or persuading the Chief Fire Officer to think again," nodded Alan. He returned to his notes.

"The Scots to our rescue," laughed Don, voicing the general view.

Alan relaxed. "John will you please fix a date with the Firemaster of Glasgow for a visit by you and Jane," he continued. "You will need to find out what their problems are and the data they are able to provide us with."

I took the hint; Alan wanted me to sketch out the basic requirements of the study.

"Well, they've told us that we need to plan for the future – the 1980s, say," I began. "Glasgow is to undergo a major re-development. That means large shifts in the population and big changes in the road network. So, from their Planning Department we need to obtain their estimates of population figures for when the redevelopment is complete, as well as the current position. In both cases, the data will have to be by each square kilometre of the National Grid."

"Why's that?" asked Alan, making a note.

"So that we can plot the future fire incidence, and discover the relationship between that and population density," I explained.

"What about the working population as distinct from the residential one?" asked John.

"Yes, that's a point," I agreed, "especially as we should be predicting fires in dwellings separately from those in other buildings."

Don made a point. "The rate of spread of fire in dwellings may well be different from those in industrial and commercial premises."

Alan looked at him with interest. "If we could incorporate the spread of fire into the Glasgow study that would please Eddie," he said. "Perhaps we could aim to minimize the extent of damage from fire."

"Actually, we could take it one stage further," I commented. "We could aim to minimize the financial loss from fire. After all, if we could predict the square footage damaged we only need an estimate of the average financial loss per square foot damaged, according to occupancy."

"What about life loss?" asked Don.

"That could be predicted in the same way," responded Alan breezily.

Don looked puzzled.

"Anyway, you and Jane can put your heads together on that one," Alan told him. "I've got enough now to draft out a research programme for Eddie to agree."

We all sat waiting to be dismissed, but Alan had thought of something else.

"A seminar is being held at the Civil Defence College in Sunningdale next month," he said after a pause. "The rest of the Branch will be there. Why don't you Jane and Don, both come too? It will enlarge your horizons and, who knows, perhaps one day you will be working on Civil Defence?"

⚘

The next morning when Alan entered our office he found Don sitting in the hard chair beside my desk.

Don greeted him cheerfully. "Hullo. We've defined a fire as one that spreads beyond the appliance of origin."

If Don expected Alan to be taken aback, he was sadly disappointed.

"Ah," Alan smiled, "you're working on a model of fire spread," and he sat down at his desk.

"It's quite simple really," I explained. "In the fire reports we are always given the final extent of damage, and from that we can see that many fires are confined to the appliance of origin. We are excluding those, on the grounds that they might never spread – if, that is, we can be certain that sensible precautions would prevent it."

Alan nodded.

"Thus we have been able to define the stages of fire spread," I continued. "A fire in stage 1 is confined to the room of origin. A fire in stage 2 has spread out of the room of origin to the floor of origin; and a fire in stage 3 has spread beyond the floor of origin."

I went on to develop these ideas in detail. Don chipped in from time to time.

Alan became very enthusiastic. He took several pieces of foolscap paper from a drawer in his desk and scribbled away busily. Don and I watched with interest as the mathematical equations flowed from his pen.

Eventually he looked up in delight. "There you are! I think that is it. A model of fire spread!"

I looked at the equations. They were a mathematical representation of what I had just been describing. But they were differential equations. I would be using difference equations.

"They should be solvable," Alan continued, "and they can then be fitted to the fire report data to obtain the estimates we need."

Don was determined to make a point. "The probability of a person at risk becoming a fire fatality can be measured in the same way," he announced. "Stage 1: people at risk. Stage 2: at least one fatality."

"Quite right." Alan got up and shook his hand. "You've got it!"

John and I flew to Glasgow from Heathrow Airport. We were met by a fireman who led us to a waiting car.

The Firemaster made us very welcome. After sherry and a meal we assembled in a conference room, together with the Brigade's most senior officers and a liaison officer. Officials from Glasgow's Planning Department and officers from Glasgow's Salvage Corps were also present.

The Firemaster gave a short introduction.

Glasgow is the third largest city in the United Kingdom with a population of 1,055 million. Its centre was to be comprehensively pulled down and rebuilt. The area affected covered roughly 30 square kilometres and housed approximately 380,000 people. This population density was to be reduced to about 250,000 when the redevelopment was complete, with the rehousing of many former residents in estates on the outskirts of the city, or in new towns such as Cumbernauld and Livingstone.

The structures which were planned to replace those that the bulldozer would sweep away, largely comprised high rise flats, well separated, and surrounded by pedestrian precincts and parks. The planned environment thus created would bear little resemblance to that which presently existed.

The Firemaster went on to point out that a vertical city would naturally pose problems in the provision of essential services. Water had to be provided in the highest flats; thought must be given to the disposal of rubbish; milk and bread deliveries had to be catered for. There was also, he continued with a slight flourish, the question of access for the emergency services; the ambulances, the fire appliances and the Salvage Corps. Obviously their needs had to be given due consideration before redevelopment took place.

John's speech came next. He described the methods we would use to find the best fire station sites to cover the brigade area. Clearly we would prefer to use the financial losses from fires and the fire brigade costs to obtain the optimal solution, and were working towards that. In the meantime we would, of necessity, use the brigade's attendance times to fires. He then went on to describe our data requirements in detail.

Glasgow's Planning Department offered to supply both present and future working and residential populations by wards. John accepted with alacrity, explaining we would have to translate these data into numbers in each square kilometre, but this was a task which SAB did frequently for Civil Defence purposes. The Planning Department would also provide maps showing the future road network with the expected speeds of travel along the various links.

Glasgow's Salvage Corps promised to add the estimated financial loss at each fire they attended to the brigade's fire report.

Discussion followed the speeches.

Later in the day John and I caught a plane back to London.

Don and I attended the seminar at the Civil Defence College. We both managed to stay awake during the lectures with considerable difficulty. We hoped fervently we would never have to work on Civil Defence matters.

To my surprise I received an invitation to a party being given by the Permanent Under Secretary of State. I had never met Sir Philip Allen so went to see our Administrative Officer in case there had been a mistake.

"There is nothing unusual in that invitation," the Administrative Officer assured me. "Every Permanent Secretary invites a sample of staff from all grades to one of his parties. You just happen to have been picked at random this time."

The party was held in the main Whitehall building one Friday evening. I presented my pass at the door, and after the usual check I was admitted. A messenger took me along a wide high-vaulted corridor, up a graciously curved stairway to the next floor. I followed the messenger along another corridor very similar to the one on the ground floor, with large windows in the outer wall, and ornate doors set at intervals opposite them.

I was ushered through one of these doors and found myself in a large room with high ceilings, elaborately and expensively furnished, with a fire burning brightly at the far end. Sir Philip Allen was standing close to the fire with a glass in his hand. Various officials were gathered around him. Elsewhere in the room more officials were standing about in desultory groups holding glasses or paper plates with cocktail savouries and sweets on them.

One of these officials detached himself from his group, took charge of me and propelled me over to Sir Philip Allen to be introduced.

"How do you like life at the Home Office?" Sir Philip asked, almost in a drawl.

I was truthful. "Not much," I told him.

"Why not?" Sir Philip sounded vaguely curious.

I searched for an appropriate answer which would be both truthful and not give offence. "There appears to be a lack of sincerity, a lack of openness about the place," I finally managed. "Everything is grey, nothing is black and white. Even when the sun shines it does not seem to penetrate the gloom."

Sir Philip smiled a small tight-lipped smile. He was a pale balding man of medium height, wearing horn rimmed spectacles. He would not have been noticed in a crowd. "However, you would regard yourself as amenable to discussion," he suggested softly.

"I would hope so," I confirmed.

A big man drifted up and began to talk to Sir Philip as if I did not exist. I lingered a moment and then, feeling a sense of dismissal, moved over to a cloth-covered trestle table loaded with glasses of wine and cocktail snacks. I looked about me. There was no one present I knew.

A very attractive young man, slightly older than me, detached himself from his group and joined me. He was Gordon Renton, a Principal in G1 Division of the Fire Department. Three G Divisions made up the Fire Department, and G1 Division had recently taken on the responsibility of liaising with SAB on the Home Office's Fire Research Programme.

Gordon Renton found me a glass of wine as I helped myself to a plate of savouries. "Your health," he said, raising his glass.

I echoed him. Gordon Renton was very polite, very gallant and showed commendable knowledge and enthusiasm for the Fire Research Programme.

"What would you do if a site chosen for a fire station turns out not to be available after all?" he asked at one point.

"If a chosen fire station is found to be unavailable we would remove it from the set of feasible sites and rerun the computer program," I told him. "That station's unavailability could easily affect the choice of other stations."

Then came the speeches; first those from Sir Philip's Department Heads; then came his reply, with his reminiscences. A toast was drunk and the guests began to disperse.

Gordon Renton turned to me. "Have you your diary with you?" he asked.

I answered in the affirmative.

"Take a telephone number will you!" The request was authoritative.

I drew my diary out of my handbag rather reluctantly and opened it at a back page marked 'Notes'. The number had a London code, but it was not far from Hemel Hempstead. I wrote it down.

Gordon Renton said, "That is my private number. I understand that you are amenable to discussion."

I smiled and nodded before making my departure in some haste, not even stopping to thank Sir Philip for his hospitality.

I never did make that telephone call.

⚒

Don and I were in his office discussing Sir Philip Allen's party while we had our morning coffee.

Don went to wash up the mugs which I settled down to work on one of the flexiwriters. On his return he picked up several sheets of joined and folded paper which contained his latest computer output, and brought them over to me.

"In all the excitement," he said, "I forgot to mention that we can run the siting program for Glasgow today. All the data are ready."

I smiled with pleasure. "That's fine, Don. I knew we already had the journey times, so these must be the predicted fires for each square kilometre."

"That's right," he confirmed.

"I think we agree that prediction of fire incidence is the main difference between this study and the Bristol one," I went on. "So what are the important features here?"

"Well," he said, "to begin with fires in dwellings. As we'd expect, these are highly correlated, in a square kilometre in Glasgow, with the residential population - in other words, the more people there are, the more fires there will be - but an interesting fact emerges. The incidence of outbreaks increases more than proportionately the denser the population becomes."

My concentration became intense. "That *is* important," I enthused. "And I suppose the greater the working population in a square kilometre, the higher is the incidence of fires in dwellings?"

"How did you know that?" Don looked surprised.

I laughed. "If more space is given up to industrial and commercial areas, there's less room for people to live in that square kilometre, and so the dwellings tend to be more crowded," I explained. "And crowding leads to an increased risk of accidents. Agreed?"

Don nodded. "I suppose it is obvious really when you think about it," he said.

"Right! Now let's have the results for non-dwelling fires." I was feeling excited.

"These are interesting too," Don continued. "Fires occur in these areas according to the density of the working population: that's straightforward enough. Strangely, though, these fires are almost equally likely to be caused by the residential population."

"Ah! So to get an accurate prediction of fire incidence in non-dwellings, it is essential to know both the numbers of workers and the numbers of residents in the square kilometre."

Don nodded again; and went on to describe the values of the correlation coefficients in detail.

I summed up. "So we shall need more data before we can make an accurate prediction of the frequency of fires in commercial and industrial premises," I said. "But, overall, the conclusion we are steering towards, must be that, in the redevelopment scheme working areas as far as is practicable should be separated from residential ones. Would that fit your reading of the facts?"

"It would indeed," agreed Don. "And it follows from these results that the computer program will ensure that the proposed stations are sited where the population is most densely concentrated."

A messenger arrived with several items for Don's in-tray. Seeing me, she pulled out a letter addressed to me, and handed it to me with a large smile.

"A letter from the United States of America," she announced.

I took it. "Thank you," I smiled back at her.

It was from the National Academy of Sciences in Washington DC. They had seen my paper on the *Siting of Fire Stations* in the latest Operational Research Quarterly, and were inviting me to contribute to the proceedings of a symposium to be held at the end of October, on the *Needs of the Fire Services*.

"That is fantastic!" I exclaimed as I showed the letter to Don. "I'll talk to them about the deployment of the Fire Services in Glasgow in 1980."

Later in the day I left Don's office and returned to the one I shared with Alan. I told him about the invitation from the National Academy of Sciences in Washington DC and showed him the letter.

"That's splendid," said. Alan. "That will give us more power to our elbow. Please write out a formal request for permission to accept, and let me have it."

"What happens then?" I asked.

"I write a covering note supporting your application and pass it on to Eddie," Alan told me. "Eddie does the same and passes it on to the Assistant Under Secretary of State at the Establishment Department. The AUSS agrees it, which means you can charge all your expenses to the Finance Branch."

"Do you know, I was so excited about the invitation I forgot all about the expense," I said. "I think I'd have been quite happy to pay all my expenses myself."

"Oh no," exclaimed Alan, "you can't do that. You can go only if you get official approval. If you get that, then you also get your expenses paid. By the way," he continued, "what will you talk about?"

"The deployment of the Fire Services in Glasgow in 1980."

"Ah, those results are through then?"

I pushed my hair back from my brow. "In so far as is possible without cost and loss data," I replied. "Glasgow has 28 pumps at present, so we have come up with a configuration of station sites which minimises the appliance journey times to fires when there are 28 pumps in operation."

"How many stations does that give Glasgow?"

"Twenty-two," I replied, "but I would recommend some merging of closely clustered ones in order to economise on station costs. That would reduce the final figure to only seventeen."

Alan grunted. "It's a pity we can't be more definitive," he muttered.

"We need the fire brigade costs and the losses from fire damage for that to be possible," I replied. "I should have the direct losses in relation to the fire brigade's attendance time by next spring, or the summer at the latest – but there are still the consequential losses to be estimated."

"Oh, that's something I forgot to mention," Alan exclaimed. "I have put out a contract to the Economic Intelligence Unit. They'll be handling those estimates."

"And when are they likely to report?"

"The year after next, I fear."

I sighed. "So in the meantime Glasgow will have to make do with the results based on appliance journey times," I said.

❧

A few days later Alan returned from a meeting with Eddie.

"Bad news, I'm afraid, Jane," he said as he handed me a memorandum.

It was from the AUSS, Establishment Department, to Eddie Benn, Director of the Scientific Adviser's Branch. There were insufficient funds in the Travelling and Expenses Account, it announced, to send Mrs Hogg to the Symposium in Washington DC.

"Does this mean I have to pay my own expenses?" I asked.

"No, I am sorry," replied Alan. "It means you cannot go at all. You will have to write to the National Academy of Sciences declining their kind invitation."

I felt like a wounded animal. The pain of having to turn down such a prestigious invitation seemed to sear into my soul. I let my head droop so that Alan would not be able to see the tears that had sprung involuntarily into my eyes. I found my handkerchief and blew my nose.

"Okay," I said, "I'll write after lunch. Now let's go and drown my sorrows."

I typed the letter myself on a machine in the office. I would not be attending the Symposium, I wrote, and I gave the reason - the British Home Office was unable to find the funds necessary to meet my travelling expenses.

I was so dispirited when the task was done that I did not feel like doing any work for the rest of the afternoon, and went home early. Don was quietly sympathetic.

Several days later, by return of post, came another letter from the United States of America. This time the National Academy of Sciences had enclosed a cheque to cover my expenses.

In my excitement I went straight to see Eddie, bypassing Alan. I handed him the cheque and the covering letter.

"May I go?" I asked.

Eddie smiled. "Yes, of course," he replied

"What about the AUSS, Establishment Department?" I persisted.

Eddie's smile grew broader. "His only objection was that there were insufficient funds. Now that funds are available there can be no further objection. I'll let the Establishment Department know the position. You may reply to the National Academy of Sciences in the affirmative."

I rose. "Thank you, sir," I said, and left his office with a bouncing step.

CHAPTER TEN

A BOMB SHATTERS JANE'S OFFICE

It was a beautiful summer's day.

The sunlight streamed through the windows of the train as it jogged along on its familiar route. At each stop cheerful passengers entered, the women in pretty summer outfits. Everyone seemed to be smiling. Such a change, so refreshing, I thought: it seemed odd in a way to be going in to work. Then, as usual, the train dipped underground and the passengers were plunged into the gloom of the carriage's electric light. With a sigh, I turned to my newspaper, neglected until then. Stations passed and people crowded on, but I was virtually oblivious to all that after a year's commuting.

At Euston, forcing my way through the standing travellers, I all but fell out of the door as I met the incoming throng of passengers trying to enter. From the platform I was borne along up the stairs, along a corridor, up an escalator, along more corridors, up another escalator to the underground ticket concourse; through the gates, showing my season ticket, along to another escalator, up to the main station concourse at ground level. I made for the swing doors at the front of the station which led to a bus terminal, and beyond that, through a small park onto Euston Road.

I breathed in the fresh air in gulps. How lovely to be out in the open again, and with the sun still shining!

It was pleasant too, to be able to vary my routine on such a day, though the reason for the change was more irksome. The 'Fire Spread Model' program was completely written at last, but it was very big, and it would take me some time to debug it. The Scientific Adviser's Branch had not got a lineprinter attached to the Branch's computer terminal and, as it was impracticable to bring the output back over the terminal in the form of paper tape and then through the flexiwriter, I had arranged for it to be printed on London University's lineprinter. I was now on my way to collect it. It was the first time I had done so, but it was clear that this was going to become a regular trip.

The Computer Services building comprised two terraced houses half way along on the left of Gordon Square. I entered with a light step. A computer operator found the print-out and handed it to me.

"Is there somewhere I can go to study this?" I asked.

"Yes, up the stairs to the first floor, turn right along the corridor and you'll see a door marked 'Computing Services' on your left."

I followed his instructions and found myself in a large room equipped with several tables and flexiwriters where I could do my debugging and prepare a corrected paper tape input. This *is* useful, I thought, I'll be able to put in another run before going to the office; and I settled down to work.

At about the same time, Don was parking his motor bike as usual in the basement of Horseferry House. He took the lift to the fifth floor, where Mr Groves let him through the double doors with a nod and a smile. Then on to the Registry, to pick up the key for the swing door; and so on to his office and terminal room.

He collected the fire loss data he was working on for the Glasgow study and carried it through to Alan and Jane's office. No Jane today and Alan invariably came in late; so he carried it back to his office.

Now for that badly needed cup of coffee, he thought – a thought, incidentally, which regularly occurred to one or other of us, before any serious work could be done. The ritual necessitated collecting the kettle, unlocking the swing door, passing through it and locking it again, then tramping up the long corridor to the main hall and the 'gents' where a drinking water tap was to be found. On the return journey the same procedure was repeated in reverse.

And so it happened that Don was engaged in locking the swing door on the way back, at the very instant when the door of my office was flung the wrong way through the aperture into the corridor behind him. The next moment he felt himself lifted off his feet by a giant force and crashed down again into the swing door, which itself gave way and flew several yards down the corridor. The floor rose to meet him, there was a roaring in his ears, and for a while he knew no more.

It could only have been a second or two later when he was aware of the sound of running feet and shouts, while somewhere at a distance shattered glass was tinkling down. He felt himself being turned over, and opened his eyes to see the worried faces of clerks from Registry bending over him.

"Are you all right?" they seemed to be saying in unison.

He struggled to sit up. The corridor in front of the office was covered in glass smithereens; the kettle was on its side, the lid off, the water flowing amongst the glass.

"What happened?" He felt dazed and shaky.

"An explosion of some sort," one of the COs replied. "We think a bomb went off in a car parked in the street."

The security men were next on the scene. They took in the damage at a glance. The office I shared with Alan was littered with glass, the furniture tossed about, but there were no papers amongst the mess. All papers, including the contents of our in-trays, were locked away each evening.

They came over to Don, who had got, rather uncertainly, to his feet.

"How are you, sir?"

"Okay. I'll be okay in a moment," he replied.

"Your office is devastated. You were lucky not to be in it."

"Yes, I suppose I was; but it isn't my office," and Don found that he could put one foot in front of the other.

"Take him away and give him a cup of coffee," somebody suggested.

The Registry clerks gathered round and tried to propel Don from the scene.

"Just a minute." He backed off from them, and crunched his way through the glass into the terminal room.

There he found his briefcase and the folder containing the fire loss data on the floor, in separate places. Picking them up he finally submitted to being swept off for that long deferred, and now decidedly necessary, cup of coffee.

❦

I noticed that quite a crowd had gathered at the top of Dean Ryle Street as I passed; but I did not stop to enquire the reason.

Scarcely had I entered Horseferry House, however, when the lady receptionist said, "Your husband's been on the phone, Mrs Hogg. He wants to know if you're all right."

"Yes. I'm all right." I was perplexed. "Why?"

"A car bomb went off in the street below your office," the security guard told me. "It was on the radio."

I felt my knees begin to fold. With an effort I straightened them.

"Mr Busby?" I asked, almost in a whisper. "How is Mr Busby?"

"He's fine," the guard reassured me. "He's been looked after by the Registry clerks."

"Oh thank goodness!" I sighed, as my knees stiffened again.

A lift arrived with a clang and disgorged its passengers. Don was amongst them with his briefcase in one hand. He saw me and came over to me.

"There is no point in going up to your office," he said. "It's a shambles. Nothing but glass and broken furniture."

"How are you, Don?" I asked anxiously.

"Just a few cuts and rips in my jacket." He turned to show me.

"My God! What happened?"

"They think a bomb went off in the street under your office windows. I was just locking the swing door after filling the kettle. I flew down the corridor on my face."

"Poor face. It looks all right now."

"It is."

"Lucky you."

We ambled out, down the steps to the street, into the sunshine. Except for the group of curious bystanders at the junction with Dean Ryle Street, nothing seemed out of the ordinary.

"What shall we do now?" asked Don.

I paused. "We might as well go to LUCS. I've just come from there. But first I must phone Jim. He didn't know I was going to LUCS today. He'll be worried."

"Did anyone know you were going into LUCS?" asked Don. "I didn't."

"No," I admitted. "I only decided as I was getting ready to go home last night."

"Lucky you," mimicked Don.

"Yes, lucky me!" and I laughed slightly hysterically, as I tried not to skip down the street.

❧

Three weeks later the bomb had been forgotten. Don and I had spent a very profitable time at LUCS. Then came another bombshell. This time it was a metaphorical one. Alan Weston brought it. Alan was making a habit of bringing bombshells.

"Problems, problems," he said, as he entered the office he shared with me one morning. It was much dimmer now, as net curtains had been fixed to the windows as a precaution, to stop glass fragments flying about the room. "Jane, I'm afraid we have to move our computer operations from LUCS to Portland Place."

"Portland Place?" I echoed, feeling stupid. "But that's where the Metropolitan Police traffic tickets are processed."

"And on an ICL machine which was not designed for scientific work," put in Don in horror. Don was sitting on a chair beside my desk as we worked together on the Glasgow station siting study.

"I know, I know," said Alan, sitting down and putting his hands on his knees, "but we will have to make the best of it. I want you to start transferring the data and programs at once."

Don and I turned to look at each other in absolute amazement, while Alan got up and left.

I rushed to the door and shouted after him, "Alan, it's impossible!"

He returned and stood in the doorway. "I tell you what," he said, "conduct an experiment. Take your 'Fire Spread Model' program, and some of the associated data programs, and see how you get on," and he turned on his heel and walked swiftly away.

I turned to Don. "Let's go for lunch and work out how to crack this one."

❦

Mr Ramsbotham, who was in charge of the Joint Automatic Data Processing Unit (JADPU) at Portland Place, was very helpful; too helpful. His staff would type up the 'Fire Spread Model' program, he assured me, and transfer the data on magnetic tape at LUCS onto magnetic tape at Portland Place. They were, of course, working under considerable pressure, and the traffic tickets took priority.

Three weeks later, Mr Ramsbotham telephoned. "Your tapes are ready," he told me. "How's that for speed?"

"Very good," said I dryly, secretly totally unimpressed. "When can we get a run?"

"At night," he said. "The traffic tickets must be processed during the day."

I stifled a growl. "Okay, Mr Busby and I will come in first thing in the morning, if that's all right."

"I look forward to seeing you," and Mr Ramsbotham rang off.

We were at the Portland Place building as soon as it opened at 9.00 am the next morning, and received our printed output and our rolls of paper tape from a charming red haired lady.

There were masses of mistakes, which was not surprising with so much to type up; by someone unfamiliar with the programs. The lady showed Don and I to two flexiwriters. We sat down side by side. We found the first mistakes and began to type up new pieces of paper tape. These came out all wrong.

"The keyboard is different!" I exclaimed.

Mr Ramsbotham had arrived, silently, and was standing behind me looking over my shoulder. "Yes," he agreed, "we had these flexiwriters designed especially for us; and our girls are trained to use them."

I got to my feet. "Good morning, Mr Ramsbotham."

"Good morning to you, Mrs Hogg, and to you, Mr Busby." Mr Ramsbotham bowed slightly. "If you give your work to Mrs Deignton, she will ask the girls to fit it in between the traffic tickets."

"We would rather do it ourselves, thank you," I told him.

"As you wish." Mr Ramsbotham seemed disappointed. He bowed again, ever so slightly, and glided away.

Don and I returned to the flexiwriters, gave up our touch typing and ploddingly searched out every key in turn. Patiently we made up new bits of tape, removed the faulty bits, and spliced in the new ones. This took all morning, with Don helping me with the huge 'Fire Spread Model'.

Finally the tapes were completed. Heaving sighs of relief, we took the tapes to Mrs Deignton, the charming lady with the lovely long red hair.

Mrs Deignton looked at the tapes in horror. "I'm afraid that no splices are allowed," she said. "The whole tape will need to be recopied."

I was flabbergasted. I heard a stifled epithet from Don behind me. There were yards and yards of the tape. Slowly I unrolled it, letting it spill onto the floor. Then, with great deliberation, I picked it up and tore it. I did this several times, leaving the tape a useless heap on the floor.

Mr Ramsbotham arrived on his silent feet and flung his hand up in horror.

I turned to face him. "The Home Office can sack me if it likes," I announced to him and to the array of startled faces, "but I am not going to use your services; not now, not ever!"

As if in slow motion I picked my way past the wrecked tape on the floor, out of the room, and out of the building, into the street. Don followed behind, like a shadow. Once outside, we looked at each other with sombre faces and without a word set off for LUCS. The afternoon was spent appreciating to the full the facilities there.

Strangely, no mention was ever made by anyone of the Portland Place episode. Alan Weston and Eddie Benn totally ignored it; and the LUCS bills were paid without a murmur.

CHAPTER ELEVEN

HOLROYD VERSUS THE FIRE SPREAD MODEL

Washington was wonderful. I walked the few blocks from the hotel the British Embassy had booked me into, to the venue at the National Academy of Sciences, past the White House. The morning air was more sparkling than in London, the boulevards were wide and there was a feeling of spaciousness and colonial grandeur about the buildings. The military precision with which the streets were laid out particularly impressed itself on a mind which had recently been grappling with the spider's web appearance of the Glaswegian road network.

I reached the National Academy of Sciences and was ushered through its imposing portals and the main enormous hallway to the conference room. There I joined what seemed like hundreds of strangers who sat listening as speaker after speaker enlarged on their specialised subjects. Lunch came and went, the delegates eating their meals off trays on the canteen tables.

Then it was my turn. The butterflies in my stomach cleared as I looked at the audience from the dais. It had become clear from what I had already heard that there were many differences between the respective political scenarios of the USA and the UK. I tried to give the audience a flavour of that in the United Kingdom. Then I launched into the likely fire cover problems of the Fire Service in Glasgow in the 1980s, and how they might best be solved through the deployment of manpower. I felt that my enthusiasm for my subject imparted itself to my audience and as they responded to me so I responded to them; so that the future of the City of Glasgow and its protection from fire seemed of paramount importance.

Other speakers followed, and it became clear that Federal Government money was being sought to set up a Fire Research Center; the Symposium was proving a great success.

A Rand Corporation team were attending the Symposium, and they sought me out. They took me to dinner and wined and dined me. They invited me to come to New York and work with them for a year. A job had also been lined up for Jim. We were offered joint salaries of $30,000 a year.

I was tempted. Then I thought of Sally-Ann. I doubted very much if Sally-Ann would like New York; and it would mean getting a nanny. Also, working for a contractor would involve working from 8.00 in the morning to 8.00 in the evening; which would leave no time for my family. I checked the working hours with the Rand team leader. "Yes," he agreed, "8.00 am to 8.00 is not uncommon." With reluctance I turned down Rand's offer. "Think about it with your husband," the team leader persisted. I promised him that I would.

The following evening I was on a plane back, taking off from Kennedy Airport. I thought how I would love to return to the USA, being much impressed with the hospitality and kindness of my American counterparts. Yes, it was a wonderful place, I decided, though the income disparities were huge. Even in such a short space of time I could see that.

My 'Fire Spread Model' was based on the fact that fires in buildings spread in stages. The first stage of a fire is when it is confined to the room of origin. A fire can be confined to a room for some time especially if all the doors and windows are shut. The hot gases from the fire rise to the ceiling and then fill the room from the ceiling downwards, like water filling a bath, but inverted. Eventually there is a 'flash over' as the gases are vented through a weak point. For some time after that a fire is confined to the floor of origin before spreading to be confined to the building of origin. Eventually the fire may spread beyond the building. During the final stages of its growth the fire is eating up more and more square metres of materials.

The 'Fire Spread Model' program debugging was completed just before Christmas, and Don too was ready to run his programs. These would give preliminary fire brigade costings and also preliminary estimates of direct fire losses according to the extent of damage. We went to the SAB Christmas party with light hearts. The Branch had been renamed the Scientific Advisory Branch, the double doors and swing doors were no longer locked and Mr Groves had retired.

The Branch celebrated with a cacophony of music and flashing coloured lights. The more senior staff stood around the food tables with glasses of wine in their hands attempting to hear each other above the din. Their juniors cavorted together on the cleared wooden floor of the map room.

Early in January, Don and I met at LUCS to run our programs. The 'Fire Spread Model' was using data from all relevant fires reported by the fire brigades in 1967, and the coded sample in 1963. The results were being combined with preliminary estimates of losses from fire for 1967, obtained from the Glasgow Salvage Corps. In addition, Don had seven years of data on the costs of County Borough Brigades in England and Wales, the point of his study being to estimate how the average cost per station changed as the number of stations in a brigade increased.

In effect, when the results came through, we would be able to analyse each brigade separately, and work out crudely whether it was over or under provisioned with fire stations. This could have far reaching consequences.

The output arrived. We checked that it was complete before taking the bus back to Horseferry House.

We were reinstalled in the terminal room and poring over the fruits of our labours, which had taken so long and so much effort to produce, when Alan walked in. He had a draft copy of the Holroyd report open in his hands.

"If you two can spare a moment," he began without any of the usual preliminaries, "what do you think of a statement which says there is no evidence that fires in buildings grow significantly after discovery; that they are either small or large at discovery?"

"Poppycock," replied Don impolitely. "You have only to look at a fire to see that it grows."

My response was to place part of my computer output onto a table in front of Alan. "Here are some results from the 'Fire Spread Model'," I told him. "Even before fitting the model to the data you can see that many more fires have spread beyond the room of origin at 21 minutes or more after discovery, than at 2 minutes."

Alan bent to examine the print-out. "Yes," he agreed. "I see that. By the way," he continued, taking off his spectacles and wiping them, "which category of fire is that?"

"Fires in multi-storey dwellings where there was no fire-fighting before the arrival of the fire brigade," I answered. "Where there was fire-fighting the fire spread is not so great," and I brought out another computer print-out and placed it on the table.

Alan got a chair, sat down, and studied these results for some time. Then I showed him the results for industrial and commercial buildings. He spent some time on these also.

"Would you like to hear what our conclusions are about fires where there are fatalities?" I asked eventually.

"Yes, indeed."

"Taking account of the average number of deaths per fire, there are roughly three fatalities for every two minutes delay in reaching the scene after the fire is discovered." I replied handing Alan the appropriate print-out.

Alan got up to go. "Let me have a note of these results, will you?" he said. "I'll show them to the Holroyd Committee."

"I would be delighted to do so," I replied.

The fire spread results were transformed into financial losses in relation to the fire brigade's attendance times, using Glasgow Salvage Corps data.

Don had already obtained estimates of fire brigade station costs. Now he used both the losses and the costs as data for a program he had written, which he had named 'Optimizing Fire Cover'.

A couple of days later he came into the office with a smile on his face.

"There appear to be too few fire stations covering the United Kingdom," he announced.

"Are you sure?" I asked, rising and following Don into the terminal room.

"Positive. Check it for yourself," and he handed me the print-out. Together we went through it minutely.

When I too was convinced that there could be no mistake, we went to Alan to convey the findings to him. Don was forthright: almost every brigade appeared to be short of cover.

Alan received the news in silence. He pursed his lips and, picking up a pencil, placed it horizontally between his two forefingers. He looked thoughtful.. After a long pause he spoke. "In complete confidence, I think I had better tell you that, as a consequence of the Holroyd report, which is due to be published next year, there will be a series of brigade amalgamations. The time to do this exercise is when these new brigades exist. Now is the wrong time."

Don and I looked at each other, shattered.

"Then why was this project on the Research Programme?" I asked pointedly.

"Er… that's a good question," he stammered.

"Well, what is the answer?" I pressed him.

"I cannot say," replied Alan. "All I can say is these results are not wanted now." And Alan left our office in a hurry.

Don made the best of it.

"It's being so cheerful wot keeps me going," he remarked.

❧

The promotion lists were up on the notice board and my name was not to be found there. I returned to my office feeling very sore.

Don arrived with two cups of coffee, one of which was for me. He sat down in Alan's chair and put his cup of coffee on Alan's desk. Alan was always late arriving for work but stayed late to make up the time.

"I am sorry to see you did not get your promotion to Principal Scientific Officer," Don said sympathetically as he put his cup to his lips.

"If I had stayed at the Fire Research Station I would have been promoted almost two years ago," I growled after sipping a badly needed mouthful of coffee. "As it is I cannot get promoted at the earliest until this time next year. That's a delay of nearly three years. It really is not good enough. I am going to resign."

I drank the rest of my coffee as I planned my letter of resignation, watched in silence by Don who was considering how the situation was likely to affect him. Then I put our office typewriter on my desk and wrote my letter of resignation, addressing it to Eddie Benn. Off I went to the secretaries' office to hand in my letter personally. Returning, I was too upset to do any work so tried to read the journals in my in tray.

That afternoon I was summoned to see the Chief Scientist, CJ Stephens.

As I entered his office, I realized to my surprise that I had never been in here before. It was a large room with good mahogany furniture and comfortable leather chairs. CJ was large too, a veritable giant of a man, with a very affable smile. Our previous exchanges had been limited to a "Good morning" or a "Good afternoon" whenever we had passed in the corridor.

As soon as I was seated, he lifted up my letter of resignation from his desk.

"I want you to take this back," he said.

"I'm sorry, sir, I cannot do that."

"Well now," and he settled back in his chair. "Have you got another job to go to?"

"No," I had to admit.

"In that case," CJ pressed me, "give us one more try."

My black mood began to lift but I was still regretting not having taken up the Rand Corporation's offer.

I said bluntly, "I should like to take a M.Sc degree in Operational Research and Management Science at the Imperial College of Science and Technology." And then, in a rush of courage, I added, "And I should like to be promoted to PSO straight away."

The Chief Scientist laughed. "I'm afraid I can't manage the latter, but I will have you granted a sabbatical year's leave of absence on full pay to take your M.Sc course," he told me. "However, you will have to promise to stay at the Home Office for two years after your return when you will have been promoted to PSO."

I was amazed. How quickly circumstances changed, I thought.

"Thank you, sir," was all I could say.

"I can tear this up then?"

I nodded my assent, and returned to my office, quite delighted.

"Well I never!" exclaimed Don when he heard my news.

Jim echoed those sentiments when he picked me up at Edgware that evening.

CHAPTER TWELVE

PETERBOROUGH & MARKET DEEPING RESULTS

I completed a draft report on the *Fire Spread Model*, and took it to Alan. As he stretched and turned over the pages, I stood sensing a negative reaction.

"I'm sorry," Alan said at last, "but this report cannot go forward at this time. Holroyd has not yet reported."

"Does that mean the Fire Department feels my report might prejudice the Holroyd Committee's findings?" I asked bitterly.

He gave me a sympathetic smile. "That should be phrased more diplomatically," he said, and returned the sheaf to me.

I stormed out of our office and into Don's. "Do you know, Don," I announced as I slammed my draft report down onto Don's desk, "I really must have been very naïve. I believed I could influence Home Office thinking by joining it."

"See no research findings, hear no research findings, speak no research findings," Don murmured, just sufficiently loudly for me to hear.

"Do you realise," I continued, as I paced up and down, "that since we have been here, and that is over two years now, the only report we have to our name is the *Planning for Fire Stations in Glasgow in 1980?*" I went and got a copy out of the cupboard. I fished something else out as well. "And this," I said, holding it up for Don to see, "is SAB Report No 1/68, dated October 1968. It was SAB's first report for 1968. That means that nothing came from the Civil Defence Section prior to October. How many reports came out of Jimmy Fry's Section at the Fire Research Station in a year? Have you any idea?"

Don blinked. "About half a dozen, I should think, not counting all the papers published by HMSO and technical journals."

I snorted. "And none of SAB's reports appear ever to have scaled those dizzy heights," I said.

I continued to pace up and down the room before stopping in front of Don's desk. "I'm thankful I'm going on the M.Sc course at Imperial College this September. It will be like a breath of fresh air. But what about you?"

Don smiled as I started to pace again. "Don't worry about me. I have my family. At work I just do what I am asked to do. It is not for the likes of me to reason why."

I stopped dead in my tracks. "That's it exactly," I exclaimed. "To reason why!"

⚜

The M.Sc course was exhilarating but extremely hard work, and the hours at College were very variable. A fellow student sold me a second hand car, which made me independent of Jim. He had become a local councillor so that, with the commuting and looking after Sally-Ann, I found that I did not have a spare moment. Except for a couple of days at Christmas I worked non-stop, all hours of the day, for eleven long months. There were compulsory subjects to take, together with a dozen voluntary ones, all of which involved considerable amounts of project work. Then came the exams, and finally the thesis – completed in August 1970.

In the middle of my course I learned that I had been promoted to PSO. It would not, however, become effective until I returned to the Home Office in September.

For my thesis I chose the title *A distribution model for an emergency service*. I had a session with my tutor about it.

"Ah! A very interesting subject," my tutor remarked. "The Americans are working on a minimax solution for their Fire Departments, did you know?"

"No," I replied. "What do they mean by a minimax solution?"

"The idea is to minimise the maximum attendance times. I think that's what you should do too."

"Why?"

"I understand the Home Office is interested in such a solution. An official was speaking to me about it on the phone the other day."

"Which official?"

"I really couldn't say."

"Well, I'm afraid that doesn't tie in with the SAB Research Programme," I explained. "The aim has always been to minimize the total cost of fire. The more fire stations there are to cover a brigade area, the higher are the brigade costs but the lower are the losses - life loss, property damage and consequential losses. The objective of my thesis is to site fire stations so that the costs of the fire brigade are more than paid for by the savings in fire losses."

"Okay, you know best," he capitulated.

As the only material I had available was that from the Glasgow study, I repeated it, minimizing the total cost of fire instead of appliance journey times.

It was a heartening experience to find that the results were very similar to those obtained in the study done for Glasgow. The 19 station solution gave the least total cost of fire at just over five million pounds a year. The 17 station solution was only £3,600 a year more costly, with the increased fire losses not being completely balanced by the lower Fire Service costs. This 17 station solution was the closest to that recommended in the earlier study. In fact, only three sites were preferred to three which had previously been recommended, the remaining 14 sites being chosen in both studies. These differences were almost entirely due to changes in the road network data.

The thesis was the last piece of work required for the M.Sc. The summer holidays were fast approaching and Jim, Sally-Ann and I were all keen to get away, but the thesis looked like holding us up. I spent hours on end hammering away at the keys of my typewriter.

As soon as I had finished, Jim whisked my thesis off to his College which had a Print Department. There it was reproduced and bound in record time; Jim returning home with six copies.

With relief, early the next morning, I travelled into London and personally handed my thesis to my tutor. By the time I returned home Jim had got the car loaded with our luggage, and Sally-Ann was dancing about in excitement. Without further ado we piled into the car and set off for Italy. We were going to my mother's home, Le Casacce, situated half way between Rome and Florence near Gubbio, up in the Umbrian hills.

I returned to the Home Office early in September. During my absence there had been a number of changes. The Chief Scientist, C J Stephens, had been early retired, SAB had been moved from the fifth floor to the seventh floor, and an internal reorganization had resulted in the new Chief Scientist being given different responsibilities and an office in the main Home Office building, now at Queen Anne's Gate. Eddie Benn had returned to the Ministry of Defence and SAB's new Director was John Culshaw who had been recruited from the Ministry of Defence Establishment at Farnborough. I was now in charge of the Fire Section, the PSOs Alan Weston and John Miles having returned to Civil Defence.

I was concerned about the departures of C J Stephens and Eddie Benn. Did they lose a metaphorical tug-of-war between the Scientists and the Administrators? I wondered.

As a PSO I was given an office of my own, with a carpet and a mirror, along with a conference table and chairs. Don Busby had been promoted to Senior Scientific Officer and was my second-in-command. He too had a large office which he shared with a recently recruited SO, Mike Mytton. Two new Scientific Officers had since joined the Fire Section and shared an office. They were Bob Barnes and Diana Morrow.

John Culshaw, the new Director, was a very amiable man who looked rather like Eddie Benn only slightly shorter and with lighter coloured hair. He was slim, of medium height and his hair was curly. John was as smartly dressed as Eddie and held himself well as all military personnel do. He arrived to see me as I was settling in, went over to the conference table and sat down. I joined him.

"I've had a project waiting for you almost the entire time you've been on your M.Sc course," he almost seemed to complain.

I wondered why Don could not have been asked to do this project, but remained silent.

"The Chief Fire Officer of Huntingdon and Peterborough has requested SAB's assistance in the siting of new stations," he continued. "There are plans for an expansion of Peterborough and the neighbouring village of Market Deeping."

"What is the extent of the expansion?" I asked.

"Apparently the city is set to increase its population from its present figure of approximately 100,000 to 200,000. Most of the new development will be around the existing city, and is intended to be completed by 1985."

"So how many stations are there at present?"

"Two," replied John Culshaw. "The headquarters, at Dogsthorpe, is a wholetime station with two pumping appliances and three special ones. The second is a retained station in the city centre, in King's Street. It has two pumping appliances." He paused and drummed his fingers on the table, frowning. After a moment his face cleared and he continued. "You see, Jane, this study area is not nearly as urbanized as Glasgow. We therefore have a choice of three manning systems to consider: wholetime, daymanned and retained. The two existing stations are to remain and all additional ones are to employ the same manning system. We will then be able to compare the respective merits of the three systems."

"But in an actual application, a mix of systems may be preferable," I pointed out. "Besides, it would only be sensible to look at the viability of the two existing stations."

John Culshaw's brow creased again. He pondered for a moment. "I should very much appreciate it if you would report as requested," he said in his most charming tone of voice. "You would be doing me a personal favour. There are political considerations which need to be taken into account."

I recalled Don's phrase. "It is not for the likes of me to reason why." I looked at John Culshaw.

"Please," he appealed to me, laying his hand on mine.

I nodded. "Okay," I agreed.

"Thanks, that's decent of you. By the way," he added, as he removed his hand, "the report is needed within two months."

"Two months!"

"You can manage that, can't you?"

"I'll try," I promised.

The Chief Fire Officer of Huntingdon and Peterborough made me very welcome. He had arranged for me to visit the Planning Department of the Peterborough Development Corporation. In effect, all the necessary data were already available. I had simply to pick them up.

"My preliminary assessment," he told me, "is that two additional wholetime stations will be required, each housing one pumping appliance and one special appliance. However, knowing that Operational Research techniques were available at the Home Office, I requested assistance from the Fire Department."

"I'm glad you did," I told him.

The data were soon to hand. They were the same as had been produced for Glasgow, except that turn-out times were required for stations according to their manning schemes. These turn-out times onto the road network were assumed to be one minute from a wholetime station, four minutes from a retained station, and two and a half minutes from a daymanned station.

By the middle of October all the computer runs on Peterborough and Market Deeping had been completed. I took the results to John Culshaw.

"The cost of a retained station is around £10,000 per year, and is much cheaper than either a daymanned or a wholetime station," I told him. "The men are employed in other occupations and are paid for each call they attend with, in addition, a small retainer. On the other hand, the turn-out time for an appliance with a retained crew is around four minutes, sometimes more, which adds considerably to the losses from fires."

John Culshaw waited politely and was all attention.

"A wholetime station costs almost £75,000 a year, the additional cost being almost entirely the men's wages and pensions; but the turn-out time is only one minute. A daymanned station costs £38,000 a year, the day-time personnel becoming retained men at night, giving an average turn-out time of around two and a half minutes."

"That sets the scene," agreed John Culshaw. "Now, how do the three types of manning compare in the Peterborough of 1985, given that the two existing stations remain?"

"That depends on the estimates for consequential losses and outdoor fires," I told him. "A conservative estimate for these is 50% of the direct losses. When these are included, daymanned stations are shown not to be viable; thus, the choice must be between wholetime and retained stations. With retained manning, the optimal number of stations is 11, at a total cost of £902,000 per year. With wholetime stations the optimal number is 5, at a total cost of £970,000 a year."

"A difference of £68,000 a year," remarked John Culshaw. "A clear demonstration of the advantages of retained manning."

"On the face of it, I would agree with you," I replied, "but there are several factors which militate against it. The first would be the difficulty of recruiting sufficient men to man the nine new retained stations. Secondly, organizational problems and administrative costs would be bound to rise as the number of stations increased. Thirdly, the fire losses would be at least £100,000 a year greater than the £687,000 estimate for wholetime stations. There is, therefore, a higher element of risk-taking involved when employing retained men rather than full-time men. Fourthly, the firefighting performance between the two manning systems is almost certain to differ; with retained manning the fires would tend to be larger at the time of arrival. The likelihood of a larger force being needed to deal with a blaze is therefore higher. Altogether, I think you would agree, a powerful argument against the cheaper system."

John Culshaw smiled. "I'm sure these points will be noted by the Fire Department," he said.

I drew in my breath; I could see that I would have to state my case again. I did so.

"Clearly," said John Culshaw when I had finished, "these are matters to be set out in your report. In the meantime let's have a look at the actual sites chosen for the two systems."

I handed him a figure showing the road network in relation to feasible station sites. John Culshaw took the computer print-out, found the chosen sites, and picked them out on the figure.

"But they are quite different for each manning system," he remarked. "That means it would not be possible to substitute one system for another at a later date, without closing old stations and building new ones."

"Yes, it's important to get it right now," I agreed," which brings me to a sensitive point." I paused.

"Which is?"

I nervously brushed my hair back from my forehead. "You will remember that there were constraints imposed on this project. These were that the two existing stations should remain, and that all additional ones should have the same manning system." I kept my eyes downcast searching for the right words. "Since it took very little additional time, I've rerun the program without these constraints, so that any site could be chosen with any manning system."

"Well, what were the results?"

"It seems certain that Dogsthorpe, the present wholetime station, should be replaced by station 4, which is northwest of Dogsthorpe on the major road network. The five station solution would then be three wholetime and two retained, at a total cost of £921,000 a year."

John Culshaw frowned at this news, and shook his head. "I'm sorry," he said, "the conditions laid down for the project included the constraint that the Dogsthorpe station should remain. This is something we will have to abide by."

"Even though the total cost will be higher by around £50,000 a year?"

"I'm afraid so." John Culshaw was apologetic. "As I believe I mentioned, there are political implications which, I am sure you will appreciate, I cannot divulge."

I wrote up the report as John Culshaw, the Director of SAB, wished. It was released later that year. The day a copy arrived on his desk John Culshaw called me into his office.

"Thank you for your cooperation." He waved the Peterborough report at me and smiled. "Thank you also for getting it out on time."

"That is my pleasure," I replied politely. However I was unhappy. I had compromised myself by putting my name to the recommendations in the Peterborough report.

CHAPTER THIRTEEN

JOHN CLAYTON OFFERS
JANE A SECOND INCOME

John Culshaw was an excellent and enthusiastic Director of the Scientific Advisory Branch. A Criminal Justice System Section was added and Immigration was added to my responsibilities. The computer facilities were upgraded so that all we required were in-house. A Deputy Director post was added and we were all very sad when our own colleague was not successful; the Deputy Director post going instead to another Ministry of Defence scientist, also from Farnborough. The new Deputy Director was John Clayton.

The Fire Section flourished. The Research Programme was expanded, and a large budget was provided for extra-mural expenditure on projects of all kinds. In addition, the Fire Department set up a Committee, chaired by an Assistant Secretary, to determine data requirements for fire research, both at the Home Office and the newly created Department of the Environment (of which the Fire Research Station was part).

My *Fire Spread Model* report was published and my thesis was reprinted, both as SAB reports; and others followed, the most important being *Losses in relation to the Fire Brigade's Attendance Time*. (Sir Ronald Holroyd's report had been shelved).

Much of my time was taken up with attending meetings, advising on technical matters, and on administration so that I had to delegate a lot of the supervision of staff to Don. He was in his element, really enjoying his work, and the team were happy and enthusiastic. The year 1971 passed very productively with the Economic Intelligence Unit reporting on *Consequential Losses from Fire* in December.

⟡

We moved house to Highclere Drive on the Longdean Park estate in Hemel Hempstead. It was a large four bedroom house on three quarters of an acre of land; and we all loved it.

It had been hard to decide to leave our home in The Wayside, Leverstock Green but Mrs Barbara Watts had decided to go out to work. We were also concerned about Sally-Ann's schooling and wanted to live close to a good school, and Longdean School had a good reputation.

We were very lucky to get Mrs Joyce Keeble to look after our home for us. Mrs Keeble's husband Mick was a British Telecom engineer and would often help us with our electricity problems.

Sally-Ann had been to swimming lessons every Saturday since just before her ninth birthday. She had begun going when a friend of hers had taken her along to the Cavendish School pool where a dedicated coach taught the children. Sally-Ann's friend soon stopped her swimming lessons but Sally-Ann was keen and stayed on to become one of the coach's star pupils. I sat up in the balcony watching progress and chatting with the other mothers.

One Saturday, at the end of the lesson, the coach came up to see me.

"So much talent is being wasted," he told me. "Sally-Ann should join a swimming club and take up training."

"Do you really think so?" I asked in surprise.

"Definitely," the coach was adamant.

Sally-Ann joined the Hemel Hempstead Swimming Club and took part in the training sessions with relish. She swam up and down the lanes as if she could go on for ever. After some weeks it was clear that Sally-Ann had a very strong kick, easily outstripping the other swimmers in her age group when training on legs only. The coach selected her for club swimming galas, entering her in the butterfly and freestyle events and the relays.

Sally-Ann's school chose her to represent them in the under-twelve freestyle event for the Dacorum Schools Championships. She won, and was automatically selected to represent Dacorum at the Hertfordshire County Junior Schools Championships. They were held on a Saturday evening at Potters Bar. Jim and I drove Sally-Ann over there and sat with lots of other proud parents up in the balcony. I overheard a snatch of conversation behind me where two mothers were chatting.

"Melissa's training has been going very well lately, and she won the under-twelve freestyle at the Watford Club Championships last month."

"How do you expect Melissa to do today?"

"She should win. She has beaten all the known names on the programme. This Sally-Ann Hogg must be new. We've not seen her before."

I looked at my programme again. Sure enough, next to Sally-Ann's name was that of Melissa Hart.

Sally-Ann's race was the last but one. I watched all the events with interest but Jim was bored and fidgeted.

At last Sally-Ann lined up with five other girls of her own age. She was in lane 4, Melissa was in lane 3. The race was two lengths of the pool. I felt my stomach muscles tighten as the girls were called to their blocks.

'Bang' went the starting pistol and the swimmers were off, straightening and flying through the air to hit the water several metres into the pool. Melissa and Sally-Ann were together. Together they tore up their lanes, arms flailing, legs kicking. Together they tumble-turned as they reached the top end; together they kicked off the tiled edge and glided to the surface. As their capped heads bobbed up they were still together. Down the pool they tore in unison getting faster and faster as they went. They were into the last ten metres and there was still nothing in it! The spectators were going wild. Five metres – and they were neck and neck! The cheering increased to a roar. Two metres left, and Sally-Ann inched ahead throwing her arm forward to hit the end fractionally ahead of Melissa. Everybody was alive with excitement. Jim and I collapsed on our seats, wiping the sweat from our brows. There was no sound from the row behind. Sally-Ann's record time stood for years.

That settled it. We took Sally-Ann to the best coach in Hertfordshire. Kelvin Juba was based at Hatfield and his squad was known country wide.

The routine in our household changed overnight. Jim and I got up at 5.00 am, dressed and breakfasted. Sally-Ann came down a little later. By 5.30 am she and Jim were in the car, and by 6.00 am Sally-Ann was in the pool at Hatfield with the rest of the squad. After two hours of intensive training Sally-Ann arrived at school by 9.00 am, having breakfasted in the car on the return journey. Jim's lecture preparations and markings had never been so good.

I commuted by train from Kings Langley to Euston, followed by a spell on the Underground and a walk (or a bus if the weather was bad). By 7.30 am I would be at work in my office.

In the evening I would return home by 6.00 pm. Jim, Sally-Ann and I would have a quick meal before I took Sally-Ann off to Hatfield for her evening training session. Much of the weekend would also be spent by the poolside, with a gala or a championship on virtually every Saturday.

In the Spring of 1972 I was invited by the Commandant of the Fire Service College at Dorking to talk to the Chief and Assistant Chief Officers' course on 'Standards of Fire Cover – Is there a need for revision?' I had spoken on this subject at the College several times before.

On the journey down, my car's clutch gave out suddenly and unexpectedly at a set of traffic lights just outside Staines. I coasted the car into a ditch, pursued by an angry cacophony of horns.

The one thought in my mind was my need to get to the lecture room in time. Retrieving my briefcase, I got out of the car and tried to thumb a lift.

I was lucky; a van driver stopped at once and drove me into Staines to the first garage there. Fortunately they hired out cars. I got one immediately, leaving the keys of my own with instructions as to where it could be found, and then I was on my way again – somewhat flustered now, in a car with controls which were strange to me.

I reached the College with only minutes to spare and was ushered straight onto the platform with the usual accompaniment of the College's top brass. As always my knees felt weak with nervousness and I wondered how I would make out. I turned to face the distinguished men, all in uniform with gold braid, and waited as I was introduced by the Course Director.

I spoke from notes. Once I started to talk I found I enjoyed it, that I was in sympathy with my audience. I would expand on a theme or pass over it in response to the interest shown by my listeners.

When I had finished, questions were taken. One was from the Chief Fire Officer of Northampton and Northamptonshire: he wanted to know if I would be prepared to undertake a siting and manning study of Northampton County Borough and a part of the neighbouring county?

I was delighted, and told him he should apply to the Fire Department.

Afterwards, at the bar, partaking of sherry before lunch, I met up with that Chief Fire Officer again.

"How do you think the Fire Department will react to a request for a study?" he asked me.

"Sympathetically."

We chatted about the proposed project for several minutes. Then the Chief Fire Officer voiced a question which I realised must be in quite a few people's minds. "How do you feel about being the only woman amongst so many men?"

Momentarily I was taken aback. Until that moment the thought had never occurred to me. I looked about me. The room was full of uniformed men. There was no woman present; or rather, no other woman, I reminded myself. I laughed.

"Everyone looks the same to me," I said. "So far as I am concerned, there is a job to be done, and we are all tackling it together."

John Culshaw, the Director of the Scientific Advisory Branch at the Home Office left for the post of Director at the Ministry of Defence's establishment at Byfleet, Surrey. He had been an excellent Director and every member of staff at SAB was very sorry to see him leave us.

The Deputy Director, John Clayton, was made Acting Director. John Clayton was a large man who wore spectacles and a full grey beard with moustache. He was in his early fifties and had a very suave manner.

A few days after he moved into the Director's office, I was called in to see him. He remained seated as I entered, and beckoned me to the low armchair in front of his desk When I sat down, it was all I could do to see above the rim of the desk and focusing on his face beyond it was a considerable strain.

John Clayton asked me to take him through the Fire Research Programme. He knew very little about fire matters, and it showed. He had been in Defence for the whole of his career and was steeped in it. He was now in his early fifties. As I spoke he nodded, but at times his eyes seemed to glaze over. His questions were few and lacking in depth. I came to the end and waited. There was a long pause. John Clayton sat in his chair at his desk absolutely still.

Eventually he spoke.

"Would you like a second income?"

I froze: and then laughed.

"No, thank you," I said. "I already have a second income my husband's."

John Clayton did not look amused.

"I intend to get to the top," he said, so softly it was almost a whisper, "and nothing is going to stop me."

The atmosphere was sinister. I felt numb. The soft voice sounded again as he left his chair and came slowly round his desk into the middle of the room, beckoning me towards the door.

"And there is no point in your saying anything. I will simply deny it."

I said not a word, but smiling vacantly went through the door which John Clayton held open.

Several days later I met the new Administrative Officer, Brian Davenport, in the corridor. I tried to pass him but he barred my way.

"I hear you have a second income," he said with a wink.

"Indeed I have," I flashed back, "my husband's."

"I see." And he stepped aside, letting me pass.

I laughed the incident off, but was inwardly disturbed. Back in my office I found a letter from the Secretary of the Manchester and District Group of the Institute of Fire Engineers. It was an invitation for me to come and speak to them in May.

"Ah, Manchester!" I thought. "That is why it all started."

I cast my mind back. The vision of Noel Halford at the Open Day in November 1960 rose in front of my eyes. What was it he had said? 'Why can't you tell me how many stations and men I should have covering Manchester?'

The vision faded.

"I can, I can!" I cried, smothering all sound within me. "But I am becoming compromised. If I'm not careful, I shall betray myself and the whole Fire Service. Indeed, I have already betrayed Peterborough."

I blushed again as I thought about it. John Culshaw had been so beguiling, but he was no longer the Director.

I replied to the Manchester Group, accepting their kind invitation. This time I wrote a paper rather than deliver my talk from notes.

My final paragraph stated: "Peterborough Fire Committee adopted wholetime manning as the better choice; but in the event the optimum solution was found not to be five stations, but four, once it had been conceded that with the additional wholetime stations the present wholetime station at Dogsthorpe would not be paying for itself. Also, allowing for a mix of manning systems gives an additional retained station."

The talk was given. The die was cast. My conscience was clear at last.

◦❧◦

On my return to SAB, I was called immediately to see John Clayton. He remained seated when I entered, and did not offer me a chair.

"I shall be doing all talks on Fire in future," he told me in his soft quiet voice, "including those at the Fire Service College at Dorking."

I was left with the clear impression that my days as Head of the Fire Section were numbered.

I wondered how I was going to be eased out.

◦❧◦

There was a knock on my door and Don Busby walked in. He sat down on the chair in front of my desk, and announced, "Bad news, Jane. John Clayton is moving me to the Criminal Justice Section."

I threw my head back, shocked. "Why?"

"He claims it will help my career by widening my experience of the work in SAB."

"And what is happening to Mike Mytton?"

"Oh, he's staying put in our big office," Don told me. "He will be completing our work on 'The Optimizing of Fire Cover in the UK'."

"My God!" I cried, "I don't know what I'll do without you. We've been through so much together – both triumphs and disasters!" And I turned on the full kettle sitting on the side table in the corner of my office, along with all the necessary accoutrements. Coffee was badly needed!

Don came and sat down by my desk.

"I don't want to move. You know that."

"Actually, it is almost certainly to your advantage: and I wish you all the best."

I paused, and continued.

"To be honest with you, Don, I am very fearful for the future of the Fire Section."

CHAPTER FOURTEEN

FIRE COVER STUDIES
FOR SPECIFIC BRIGADES

John Clayton, as Acting Director, had no Senior Principal Scientific Officer to undertake the tasks of Deputy Director, and I increasingly found myself being called upon to fill this role. I was sent to the Civil Service Commission, first to shortlist recruits to the Scientific Civil Service and then to represent the Home Office on the interviewing board. I acted in a similar capacity on a Committee on Operational Research in Government chaired by a Deputy Chief Scientific Officer from the Civil Service Department. This involved going to conferences, symposia, and working party meetings both at home and abroad; and undertaking a milk round of universities. In addition there was a lot of report vetting and advisory work of a general nature. Somehow, I found time to supervise my staff in the Fire Section, and complete the report *Losses in relation to the Fire Brigade's Attendance Time,* which was published in December 1973.

Don, before he was moved, had been compiling a new set of loss data. This exercise, in which all Scottish brigades and 53 English and Welsh ones had taken part, added two further categories to the analysis of all relevant fires for the years 1970/71: the area damaged and the estimated direct loss resulting from that damage. Also, in December 1971, the Economic

Intelligence Unit had reported on consequential losses. They went further than anyone previously had done, in urging that losses caused by the disruption of production and trade, should be taken into consideration along with losses of life and material damage. The long term disruption that fires could cause, affected not only the firm concerned, they said, but could hit the national economy.

I was weighing these matters one afternoon when Diana knocked and came in.

Diana was a petite, dark haired girl with a fringe and dark blue eyes. She had married a fellow student on graduation, at about the same time as she had joined SAB. All had seemed to go well with her at first, but in recent months she had been looking more and more unhappy.

Diana was working on the siting of fire stations in Northampton study, and I, joining her at the conference table, waited to hear what her problem might be.

In a rather flat voice, Diana said: "The brigade has provided data on accidents on the M1 and M45 motorways, and I'm not sure how to include this information in the siting program."

I pondered for a moment or two. "You'll need to carry out a sensitivity analysis," I decided, and went on to describe how this could be done. While I was talking I was more than usually aware of Diana's downcast expression.

"Are you happy with that?" I asked as I finished.

The girl nodded.

"How's the study progressing?" I went on.

"Well, I have the travel times along the road network now, and yesterday Bob provided the fire incidence predictions. He gave me the station costings some time ago. There are just the loss figures to come."

I smiled. "And you are waiting for me to provide them." I brought the papers from my desk. "Here they are. I wasn't sure which consequential loss factor we should use. The EIU says a factor between 1.38 and 4.0 of the direct losses according to economic conditions. On balance I think we should use the conservative estimate of 1.38. There has been very little unemployment on average in recent years in the UK. Also, we don't want to recommend more stations for the study area than is absolutely necessary."

I paused.

"What do you think?" I asked Diana.

Diana nodded woodenly. "I agree," she said.

I turned back to my notes.

"A loss figure of £60 is my best estimate for the loss for each additional minute spent by the brigade travelling to a dwelling fire. For non-dwellings, a conservative estimate of the loss for each additional minute's delay starts at £1,000. This is for attendance times of two and three minutes. For longer attendance times, around 20 minutes, the loss is getting on for £2,000 per minute ...."

I stopped, aware that I no longer had Diana's attention. The girl's head was in her hands and tears were pouring down her face. I went over to her and put an arm around her shoulders.

"What's wrong, Diana?" I asked.

The sobbing got worse. I drew several paper handkerchiefs from the box I kept on my desk and handed them over. Sitting down beside Diana, I waited for the storm to subside.

"It's my husband," Diana stammered at last. "He doesn't love me anymore. He wants a divorce."

She bowed her head almost to her knees and the tears flowed afresh.

I was genuinely moved. "You poor thing! I am sorry. You have my deepest sympathy."

"What shall I do?" Diana's tears were a flood. "I love him so."

"Of course you do. No wonder you have been looking so miserable," and I did my best to comfort Diana while she poured out the story of her failing marriage.

Forty five minutes and a cup of tea later, Diana felt strong enough to return to her office. There was no point in her going home. Her husband was there. She was not crying now, but her eyes were still red from weeping. Moments after she had left John Clayton came through the door.

"What is the matter with Diana?" he asked.

"Marital problems, I'm afraid," I replied.

A few days later Brian Davenport came into my office and shut the door behind him.

"Rumour has it that you've been ill-treating your staff," he announced.

"What!" I could hardly believe what I was hearing.

"I understand the lovely Diana was seen leaving your office in tears."

"Marital problems," I replied.

"That is difficult for you. You have obviously got to respect her confidence," Brian remarked.

"Quite. It's a personal matter. I'll just have to appear to be an ogre. From whom did the rumour originate, do you know?"

"The head man," Brian told me. "He seems to have got his knife into you."

Diana resigned soon afterwards and went home to her mother. The annual leave due to her took care of her month's notice. I had to take over her study on *The Siting of Fire Stations in Northampton and Northamptonshire*, and write the report.

Don's place had still not been filled, and with Diana's departure, the problem of staff shortage had become acute. I could not understand why John Clayton had so signally failed to act. I decided to put in a formal request for an SSO, and for another SO.

Ralph Shuffrey, the Assistant Under Secretary of State in charge of the Fire Department was holding an internal meeting in the large conference room on the sixth floor of Horseferry House. Ranged on either side of the table, the other officials descended from him in order of seniority. Two of his Assistant Secretaries faced Her Majesty's Chief Inspector for the Fire Services (HMCI) and SAB's Acting Director, John Clayton. I sat next to John Clayton, opposite the Principal and his assistant from G1 Division, with an Inspector from the Fire Inspectorate beside me.

The Chairman had worked his way through every project on the Fire Research Programme. The one he had spent most time on was 'The Optimizing of Fire Cover in the United Kingdom'. It had been a study dear to Don's heart, and Mike had just brought it to completion.

Finally, the Chairman moved on to 'any other business'. Ralph Shuffrey turned to the Principal.

"The Chief Fire Officer of Manchester has written to the Fire Department," the latter told the meeting. "He would like a study on siting and manning in Manchester, and his request has been granted."

Interesting, I thought. But now Ralph Shuffrey was speaking again.

"As we saw from our review of the Research Programme, SAB has produced a ranking of all brigades in the UK by their degree of provision of fire cover using a crude model. This list will be used as the basis for a new project to be included on the Research Programme. It will be called 'The Testing of the Fire Cover Models', and will be carried out extramurally."

I choked back my urge to protest. The project to go to outside contractors! My own staff needed the experience and knowledge which would be gained from such a study. They already had a clear understanding of the background which the contractors would have to spend weeks learning – all at the taxpayers' expense.

"The six brigades at the top of the list may be overproviding cover," Ralph Shuffrey was saying, "and the six brigades at the bottom of the list may be underproviding. Their Chief Fire Officers will be invited to participate in the project. Ah, wait! I see that the six at the bottom includes Manchester. As Manchester's request for its own study has already been acceded, Manchester will not be included in this project. The seventh brigade from the bottom will be included instead."

The meeting ended soon afterwards. John Clayton, appearing quietly at my elbow, asked me to accompany him to his office.

We arrived there to find a young man sitting with his back to the door, leafing through journals. He rose as we entered, and I recognised a familiar face.

Dr Ron Rutstein – Mrs Jane Hogg," John Clayton introduced us to each other.

I shook Ron's hand. "How nice to see you again," I said.

"Do you two know each other?" asked John Clayton somewhat slyly.

"Yes, indeed!" I responded. "Dr Rutstein was a lecturer on the M.Sc course I attended at Imperial College. He lectured to us on queueing theory and on experimental design. Two very difficult subjects."

"Not at all, not at all," remonstrated Ron modestly.

John Clayton went round his desk and sat down. Ron and I were left standing.

"You may wish to introduce Dr Rutstein to your staff," he told me.

I looked from one to the other of them, and then back again, perplexed. John Clayton gave a hollow laugh.

"Dr Rutstein is your new SSO," he informed me. "Brian Davenport has assigned him Dr Busby's old office and sorted out the administrative side. I gave Dr Rutstein a brief introduction to the work of the Branch on his arrival this morning. I'll leave you to fill in the details of the Fire Research Programme."

We left the office together, and I could hear John Clayton chuckling as I closed the door.

"Well, what a surprise!" I said to Ron as we walked down the corridor to my office. "And here we have role reversal with a vengeance. There was I deferring to you as one of the staff on the M.Sc course; and now you find yourself with me as your boss! I hope the shock is not too bad."

"Not at all," he replied politely. "The pleasure is mine."

We reached my office where I deposited my files and papers.

"Would you care to have a pub lunch with me?" I asked.

"Delighted."

"Good! Then you can meet the staff and talk shop this afternoon."

I was summoned to see Ralph Shuffrey. The call was put through from his secretary. I went, faintly surprised. The walk from Horseferry House to the new Home Office building in Queen Anne's Gate kept my adrenalin flowing.

"How far have you got with the Manchester study?" was his first question.

I explained that we had been to Manchester, given a presentation to the senior officers, and were now in the process of collecting the data for the Fire Cover Models. These consisted of the Station Siting program, the Manning program and their peripheral programs. Ron Rutstein was working on the Manning program, while Bob Barnes and a new Scientific Officer, with new and different data, were seeking to determine the loss in relation to the brigade's attendance time for the second and third pumps, as well as for the first pump.

"The Standards of Fire Cover," Ralph Shuffrey said, bringing me back to the matter at hand. "How do they fit into the Fire Cover Models?"

"They don't, but they can be made to," I replied.

"How?"

"If we run the siting program in the normal way," I told him, "we get the least total cost solution. If this does not conform to the Standards of Fire Cover, we can rerun the program with artificially high losses assigned to those areas which are outside the Standards' limits. Thus, we will ensure that the sites chosen as fire stations will give the attendance times to the various Risk Category areas as specified by the Standards. However, this solution will cost the nation more every year, either in increased station costs or in increased losses from fire."

"Nevertheless the Standards of Fire Cover are the Home Office's means of guidance to the Local Authorities," said Ralph Shuffrey firmly.

"They are recommendations only," I reminded him.

He looked at me thoughtfully for a moment. I suspected I was not being amenable enough for his liking. I consoled myself with the thought that I was not there to be amenable but to put the scientists' point of view.

"I want you to impose the Standards on the Manchester station siting study," Ralph Shuffrey insisted bluntly.

"I'm afraid I can't do that," I responded, equally bluntly. "The Chief Fire Officer has asked for the least cost solution."

There was a Local Authority reorganization. Manchester was enlarged to become the Metropolitan County of Greater Manchester. The Chief Fire Officer of Manchester was retired early and the Chief Fire Officer of Lancashire was appointed the Chief Fire Officer of the new Metropolitan County of Greater Manchester. When the reorganization had been completed, I made a special journey to see the new Chief Fire Officer. I put on an individually designed presentation on the methods of fire station siting and manning, with special emphasis on the savings to life, property and consequential losses which the project aimed to achieve.

The new man was endlessly polite. He acted the gracious host over drinks at the bar and over lunch in the officers' mess. But when I took my leave, shaking my hand, he said, "I am sorry you have had a wasted journey. It would embarrass me to continue with the study."

In due course this Chief Fire Officer of the Metropolitan County of Greater Manchester was to become Her Majesty's Chief Inspector of Fire Services at the Home Office; taking over from Bill Holland, erstwhile Chief Fire Officer of Bristol.

The outside contractors who had won the project 'The Testing of the Fire Cover Models' called themselves the Local Government Operational

Research Unit (LGORU). Their team was led by Frank Jenner. He arrived one day to see me, full of enthusiasm. He was of medium height, slim and had mousey straight short hair and light blue eyes.

He sat down with a thump at my conference table and gratefully accepted a cup of coffee. The journey by train from LGORU's office at Reading and then by Underground to Victoria followed by a fairly long walk to Horseferry House had generated a thirst.

When Frank had finished his coffee he turned to me. "We have all your programs inside the computer now, being debugged."

I nodded my approval as Frank continued, "As a matter of interest, LGORU have a general purpose hill-climbing curve-fitting program which we used on your fire spread data. You may be glad to hear that it gives the same results. If we had obtained a better fit, we would have used it instead of your Fire Spread Model, but unfortunately it doesn't, so your model is still the best. However, we've gone one better than you on our program to find the quickest route through a road network. The time taken in the computer is some 60% quicker."

"I'm glad to hear it," I remarked dryly, wondering whether the small saving in computing time really mattered.

"So we will use LGORU's quickest route program, and we will see what we can do by way of speeding up the Fire Cover Models once we have got the typing debugged," he went on.

"Thank you," I managed to say. "In the meantime, I had better organize a meeting here with the brigades' liaison officers. They will be looking forward to a presentation from you."

"Yes, indeed," he agreed. "The presentation is very important," and he and I spent some considerable time going over the relevant points which he should make.

When we had finished, I remarked, "The better the presentation the easier it is to obtain the data; and you will need that soon, if only to check that your versions of the Fire Cover programs are working correctly."

"Oh, there is no need to worry about that," he assured me. "We've already got all the data we require for that purpose. We are doing a Fire Cover study for the Chief Fire Officer of Greater Manchester."

I felt as though I was falling from a great height flat on my back, through a void into space: falling and falling, spinning as I went.

"Are you all right?" I heard Frank say.

I pulled myself together. "Oh yes! I just need some fortification. We could both do with some. Isn't it hot in here? Let's go to lunch."

CHAPTER FIFTEEN

JANE IS
LOANED TO THE DOE

John Clayton's promotion to Deputy Chief Scientific Officer and Director of the Scientific Advisory Branch was announced. At the same time the post of Deputy Director, carrying the rank of Senior Principal Scientific Officer, was trawled. Unusually, the net was cast wide to include all Government Ministries with Operational Research or Systems Analysis Sections. At the Home Office, I was the only Principal Scientific Officer to be short listed from all those who had applied.

The interviews were held. The Chairman and the Board generally, did not put me at my ease. They appeared to be less than sympathetic towards me. My spirits drooped.

A few days later the year's promotions to Principal Scientific Officer were announced. Dr Ron Rutstein was on the list. I had been his reporting officer and John Clayton his countersigning officer.

Three weeks passed, and at last the letter from the Establishment Department arrived. With trembling fingers I tore open the envelope and extracted the single folded piece of paper. My application for Deputy Director at the Scientific Advisory Branch had not been successful.

John Clayton chose that moment to enter my office. He sat down on the chair beside my desk. I tried not to let him see the tears that were welling up into my eyes and threatening to course their way down my cheeks. I blew my nose in desperation.

"I did short list you," John Clayton said. "You should be grateful to me for that."

"It is the promotion that matters, not the short listing," I replied.

"Yes, it's very unfortunate," John Clayton agreed stroking his beard and looking pleased with himself. "Now that Dr Rutstein has been promoted, we have a Section Head surplus to requirements in the Fire Section."

I waited. I knew what was coming.

"And the surplus Section Head is you."

John Clayton rose from his chair and walked to the door, turning round to face me at the last moment.

"The new Deputy Director will not be taking up his duties for a month. I want you to continue as you are for the time being."

He opened the door and turned around again. "You know, Jane, women get their power in the home."

Then he was gone, shutting the door behind him.

That afternoon I went over to the Civil Service Department to attend a meeting of the Operational Research in Government Group. John Clayton was there, although he had never attended before. When I arrived, he made his apologies to the Chairman and departed. I took my seat amid an atmosphere of embarrassment.

The following day I asked to see the AUSS, Establishment Department, and the Chief Scientist. I wanted to know why I had failed to get promotion to Deputy Director, especially as I had been acting in that capacity for almost six months.

The AUSS was very charming. He got out my latest Annual Confidential Report.

"This is an outstanding report," he told me. "It is full of As and Bs - mainly As."

"Then why did I not get the promotion?" I asked.

"Ah, I'm afraid there is one D," he said. "It's for 'relations with others'. It puts you out of the running for all further promotions."

"But that is ridiculous!" I cried. "I get on very well with people. What proof is given?"

"None," he replied. "It is a subjective judgement. Presumably John Clayton, your reporting officer, has his reasons."

"He has never given me any warning to that effect," I protested. "Surely if he felt like that he should have done so, and so allowed me to correct the impression."

"That may be," the AUSS hedged, "but I fear that is the situation."

"Who was the countersigning officer?" I demanded.

"The Chief Scientist."

"But he doesn't even know me! He would not recognise me if he saw me!"

"He would have to rely on his Director," replied the AUSS.

There was clearly nothing to be done.

The Chief Scientist, when I eventually saw him, remained noncommittal throughout the interview. There was no explanation as to how I had come to score a D for personal relations.

◦✄◦

The new Deputy Director arrived. His name was Sid Butler and he was yet another Ministry of Defence scientist from the establishment in Farnborough.

Sid and I had a meeting in his office. It was very cordial. I gave him a full explanation of all the work, reasoning that he was not to blame for my predicament. Then I got onto the extramural contracts.

"There's a meeting of the Project Steering Committee on 'The Testing of the Fire Cover Models' contract next week," I told him as our session ended.

"Fine," said Sid. "I'll take over as Chairman. Please prepare the Agenda and send out the papers in the normal way. I'll want you at the meeting taking the minutes."

My humiliation was complete. The meetings I used to chair were now chaired by Sid Butler. Ron Rutstein was present in his capacity as Head of the Fire Section. I was just the minutes secretary. The Fire Service brigades' liaison officers were there to witness my downfall.

"I want a transfer," I told John Clayton.

A month had passed, a month during which I had been left with no work, other than to act as minutes secretary to the various extramural project steering committee meetings. Ron clearly felt the awkwardness of my situation. He had been asked to produce a research report on the *Methods of Planning Fire Cover using Cost Effectiveness Criteria*. This Ron had done, praising my work at every opportunity.

"You want a transfer to another Ministry." John Clayton looked at me, keeping me standing as was now his habit. "Very well. I'll pass the request on to the Establishment Department and let you know the outcome."

I was clearly dismissed. I returned to my office to read the journals in my in-tray – and to do some thinking.

Now was not the time to quit the Civil Service, I reasoned. Pensions were not transferable, and I did not wish to be penniless in my old age. I would have to try and find a suitable job in another Ministry.

How I wished the Department of Science and Industrial Research (DSIR) still existed so that I could return there. Unfortunately, Lord Victor Rothschild had believed in his concept which he called the 'customer/contractor relationship'. This took the scientists away from their own Department and placed them at the mercy of the administrators in each of their respective Departments. (Lord Rothschild headed the Central Policy Review Staff from 1971 to 1974. The CPRS known popularly as the 'The Think Tank' – researched policy specifically for the Government. (It was disbanded by Margaret Thatcher when she came to office.))

I was so bored and depressed that I decided to take a week of my annual leave. I spent the time in my garden, regaining my peace of mind.

A letter from the Establishment Department awaited me on my return. The Department of the Environment would consider taking me on loan. I should arrange to see Dr Penrose of the Central Unit of Environmental Pollution (CUEP).

I saw Dr Penrose. He headed a small team writing reports for a proposed reorganization of the bodies concerned with environmental pollution. It was this group that I would be joining, if Dr Penrose was prepared to have me. He was. I was so desperate for some work that I would have taken anything which appeared to be reasonable. CUEP and Dr Penrose appeared to be that.

SAB held a farewell party for me. It was the kind of party normally reserved for people leaving permanently. I was given a couple of crystal vases.

"But I'm only going on loan," I protested in my 'thank you' speech.

❦

Number Two Marsham Street was less than a hundred yards from my former place of work at Horseferry House. It consisted of three huge tower blocks connected at the base by the first three floors. The Central Unit of Environmental Pollution was housed on the tenth floor of the Central Tower; but Dr Penrose's splinter group had been assigned three rooms on the eighth floor of the South Tower; amongst the road transport engineers.

I shared an office with Keith Jones, a Higher Executive Officer; while, further down the corridor, was the suite of two rooms occupied by Dr Penrose and his secretary.

The CUEP Administrators and the Scientific bodies met under the umbrella of a set of Management Monitoring Groups. There was one each for land, air, fresh water and marine water pollution, and the hybrid pair, Biological Health and Environmental Health. Dr Penrose was the Scientific Adviser appointed to each of these Groups.

A massive reorganisation of the scientific work was being proposed. The task was to garner information from throughout the United Kingdom, collate it, and ensure that it was compatible with the data required for standards devised by the European Economic Community (EEC).

The remainder of 1975 and the first few months of 1976 passed quietly enough. Dr Penrose wrote reams of beautiful prose describing the current organizational system for administering environmental pollution, and his proposals for improving the information flow and control. Keith and I collected material for him as required, occasionally drafting a section for him.

One morning, just before lunchtime, Dr Penrose came into our office.

"Time for lunch, young man," he said.

Keith took the hint and left. Dr Penrose sat on my desk and looked down at me. "I'd like you to go and see Professor Stewart at MARC Chelsea," he told me. MARC, he explained, was the name of a Unit at Chelsea College, run by Professor Stewart with a staff of three research fellows. Funded by the DOE, they undertook research on environmental pollution, gathering data and collating it. "I want you to do an inspection of their organization and work, and report back to me in writing."

I blinked in surprise.

Dr Penrose leaned forward and looked straight into my eyes. His were green with hazel specks. The thick horn-rimmed glasses he wore for long sight made them appear enormous. I felt as if I was being hypnotized by a snake. He was virtually bald with a beaky nose, receding chin and round cheeks. The snake-like impression grew stronger. Strangely, a snake's scent seemed to fill my nostrils. I lent back in my chair, trying to escape the hypnotic effect.

"And you are to find Professor Stewart and his team inefficient," he seemed to hiss, almost in my face.

I did not reply. I returned the stare with a stare.

The position remained static for several moments. Then Dr Penrose appeared satisfied. He withdrew his head, rose and glided from the room; the snake-like impression persisting to the last.

I had my lunch at my desk. I had taken to bringing in sandwiches. As I munched away, I pondered on this new problem. Then a thought came to me. I went to the filing cabinet and found the MARC Chelsea file, which I brought back with me to my desk. Leafing through the papers, I found what I was looking for, the name of the project officer - one Stanley Hall. He was in the Research Projects Department.

I went for my usual lunchtime walk. I was getting used to being a 'loner'.

On my return, I looked up Hall's telephone number in DOE's directory and telephoned him.

"My name's Jane Hogg," I told him. "I work for Dr Penrose in CUEP. He wants me to go and see Professor Stewart at MARC Chelsea. I see from the file that you are the project officer. May I come and have a word with you?"

He agreed, and I climbed the stairs to the tenth floor of the South Tower and found his office. I was at my most persuasive. Stanley Hall agreed to take part in the 'staff inspection'.

Together we spent several weeks with Professor Stewart and his staff. All three research fellows - a woman and two men - were first-class academics, enthusiastic and devoted to their work. We talked to them, studied their files, examined their computer print-outs, checked their accounts and went for lunches with them in a nearby pub. The team's initial reserve soon melted, and as time passed they became more and more expansive. Eventually Professor Stewart confided in me.

"I'm so worried about the future of this Unit I can hardly sleep at night."

With Stanley's help, I wrote my inspector's report as requested. The conclusion: the Unit was doing an excellent job and DOE funding should continue into the foreseeable future.

The report was almost complete when Stanley asked me to remove his name as joint author.

"My Assistant Secretary has ordered it," he told me.

The erasure was duly made.

The report was typed, copied and dispatched to all interested parties, including Dr Penrose.

As I awaited what I knew would be a traumatic outcome, the inter-departmental post brought me a Home Office SAB report. It was Fire Research Report No 2/76, *An Assessment of the Fire Cover Models* by Dr Ronald Rutstein. There was a very nice covering note from Ron, together with another report.

With interest I picked up Ron's report, opened it, and was soon thoroughly absorbed in it. I noted with satisfaction that Ron, using new brigade data, had obtained the same results as I had for the losses in relation to the fire brigade's attendance time for the first pump. I continued to study the report and noted the conclusions with even greater satisfaction. Twelve brigades had been studied in depth. They were the six considered to have the highest density of fire cover and the six (without Manchester) considered to have the least density of fire cover. The results showed that only one of the brigades had sufficient stations. These results implied that scarcely a brigade in the whole country was providing enough cover. In addition, Ron wrote, "the Fire Cover Models tended to place a station in the centre of the town where the fire incidence was highest, rather than on a bypass outside, which was often the existing arrangement."

I studied Ron's report with great satisfaction; and then picked up the second one.

Emergency Services Research in Great Britain dated August 1975 was a report by Edward H Blum of IIASA (International Institute for Applied Systems Analysis).

I turned the pages and came across a paragraph which really cheered me up.

"Jane Hogg established her group, against much opposition from administrators in the line Fire Department part of the Home Office, in 1968. It quickly received the blessings of several top-level commissions that examined British Fire Services between 1968 and 1972, and is always noted favourably in the Annual Report of the Chief Fire Inspector, yet a third part of the Home Office concerned with fire protection. But her work has been part of a continual uphill battle against the old-line administrators, who are fighting against 'encroachment' by scientific civil servants throughout the British government. As a result, though her group has produced much technically first-rate work, among the leading work in its field internationally, it has yet to gain a secure footing in the civil service or to make much headway against the national fire administrators, whom it seems to make insecure."

Further on I found another paragraph which made my mood even better.

"As we discussed our various experiences in implementation, it became clear that Britain has two important structural influences making implementation relatively more difficult than in the U.S. (and some continental European countries). First is, of course, the rift between administrators and analysts, and the extreme defensive steps taken by the national administrators to 'protect' their positions. Second is the relatively low level of education among top fire officers. In Britain, few top officers seem to have any college education at all, whereas in the U.S. many top officers of major fire departments have at least taken formal education in fire sciences or public administration and a fair number have quite good technical education."

My handkerchief was in my handbag. I scrabbled for it and dabbed at my eyes. I wondered why I wanted to cry when I was so happy.

The telephone rang. An official from the Home Office Establishment Department was on the other end. I was to pack up immediately and go on indefinite 'gardening leave', while my future was being considered.

CHAPTER SIXTEEN

JANE IS
LOANED TO THE DHSS

'Gardening' leave lasted only a week. At the end of it the official from the Establishment Department contacted me again with instructions to report to Dr MacDonald at the Department of Health and Social Security (DHSS) on Monday morning.

I did not need to ask for details. Dr MacDonald was familiar to me from my Operational Research in Government days. He was the Head of the Operational Research Unit at the DHSS, which was based at Great Titchfield Street, not far from the Post Office Tower, north of Oxford Street. I made some swift calculations. The journey to work would be easy: train to Euston and a walk from there.

Mac set me to work on an Anglo-Russian project. (Anglo-Russian projects were all the rage under Prime Minister Harold Wilson at the time.) The objective was to build a crude general model of the Emergency Medical Services to be applied to Moscow or London.

I was assigned a desk in an office with a Higher Scientific Officer who was dying from leukaemia, but was bravely staying at work; walking about on crutches. His friends were in and out of the room all day giving him moral support. They were a nice bunch of lads who took me with them to the canteen for lunch and treated me as one of their group. I was also invited to the Unit's special Christmas party held in a pub near Richmond.

After the Christmas and New Year break, I returned to find that the lad with leukaemia had weakened considerably. Mac was concerned for the lad and decided to move me from his office so that one of his friends could be installed with him to look after him.

I was to share an office with another PSO, a Dr Ackroyd. When I saw the office I was appalled. The place was a shambles! There was a coating of dust an inch thick over everything. The mere placing of my files on the spare desk drove dust up in clouds.

"Please may I see Dr MacDonald," I asked his secretary on my almost immediate return to her office.

"I am afraid Dr MacDonald is in a meeting," the secretary told me.

"It is about Dr Ackroyd's office," I explained. "I cannot stay there. It's filthy."

The secretary was sympathetic.

"Yes, I know," she said. "Dr Ackroyd will insist on leaving his papers and books out all over the place - on his desk, the tops of cupboards, the window sills; in fact, anywhere there is a flat surface, including the floor around his chair. The cleaners refuse to clean his office. Unfortunately, there is nowhere else to put you."

I moved in disconsolately. I swept the dust off my desk with a paper handkerchief, put all my things out of sight and tried to settle to my project. My asthma flared up. I started to wheeze, my eyes and nose dripped, there was a pain in my left lung, and my head felt like cotton wool. Dr Ackroyd was totally oblivious to my state of health. I left work early, feeling that I was getting a bad dose of 'flu at best and double pneumonia at worst.

The next morning I had recovered, but the sight of the office brought back vividly the misery I had endured the previous day. Dr Ackroyd was a late starter. The cleaners were just leaving. I could see two of them putting away their mops and pails.

I went up to them.

"Is there any chance of you cleaning Dr Ackroyd's office?" I almost pleaded.

They gave me a wary look.

"Dr Ackroyd won't put his things away, and he won't let us move them," one of them said. "We ain't been in there for over a year. Have we, Doris?"

Doris shook her head. "No more we ain't," she agreed.

I returned to the office and did my best to work. The wheezing began, my nose started to run, my eyes smarted. I could hardly think. What was I to do? In desperation I went to the cleaners' cupboard. Armed with a bucket, a mop, soapy water and a sponge, I proceeded to clean my half of the room. The other half was impossible. It was covered with books, papers, dirty cups and saucers, old bags, shoes, tennis rackets, paraphernalia of all kinds.

An hour later the job was done and I poured the final bucket of greasy black water down the sink, put away the cleaning equipment, and walked back to the office. I could see the junior staff all agog; heads poking out of office doors. Loud whispers were exchanged. My constant toing and froing with a clean pail of water, then a black pail of water, then clean water, then black water, …, had caused much speculation.

Sitting down at my desk at last, I blew my nose. Black dirt formed on my handkerchief. My head felt as though it was splitting in half.

A large figure loomed in the open doorway. It was Dr Ackroyd, beside himself with fury! He could not speak, he could not move. The suspense lasted just a moment. Slamming the door, he stamped over to his desk and threw down his briefcase. A cloud of dust rose, like a mushroom. He picked up a book and blew more dust all over me.

"What is all this?" he almost screamed at me. "You might have asked me. It is *my* office."

"You were not here to ask," I replied quietly.

He picked up another book and banged it down on his littered desk. A fine haze surrounded him. I sneezed and coughed. That was too much for him. Out he stormed and I could hear him marching down the corridor. A door slammed. Then all was silent.

Half an hour later Mac showed up.

"I'm having you moved," he said. He turned on his heel and departed.

There was a lull of about ten minutes, and then a porter with a trolley appeared. My things were loaded onto it. The porter wheeled it to the lift with me following. The Unit was situated on the sixth floor. The small lift clanked downwards to the ground floor. Porter and trolley emerged, and set off down a bare stone-floored corridor. Three doors along the porter stopped before a small cell-like room, about seven feet by seven feet square.

I stood in the doorway surveying it. An uncarpeted floor. A metal desk and a single chair for furniture. In the centre of the bare brick exterior wall, high up, was a small barred window, the glass smeared with dirt, through which the light filtered wanly. A single bulb hanging from the ceiling at the end of a long flex.

The porter lifted my things off the trolley, heaped them on the desk, and left, shutting the metal door behind him. Clang! I felt as though I had been shut in a prison.

The months slipped by as I concentrated on my project. No one visited me. I arrived in the morning, had a walk in Regents Park at lunch time, and went home in the evening. It was a very solitary cloistered existence.

My report completed, I telephoned my official contact at the Home Office Establishment Department. He sent me on 'gardening leave' again. It was July 1976.

I forgot my sorrows by concentrating on Sally-Ann and Sally-Ann's swimming. I was invited onto the Hatfield Swimming Club Committee and given the job of Entries Secretary.

Early in September the official telephoned again.

"You are to return to SAB. On the 13th," he told me.

I sighed. Actually, I had been enjoying 'gardening leave'.

John Clayton greeted me with no great show of emotion, leaving me standing as usual.

"You will nominally be the project manager on the 'HOT SEAT' project," he told me, "but I will still be running it."

"What is 'HOT SEAT'?" I enquired.

John Clayton looked at me as though I was an imbecile, then got up and went to his cupboard.

"It is a training game for local authority officials. It simulates the run-up to and the aftermath of a nuclear strike. The Home Defence College will be using it on its 'Chief Officers' course. You'll find all the details here." He handed me a set of files. "Good day."

I was dismissed. I stood for a moment with the files in my arms, then turned and made my way to the door.

"You are assigned Room 718," he called out, just as I was leaving.

Room 718 proved to be another tiny office, just large enough to contain a desk, a chair, and a cupboard. I was being treated as an outcast of junior rank. I looked at the Home Office directory which had been left on the desk. My name did not appear in it.

I made my way to Ron's office. He was not there and the room looked unused. I looked in at the office which should have contained his staff. Again there was no sign of anyone. On I went to see Brian Davenport, the Administrative Officer who made me welcome, offering me a chair.

"Where can I find Ron Rutstein and his staff?" I asked.

"They have all left," Brian replied. "The Operational Research work on fire has been discontinued."

"What happened?" I managed to croak, in surprise and alarm.

"The emphasis is now on computerised command and control, on thermal imaging and other equipment research. Much of it is based at the Fire Service College at Moreton-on-the Marsh," Brian explained.

I returned to my tiny office. I was desolate. I felt as though my life's work had been destroyed.

◦✕◦

I did not know how I was going to bear the pain. My dreams were shattered. My staff had gone. I had learned that Jimmy Fry was dead. He had suffered a heart attack in the street just before Christmas, had been taken to hospital, and had died there shortly afterwards.

'HOT SEAT', the project of which I was nominally in charge, was being developed by a team from the Royal Military College of Science, at Shriven-ham. I sat in on the meetings at Horseferry House, which John Clayton chaired, and took the minutes – as I did also when rehearsals of the Game were played through at the new Home Defence College in Easingwold, North York-shire. For most of my time I had nothing to do. So I read up on Civil Defence.

I now became acquainted with all those factors that had seemed so tedious and external to me at the seminar at Sunningdale all those years ago. I studied the stages of a nuclear attack, the after effects, the fall-out and all its attendant horrors. I understood, finally, what was meant by EMP or electric magnetic pulse. I probed the preparations that local authorities were making to cope with such a calamity.

John Clayton sent me on courses at the Home Defence College. Alan Weston, who was in his element, was instrumental in ensuring that I was very well trained. But I still had no project of my own.

Alan brought up the matter of my employment at a Section Head's meeting.

John Clayton told the gathering, "Mrs Hogg will become an expert on gaming. Besides 'HOT SEAT', she will be concerned with a Probation Officers' game and with a Fire Officers' game. It is where her talents lie." And at the prospect he gave a long chuckle.

But the Probation Inspectorate were not interested in a training game for Probation Officers; while fighting simulated fires through the medium of a training game was only toyed with by the Fire Inspectorate.

Finally I got some work: a simulation study of the case working groups of the Police Complaints Board. At last I had something to which I could apply my mind, and I did so with enthusiasm.

ⱽ

It was 13th July 1977.

I, at work in my small office on the Police Complaints Board project, received a surprise visitor. Nigel Lomax, the Director of the Police Scientific Development Branch (PSDB), came in breezily and shut the door. He had to stand as there was no chair for visitors.

"I've a job for you," he told me. "I want you to head one of my Operational Research groups. If you're interested, why not come and see me at three o'clock this afternoon? We can have a chat about the work over a cup of tea," and he opened the door and departed.

A few minutes later John Clayton arrived. He too had to stand.

"I understand Nigel Lomax of PSDB has been to see you."

"Indeed, yes." I was fairly certain that no traffic to and from my office would go unnoticed by him.

"A job for you," John Clayton continued. "Economic modelling of the conditions after a nuclear attack. With your economics background it should be a project you would enjoy; and it's one which badly needs doing."

"That project has already been done twice while I have been in the Branch," I answered, trying to match his soft tones. "I was very impressed with the approach and the results both times."

"There are some new factors to be considered now, and I'm sure that you are just the person to incorporate these, and perhaps try a new approach."

John Clayton was being his most persuasive. His personality always did seem to light up when he was involved with Civil Defence. He would not let Sid Butler, the Deputy Director, play any part in it. He supervised the Research Programme himself, looked after the entire Scientific Advisers' countrywide network and managed the Home Office Scientific Advisory Council (HOSAC).

"Nigel Lomax has invited me to discuss the possibility of my heading one of his OR groups," I told John Clayton, virtually certain he already knew. "I am to see him in his office this afternoon. I should like to consider these two options for a few days. May I let you know then?"

"Of course," John Clayton bowed to the inevitable. "But I hope you will not leave us."

I watched him depart. The door closed on my solitude. Why, I wondered, was he so anxious that I stay in SAB?

I presented myself in Nigel Lomax's office on the fourth floor at 3 o'clock precisely. He came out of his inner sanctuary to usher me in to it, and into an easy chair. He handed me a glass of sherry, and took one himself to a seat opposite.

"So much more enjoyable than a cup of tea, don't you think?" he said, flashing me a welcoming smile.

He had lovely teeth, I noted.

Nigel leaned forward. "I'm so glad you accepted my invitation for a chat," he said. "That means you are interested."

I smiled and gave a small nod.

"As you may know, I have lost Daniel Storey to a SPATS course and need a good man – er, PSO – to take his place. Daniel has just started the development of a training game for the Police College at Bramshill. This game is aimed at potential ACPO officers. ACPO, as you will know, stands for Assistant and Chief Police Officers." He paused, and sipped again at his sherry.

"No, I'm afraid that I did not know," I murmured.

"Anyway, Daniel's group also deals with MIS – that is, Management Information Systems – and his staff are putting these in at Strathclyde at the moment. Another of his responsibilities is preventive policing: just up your street, wouldn't you say?" That smile again.

"What staff does Daniel have?" I asked.

"I'm glad you asked that," said Nigel. "Elizabeth Neve and Penny Stevens are the MIS team, while Max Perry is the Command and Control expert. They're a very high powered trio, I'd have you know, and much respected by the police forces. They will give you every assistance. Elizabeth and Max are SSOs. Penny is an HSO," and Nigel launched into the work they were doing. His enthusiasm was catching. I had heard that Nigel created an immense feeling of *esprit de corps* in his staff.

He broke off as a thought occurred to him.

"By the way," he said, "you would be reporting to Roger Munn. Do you think you'll get on with him?"

"I don't see why not," I replied; and realised I had committed myself.

"Good!" Nigel exclaimed. "Then you will be joining us?"

"Thank you for asking me," I said. "I should like to give it a try."

"Splendid! By the way," he added conspiratorially, "I don't think John Clayton wants to let you go."

"No, I don't think he does," I agreed.

CHAPTER SEVENTEEN

JANE
MOVES TO PSDB

I joined the Police Scientific Development Branch on September 1st 1977. The Principal in charge of Administration welcomed me and showed me to my office.

What a change of surroundings! It was a big, light, airy corner room with conference table and chairs, and an easy chair, as well as all the usual furniture and fittings.

My staff came crowding in to meet me. Max, Elizabeth and Penny had been without a PSO for some months and had been going to Alex Mason, the PSO in charge of Systems I Group, for advice and guidance.

My group was known as the Systems III Group and worked on police operations. Other groups dealt with traffic, CID, fingerprint matching, human factors and equipment.

Max and Elizabeth gave me a briefing on the 'state of the art'. Max had been installing a 'command and control' computerized system into Strathclyde Constabulary's control room and advising on the manpower requirements to run the system. Henceforth all incidents, changes of personnel and messages were logged into the computer, so that the control room staff could instantly locate any resource, traffic car, panda car, footman, dog van, etc. The computer reported the resource's state (whether it was 'busy' or 'idle') thus facilitating rapid redeployment if necessary.

It had been Elizabeth's and Penny's task to write computer programs which collated all this information and turned it into statistics for management purposes, known as 'Management Information Systems' or MIS.

The project was now virtually complete; there would be a few 'bugs' in the systems which would emerge with use. Max or Elizabeth, or both, would then need to go to Glasgow to eliminate them.

Elizabeth put in a plug for MIS.

"Nigel Lomax is very keen on MIS," she told me. "He says they have three uses; first, to tell you what has happened in the past; second, what may be expected to happen in the future; and third, what is likely to happen if some change is made."

"Our MIS are doing the first two," chimed in Penny. "Max has done some modelling for the third. He can tell a Chief Constable how many Control Room staff are required according to the area to be covered and the number of occurrences to be handled."

"I think Nigel is particularly interested in how force manpower should change if Divisional Boundaries change," said Max.

"Perhaps that's why he has recruited you, Jane!" exclaimed Penny.

I laughed.

"Maybe," I replied, "but in our discussions, he put particular stress on the importance of the Senior Police Management Game for the Police College at Bramshill. He is keen that MIS be incorporated into it. We also have a project called 'Preventive Policing', the results of which will hopefully give us some 'cause and effects' which we can use in the Game."

"How's that?" asked Elizabeth.

"Well, in any game," I explained, "the players make decisions. These decisions result in 'outcomes'. In a learning game, as is required for Bramshill, these 'outcomes' should reflect situations in real life; so that the players can learn from experience."

"We know practically nothing about the Game," said Max, "just that we have to develop one. Can you tell us more about it?"

"I wish I could," I replied, "but I've got to read the files first and formulate some ideas. I should have done this by Thursday. Shall we have a meeting then to work out a skeleton plan? Would that suit you all?"

They all consulted their diaries, and agreed that would be okay. The first meeting of the new Systems III Group was to be held on Thursday at 10.00 am in my office.

I was sorting out my belongings and putting them away when I received another deputation, this time in the shape of three men. They introduced themselves as Superintendents Charles MacKinnon, Damien Grant and Jeremy Bright, police officers on two year secondments to the Home Office, liaising between Nigel's Police Scientific Development Branch and the forces. They were based in the Police Research Services Unit (PRSU) headed by Chief Superintendent Albert Walton. They were affable and courteous, and urged me to let them know if they could do anything for me.

I promised that I would.

Soon after they had left, Elizabeth poked her head round the door.

"May I come in?" she asked.

"Of course, have a seat."

"No, thank you, I won't be staying. But I thought you ought to know ... ." She paused.

"What ought I to know?" I asked.

"Well, er ... the police officers ... they all try it on, you know," Elizabeth stammered slightly.

"Try what on?" I was slow on the uptake; then I tumbled to it. "Oh! You mean propositioning."

"Yes," said Elizabeth. "Ann Davidson, of the Human Factors Group, had a terrible time from one of the Supers last year. He tried to convince her that she couldn't manage without him. Penny and I have both had similar experiences."

"You poor things," I sympathized.

"Well, I should watch out if I were you," warned Elizabeth.

"I will," I promised. "But I'm sure they'll regard me as much too old for that sort of thing."

Elizabeth left looking as though she was not convinced.

It occurred to me to go and see Nigel Lomax and Roger Munn if only to let them know that I was 'in post'.

Nigel received me with his beautiful smile, shook my hand and hoped I was settling in all right. A telephone call cut short the exchange of pleasantries.

I went on down the corridor to Roger Munn's office, and knocked on the door.

"Come in," said a clear voice.

I did so. The office was dark, the furniture was dark, and I looked for Roger a little unnerved.

He was a small, clean shaven man with straight short light brown hair and light brown eyes behind a pair of very expensive gold rimmed spectacles. Most male scientists in PSDB looked like police officers in mufti. Roger Munn was no exception. He remained seated behind his desk as I walked towards him.

I introduced myself. "I am Jane Hogg. I have just joined your Division."

Roger Munn's unsmiling expression did not alter. "Don't come and see me," he growled. "I will call you when *I* want to see you."

"Sorry, sir," I said, backing out of the door.

Out of the frying pan into the fire? I wondered.

It was another month, on 13th October, before I heard from Roger Munn. The telephone rang in my office.

"Mr Munn will see you now," his secretary said.

Roger Munn rose from behind his desk as I entered and beckoned me to his conference table.

"This arrived today," he told me without any preliminaries. He passed a file over to me. It contained a single document, a minute from the Assistant Secretary, F3 Division, headed *Research into Preventive Policing – Proposed Force Schemes – Additional Manpower*. A request had been received from the Chief Constable of Humberside for a research project on the deployment of the additional men his police authority had recently decided to provide. I particularly liked one sentence which caught my eye: 'The Chief Constable is anxious that any research should be practical, down-to-earth research which he could put into operational effect'.

I looked up and met Roger Munn's gaze. "I should like to take this work on," I told him. "It'll complement our gaming activity and keep our feet firmly on the ground."

"Good," he said. "I want you to visit Mr Hunt in Hull," continued Roger Munn. "His staff officer is Chief Inspector Briant. Telephone him and arrange a suitable date."

He rose. I picked up the file and followed suit, making for the door.

"Mrs Hogg," he called after me in his clear voice. I half turned towards him. "You will find yourself in a Kafka-like situation, where only the victim knows the truth."

The statement came out of the blue, like a bombshell. I was shattered. I wanted to say, 'That's not Kafka! Kafka's victim had no idea what was going on!' But I could not get it out. My mouth just opened and shut.

Roger gave me a dismissive wave. I thanked him politely and turned back to the door. Somehow I found the handle, let myself out of Roger's office, and made my way back to my own.

I returned to my office feeling more than a little shaken. Ron Davis followed me in and settled himself in my easy chair. He accepted a cup of coffee from me. Ron was the Chief Superintendent in charge of Traffic projects. He had made a habit of having his morning cup of coffee with me. Most of the police officers liked to come in to chat me up. None more so than Ron. I had taken it in good part and made use of their presence to learn about policing. It surprised me to find how little I actually knew.

He must have seen from my face that I was troubled, for he did some prodding; but I did not respond, preferring to consult with him on policing matters.

Ron finished his coffee and got up to leave. He stood looking down at me from his great height of around six foot eight inches.

"Did you know," he asked, "that you have a very bad reputation?"

I could only stare at him in astonishment, until I felt my cheeks flushing an angry red. The jangling in my head seemed to get worse.

Someone else came in – it was Chief Superintendent Albert Walton, Head of PRSU. He paused a second in the doorway, giving us a significant look. Ron made his excuses and left.

Chief Superintendent Walton advanced into the centre of the room, waving aside my offer of the easy chair.

"Superintendent Damien Grant will be the PRSU liaison officer attached to your Group. He will work on all your projects," he informed me.

Then, turning sharply on his heel, he departed, shutting the door behind him.

I shook my head – several times. It seemed gradually to return to normal. I found the Humberside Constabulary Headquarters telephone number and spoke to Chief Inspector Briant. A meeting with the ACC(Operations) was arranged.

❦

Superintendent Damien Grant sat – sprawled, rather - in the easy chair facing my desk. He was tremendously tall; almost as tall as Ron Davis whom he had ousted in the coffee time stakes with me. Being the Systems III Group liaison officer gave Damien a head start.

I, sitting at my desk, was working on an outline plan for the Senior Police Management Game. It was like constructing a skeleton. Once the bones were correctly in place, the organs and flesh could be added. Then life had to be breathed into it, by metaphorically injecting air to the lungs, and blood to the arteries and veins.

"PRSU would particularly like some specific aims built in," said Damien.

"Certainly," I responded. "What sort of thing have you got in mind?"

"Teaching the students the likely effects of alternative resource allocations and deployments is one," he told me.

"Like what, exactly?"

"Well, initially there could be a fairly sizeable decrease in the annual police budget. Or a need to change police boundaries might arise; or a vast amount of manpower might have to be brought to bear on a single problem."

"And what *would* the likely effect of such changes be?"

"They could affect rates of reported occurrences, clearances, arrests, summonses, etc. There could also be confrontation with funding authorities; the need to cooperate and coordinate with other services; grass roots problems with morale and the level of public complaints." Damien stopped. He had been ticking the points off on his fingers.

"Yes, I see that," I said. "But how are we to discover the magnitude of the rates you mention, and the direction in which they are likely to change? What are they again so that I can make a note?"

"Reported occurrences, clearances, arrests, summonses," dictated Damien. "Of course what the players can do with their resources may be constrained by personnel or equipment availability, or by management policies and priorities."

I put my head in my hands. There was rather too much to note at once.

Damien was sympathetic. "Don't worry," he told me. "I'll let you have a note on my suggestions."

He rose and, placing his hands on my desk, he leant on them, bringing his head more on a level with mine.

"By the way," he announced, "your meeting with Mr Hunt, the ACC of Humberside: it's had to be cancelled."

"Why's that?"

"Firemen's strike," said Damien. He straightened himself to his full height. "Mr Hunt will get in touch at some later date. But in any case I'd rather you didn't go without me."

"But Damien, I don't need you in attendance wherever I go," I protested.

"As your liaison officer," Damien's tone of voice was humorously severe, "I must insist on accompanying you to all meetings with ACPO personnel."

"Very well." I was not too pleased.

He made his way to the door.

"Damien!" I called after him. "Before you go, tell me how we are to estimate the magnitude of the rates of all those things you said, according to players' decisions."

"That's where preventive policing comes in," he smiled at me. "Albert Walton will be arranging a meeting shortly."

And he departed, closing the door behind him.

What a very helpful, clever man! I thought. I was beginning to feel a great deal of admiration and respect for Damien Grant. Perhaps it would be an advantage to have him on force visits after all.

⁂

It was a cold day in January. Chief Superintendent Albert Walton was chairing a meeting of the *Working Party on Preventive Policing – Force Visits*, in his office. Others present were Superintendent Damien Grant, Superintendent Mike Vickers, Dr Ian Jamieson of the Home Office Research Unit (HORU), and me.

"I have called this meeting," the Chief Superintendent announced, "to discuss PRSU visits to forces who might welcome Home Office assistance in evaluating their preventive policing projects. I have to say," he continued, "that the response so far has been disappointing. Nevertheless, we have a list of half a dozen possible forces who have expressed a willingness to be involved. Superintendent Damien Grant will be in charge and will arrange the visits."

Damien looked up from his notes. "The purpose of the visits," he said, "is that they should provide information: first, whether there is a scheme which seems worth investigating; second, the nature of such a scheme; third, how far it has developed; and fourthly, the nature and extent of the Home Office assistance which might be required."

"What form might Home Office assistance take?" asked Ian Jamieson of HORU.

"Help may be required with the methodology for evaluation, the evaluation itself, or the subsequent preparation of a report assessing the scheme," responded Damien.

Chief Superintendent Walton added from the Chair, "The objective of any research which followed the visit, however, would be to discover whether particular preventive policing measures are effective. In addition, you, the team, are charged with reporting on whether forces are likely, or are willing to introduce variations in policing methods so that the effect of variation can be measured."

He paused and looked around at the people at the table.

"Any questions?" he asked.

No one responded.

"In that case," he went on, "the following are the forces to be visited: West Yorkshire, Devon and Cornwall, Greater Manchester, Humberside, and West Midlands."

"And Lancashire," added Damien Grant.

"Ah, yes! And Lancashire." Chief Superintendent Walton collected his thoughts. "The sortie team will consist of two pairs, both going together initially. They are Superintendent Damien Grant with Jane Hogg for the Operations side, and Mike Vickers with Ian Jamieson investigating sociological aspects. Both teams are to take notes and write a combined report on all visits."

He got to his feet and ambled over to his desk. The meeting was over.

I returned to my office, feeling pleased. It would be good to be associated with Damien Gant, and have his leadership and guidance on the project, I thought.

CHAPTER EIGHTEEN

SUPERINTENDENT DAMIEN GRANT PROPOSITIONS

A progress meeting of the Systems III Group, with Superintendent Damien Grant sitting in, was in full swing. Having cleared the preliminaries out of the way, we had settled down to discussing the Senior Police Management Game itself.

I explained how the Game's construction fell into three parts.

"The first part," I said, "will require gaming expertise, being concerned with the scenario, the story, the Game rules and the intervention of the Directing Staff."

I paused and looked at the enthusiastic young people around me. They were all attention. "The second part is the construction of the Game drive. Here, computing and modelling skills will come into play, to produce the outputs for the players' information as the Game progresses through Game time. Elizabeth and Penny have already started work on this." Elizabeth and Penny both nodded in agreement

"The third part, the research and implementation packages, is the collection of actual data and the estimation of how the variables are likely to change as Game time progresses."

"That's a huge task!" commented Max.

"The original plan was that the Game should be completed by Christmas," pointed out Elizabeth.

"Which Christmas?" asked Penny.

Everyone laughed.

"We have £100,000 in our budget for the year 1978/79," I told them, "and all of that, I am glad to say, can be spent on contractors for the Game."

"That's more realistic," said Max. "Perhaps we should start by getting in a gaming expert. None of us have that kind of expertise."

"I agree," I said. "And I should like to propose Professor Douglas Holden of the Royal Military College at Shrivenham. Professor Holden and his team did a very good job on 'HOT SEAT' for the Home Defence College."

"You should get the agreement of the Police College to this plan," put in Damien. "You might ask Professor Holden to lay on a presentation for the senior officers."

I smiled at him. "Thank you, Damien, I'll do that. I'll get in touch with the College right away." And I made a note of it.

"RMCS, being part of the Ministry of Defence, should not be too expensive," I continued. "So we'll still have plenty of money for another contractor to help with the data collection and model building. LGORU would be ideal. They have plenty of experience with the Fire Service, and the effects of alternative station boundaries and manpower allocations. They would also be very good on the budgeting aspects."

"But so would we," protested Elizabeth. "We don't need to draw in a contractor for that."

"Come now," said Max, "there's far too much for us to do. At least LGORU could collect the basic data, and construct a budgeting model and a manpower planning model for us."

"Is that agreed then?" I asked.

Everyone expressed assent.

"Good. In that case, I'll seek Roger Munn's approval, and then contact Professor Holden and the LGORU people."

The Preventive Policing team, consisting of Superintendent Damien Grant and me, Superintendent Mike Vickers and Dr Ian Jamieson, went on a whirlwind tour of police forces. Devon and Cornwall was the first to be visited. The force had already made its own arrangements for the evaluation of its projects. Then came Lancashire, with Humberside the following day.

Mr Philip Hunt, the Assistant Chief Constable (Operations) chaired the Humberside meeting. Several Divisional Commanders were present as well as his Staff Officer. Ian Jamieson of HORU was in his element, referring authoritatively to the Ditchley Conference and to split-level schemes in the States. I remained silent throughout. Mr Hunt noticed this and attempted to draw me out.

"I'm afraid that I'm a newcomer to policing," I confessed. "I know very little about it."

"In that case, may I invite you to spend seven days on the beat in Humberside?" asked Mr Hunt. "I would lay on foot beats, panda cars, Team Policing Units, traffic cars, the Vandal Squad. You would experience a wide range of different policing problems on different beats, different shifts. What do you say?"

I could not resist such a splendid offer. "Thank you very much, Mr Hunt. I shall be delighted to accept."

"Good!" He was pleased. "My Staff Officer, Chief Inspector Briant, will liaise with Superintendent Grant on the dates and programme for your visit."

On Monday 13th March, to my surprise, a new Scientific Officer named Adam Tyler joined the Systems III Group. I decided to put him under Max's wing and he was given a desk in Max's office.

Establishment Department seemed to be very fond of the 13th, I noted.

The next day the Preventive Policing team was back on the road. West Midlands was followed by Greater Manchester, and so on to Strathclyde. Finally the members of our team were able to go home, at which point in time Superintendent Damien Grant fell ill.

In Damien's absence, Superintendent Mike Vickers took over the leadership of the Preventive Policing project. He wrote a draft report and persuaded Dr Jamieson and me to submit separate recommendations on behalf of the Home Office Research Unit and the Police Scientific Development Branch respectively.

Superintendent Damien Grant returned to work in April and immediately set about arranging my seven day visit to Humberside. The dates he fixed were 3rd May to 10th May.

I was aghast. "I am sorry," I exclaimed, "I can't go on those dates!"

"Why not?"

"Because my husband's birthday is on the sixth of May. I can't be away then."

"I'm sorry," he said, obviously feeling anything but, "the programme has been arranged. It would seriously inconvenience the Humberside Force if you were to withdraw. There would also be little likelihood of being able to arrange another set of dates."

I sighed and was forced to acquiesce. Jim had been very good about my previous trips; but he was bound to be hurt by my absence on his birthday.

"The Chief Constable of West Midlands has invited us to a presentation of the new Leasco Command and Control system," continued Damien. "It's being held at the Force Headquarters in Birmingham on Tuesday the second of May. I have accepted on behalf of us both. I will meet you there; and then I should be grateful for a lift in your car to Hull immediately afterwards."

I gasped. I got out my diary and made a note of the dates. I was not at all sure that being in Hull with Damien, perhaps for several days, would be advisable. I decided to fix him up with a meeting, or two.

The opportunity soon arose. Roger Munn called a meeting of the 'Computer Gaming Working Party' as he termed it. I attended along with Damien Grant and Superintendent Roland Baxter of the Police College. We discussed the terms of reference the Working Party should construct in order to choose the police force on which the Senior Police Management Game would be based. A further meeting was arranged for Thursday 4th May, during my visit to Humberside. Roger agreed that I need not be present as long as Superintendent Grant was.

As we left Roger's office, Damien turned to me. "By the way, Jane, I'm seeing my Chief Constable on Friday about my next job."

"Your next job?" I was surprised. Damien was not due to complete his two year secondment to PRSU until the end of September.

"Yes," said Damien. "I'm being recalled to my force early."

"I'm sorry to hear that, Damien. The team will miss you."

Superintendent Damien Grant was sitting in the front passenger seat of my car. We were on our way from Birmingham to Hull.

I had met Damien Grant in the foyer of the Police Headquarters. We had then gone to the preliminaries of the presentation of the new Leasco Command and Control system, where I had been amazed to discover that we were attending a VIPs' drinks and lunch, and that among the dignitaries present were my AUSS and my Director, Nigel Lomax. Roger Munn, apparently, had not been invited. Worse still, Sir Philip Knights, the Chief Constable, had taken me to sit beside him at the top table at lunch, while my AUSS and Director sat elsewhere.

I was still remembering the embarrassment I had been caused as I motored up the M1. I wondered how Roger Munn was going to react.

"Friends of mine swapped wives some time ago," Damien mentioned casually beside me.

I came back to the present with a start.

"Oh, really!" I murmured. "And how did they manage?"

"Very well," Damien told me. "The two families had been very friendly. The kids accepted their new fathers without a murmur. One of the families did however move away," he conceded.

I concentrated on my driving and said nothing.

We arrived in Hull around 6.00 pm and drove to the Police Headquarters in Queen's Gardens. Damien went in, collected our detailed programme and discovered which hotel we had been booked into. It turned out to be the Centre Hotel in Paragon Street. We washed, telephoned our respective homes, and went for a steak dinner at the nearby Berni Inn.

Returning to the hotel, we started up the stairs. A notice at the top forbade non-residents beyond that point.

"Would you like a coffee and brandy?" Damien asked.

I stopped. "Yes, indeed I would," I said and began to retrace my steps down the stairs.

"No need for that," he called after me. "There is coffee and a fridge full of drinks in my room."

I came back and followed Damien, wondering if I was being wise. It would be churlish to back out now, I decided.

Damien took a key out of his pocket and opened a door.

What a nice room Damien has, I thought. It was almost twice the size of the room I had been given, and was furnished with two armchairs and a round table. The bed was tucked away discretely in a corner.

Damien made the coffee and brought it in two cups to the table. He then got the brandy out of the fridge and filled two tumblers. His hands were strangely unsteady. He seemed to be sweating slightly. Placing the tumblers beside the coffee cups, Damien sat down.

Suddenly it struck me: Damien was nervous!

We drank our coffee. Damien asked me about my taste in novels: had I read any Dick Francis? I had to admit I had not.

"They make excellent reading," Damien assured me, "and are very true to life. Let me lend you some."

He was very eager. He got up, searched in one of his bags, produced three paperbacks and placed them on the table in front of me. He sat down again but not in his chair; on the carpeted floor beside my chair.

In my more naïve moments I had been under the impression that the presence of a police officer provided me with protection. Now I began to suspect that I myself was in need of protection; and from the very police officer whom I had trusted - and, yes, I had to admit it, was attracted to.

I raised my brandy tumbler, downed the contents, and got up to leave. Damien jumped to his feet.

"Another brandy, I insist."

He rushed over to the fridge. "It will make you sleep well."

I hesitated.

As if by magic Damien was back with a full tumbler. He thrust it into my hand.

"There's your nightcap."

"Thank you."

I sat down and began to gulp the brandy. It burned my mouth, throat and stomach as I swallowed it.

Damien laid his long frame down by my feet again and looked up at me. Desperately, I gulped the brandy. Only one more gulp to go. Damien was getting closer. I could hear his fast breathing. I emptied the glass.

Gathering up my handbag and the three Dick Francis novels, I rose to my feet and rushed to the door. I was turning round to thank him for his hospitality, when I found myself enveloped in Damien's arms.

My head was thrust back and Damien's lips were over my mouth, his tongue flicking in and out. My knees gave way under me, and the books went flying in all directions onto the floor.

He picked me up and carried me over to the bed. Laying me gently down on it, he climbed on top of me, showering my face with kisses. I struggled to return to my right mind.

"But Damien, I'm years older than you!"

"That doesn't matter," he breathed, covering my lips with his and fondling my breast.

"What about your wife?" I insisted.

"She won't know."

God give me strength, I thought, as the implications sank into my bemused brain. Summoning up a tremendous effort of will I sat up on the bed. Damien lay back in surprise.

"I want to, but I won't," I told him.

He watched in silence as I retrieved my handbag, my shoes and the novels; and virtually flew out of the room.

Back in my own small room, I undressed, had a shower, got into my nightdress and sat down by the dressing table. I stared at myself in the mirror as I put on my night cream and combed my dark blond hair. My pale face and haunted blue eyes looked back at me reproachfully.

For hours that night I lay awake in bed, totally unable to sleep.

My mind was in turmoil – and so, I had to admit, was my body.

I had looked up to, and trusted Damien Grant. He had provided leadership and guidance on the Preventive Policing visits Chief Superintendent Walton had sent us on. He provided my Systems III Group and myself with guidance and was my liaison officer when I met ACPO personnel. When he was on duty his behaviour was impeccable. He had given me no indication that this would differ when he was off duty.

I remembered Elizabeth's warning, but still could not believe that Damien meant me any harm. After all, if my understanding of police language was correct, he was warning me that something serious was underfoot when he lent me the Dick Francis novels. Nevertheless, I had been very stupid going into Damien's room. I resolved to take much more care in future.

CHAPTER NINETEEN

POLICING
IN HUMBERSIDE

The next morning when I woke I knew something was different. Then I remembered Damien and the night before. I blushed at the memory, got up and washed and dressed. Walking down the corridor past Damien's room, I took the lift to the dining room. I had almost finished my breakfast when he arrived. His face and demeanour displayed no emotion whatsoever, and apart from a polite, "Good morning," he made no conversation.

"When's our meeting with Mr Hunt?" I asked Damien.

"It was to be at 9.00 am, but has been postponed to 10.00 am," answered Damien.

At 9.00 am we met in the hotel lobby and went out into the street, wandering around the shopping areas for a time before going to have a coffee at one of the stores' restaurants; just for something to do. Beyond the barest necessities of speech we remained silent throughout.

Mr Hunt and Chief Inspector Briant were waiting for us at Police Headquarters when we arrived at 10.00 am. After the normal pleasantries, Mr Hunt remarked, "We were expecting you at 9.00 am."

"I'm sorry, sir," responded Damien, "there must have been a mistake. I have 10.00 am down on my programme. We have been kicking our heels for over an hour."

Mr Hunt opened the proceedings by giving me an introduction to the Humberside Police Force, the areas it covered and some of the problems with which it was faced. I was then shown the Force Operations Complex consisting of the Communications Room, the Operations Support Echelon and the Criminal Intelligence Unit; with a break for lunch with Mr Hunt in the officers' mess.

Inspector Brian Nesbit was in charge of the Criminal Intelligence Unit. He was a very intelligent and enthusiastic officer who went to a great deal of trouble explaining to me the workings of his unit. I was left in no doubt that all the known villains in Humberside were thoroughly documented and could be easily matched with any crime they might commit.

At the end of the session Brian Nesbit enquired which hotel we were booked into. When I told him it was the Hull Centre, the Inspector frowned.

"On behalf of the Humberside Police Force, may I apologize for the environment and the clientele in Paragon Street." He continued, speaking with emphasis. *"Unfortunately, Hull is very short of hotels."*

I made light of it, and asked which hotel he would recommend. The choice appeared to be limited, but he did mention a small family hotel which I might note for future use. I jotted it down in my diary, and at the same moment had a mental image of the big modern building I was in, which overlooked the beautiful public gardens and had behind it a multi-storey NCB car park of five or six levels. I was good at thought transference, I knew, but who had put the idea into my head that the building I was in would make an excellent hotel?

The next interview was to be with Chief Superintendent Ralph Todd, the Commander of 'C' Division. Damien excused himself; he had a train to catch so that he could attend Roger Munn's meeting the next day.

"I'll see you on Monday evening," he told me as he departed.

The 'C' Division Headquarters was also housed in the same building in Queen's Gardens. Chief Superintendent Ralph Todd was a delightful person, most anxious that I become well acquainted with police work. It was also clear that he was extremely concerned about the future of 'C' Division.

I was then sent out for a couple of hours, accompanying a police constable on his beat, so that I could witness the incidents with which he had to deal. Later, after a snack in my room, I was taken out on patrol in two different panda cars until 2.00 am, during which period a prison break exercise was suddenly staged.

Amazingly, on my return to my hotel, I found that I was not at all tired. I sat on my bed and mulled over the information I had gleaned during the day.

P A Management Consultants were being brought in by the Chief Constable, at a cost of £100,000, and were expected to report that there should be only three Divisions in North Humberside; and that 'C' Division should be split between 'B' and 'D' Divisions. As there were already moves to relocate the Force Headquarters at Beverley this would mean that there would no longer be a need for the beautiful large building in Queen's Gardens in the centre of Hull.

I cast my mind back over the day's events. Something one of the police officers had said, stuck in my mind. "We know we can trust you, Mrs Hogg."

✣

The next day Mr Hunt motored me over to Scunthorpe to talk with the Chief Superintendent in charge of 'E' Division. After lunch, I went on patrol in a panda car, then with the Vandal Squad, and after that with a Team Policing Unit.

I was called in by Control during the afternoon to learn that Superintendent Grant wanted me to telephone him. I was given a London number, which was not a Home Office number. It had to be where Damien lived in London during the week.

"May I use a telephone?" I asked one of the Control Room officers. I would call Damien now at the office; I certainly was not going to ring him at home in the evening.

The officer assigned me one, and I got through to Roger Munn.

"I'm sorry to bother you," I told Roger, "but Control here has told me that Superintendent Grant wants me to contact him, and I do not have his office number."

Roger grunted and transferred me to Damien.

Damien sounded surprised to hear me. "I'm sorry," he said. "I won't be coming back to Hull on Monday after all. I have to go to Bristol on Wednesday. It would mean too much travelling."

On Friday, I was on duty for twelve hours at a stretch in Grimsby and Cleethorpes in GP (General Purpose) cars and a Team Policing Unit. On Saturday, Jim's birthday, I was out again for another twelve hours, this time in the Immingham Sub-division. I rang Jim before I went and he sounded a little unhappy.

On Sunday morning I was transported from Cleethorpes to Hull in five traffic cars. Each car took me to its area boundary where the next car was waiting, and into which I was transferred. I had lunch at the Centre Hotel, and then spent eight hours with 'D' Division in East Hull; talking first to the officer in charge at Tower Grange and afterwards patrolling in a panda car. On my return to the Centre Hotel I found I had been assigned a twin-bedded room next to the stairs. It made me feel uneasy. I arranged to take all my meals in my room.

On Monday, I was with 'B' Division at Priory Road Sub-Division and the Hessle Road Sub-Division. I was talking with the Chief Inspector in charge of Priory Road Sub-Division when his telephone rang. It was Roger Munn.

"I have just learned that you were at the VIP reception and Leasco presentation in Birmingham on 2nd May," he said crossly. "Can you explain that?"

"I'm sorry, sir," I replied. "Superintendent Grant accepted an invitation from the Chief Constable. I had no idea that it was a VIP affair."

"Huh," he grunted. "I want you to see Superintendent Leslie Rainer at the Force HQ tomorrow. He is preparing some suitable questions to ask of potential forces on which to base the Senior Police Management Game. As soon as you have them, I want you to telephone them through to my secretary."

"Yes, sir."

"There will be a meeting of the Working Party to select the force for the Game. In my office at two o'clock on Friday afternoon. You are to be there."

"Yes, sir," I repeated.

Superintendent Leslie Rainer was very handsome and debonair. He had Chief Inspector C R Donaldson with him. The three of us together drafted a questionnaire which concentrated on major incidents, manpower required for major crimes, variability in topographical features, and likely changes in demographic factors. When it was completed, I telephoned it through to Roger Munn's secretary, as requested. Superintendent Rainer than took me to lunch in the officers' mess.

We were having coffee afterwards when Superintendent Rainer, seeing a group of officers just settling down to their lunch, said, "Ah, there are some of your friends."

I turned round to look. "I don't see anyone I know," I replied.

"That group of police officers over there at the table by the windows. They're on the Senior Command Course at the Police College. They, like you, are staying at the Hull Centre Hotel."

Ah! How wise I had been to have all my meals in my room.

"Well," I responded, "I wouldn't have seen them there because I have a continental breakfast brought to my room, and when I am taken back to the hotel for my evening meal, I always have sandwiches brought to my room."

Superintendent Rainer looked disappointed.

For the rest of Tuesday I was on duty in the centre of Hull on two separate footbeats; on the first of which I and my police constable could be seen accompanying an elephant.

This was my last day, and the following morning I went to take my farewell of Mr Hunt, and to thank him for his generosity. We discussed my impressions of policing and I recounted these, being careful at no stage to mention possible changes in Divisional boundaries.

Then I was off home, motoring the whole way. Thursday I took off on leave. I had lost over half a stone in weight. I was glad to be back with my family. Jim and Sally-Ann had given me a great welcome.

On Friday I arrived at my office early, as usual. Two minutes from Roger Munn, both sharply worded and unexpected, sat waiting for me in my in-tray. I settled down to read them.

The first was on the report on Preventive Policing. Nothing in that pleased Roger. The second was on the proposed appointment of LGORU as contractors for the Senior Police Management Game. LGORU's proposals were suddenly no longer acceptable to Roger, although he had agreed to them earlier and minuted the file to that effect. I responded to both minutes in my most soothing manner, wondering what had caused Roger to be so upset.

As I worked I found myself being interrupted by Damien. He was in and out of my office all morning.

In the afternoon, I attended the meeting of the Working Party in Roger's office, together with Superintendent Damien Grant and Superintendent Baxter of the Police College. Roger went through the questionnaire I had telephoned in and a list of potential forces was agreed. Letters were to go out to each Chief Constable immediately. A further meeting was arranged for the following Tuesday, at the Police College.

As we got up to leave, Damien announced, "Jane, I shall be in Sussex on Monday."

I was embarrassed. Damien's whereabouts were not my concern. Superintendent Baxter looked at me with one eyebrow raised. Roger appeared not to have noticed.

Back in my office, I decided that I would have to get matters sorted out with Damien. The situation could not be allowed to continue as it was. If I myself chose the place and time, I thought, I would be quite safe.

Context

Humberside Police News
October 2nd   Number 47

Chief at new style divisional meeting

THE FIRST of a new style Divisional Meeting, attended by the Chief Constable, was held at Grimsby on the 20th September.

This meeting, which was the forerunner of others to be held throughout the Force during the next twelve months, was well attended by representatives of all ranks within the Division.

Whilst matters of particular interest to F Division were discussed, Detective Inspector Lamb (CIU) and Superintendent Thomas (Communications Officer), were also invited to speak regarding their specialist departments.

The emphasis was on informality and it was in this light that the Chief Constable elaborated on matters of Force Policy currently under consideration. Subjects such as the workings of the Policy Group, the possible Force Review, Training

OUR FORCE CHOSEN FOR COMPUTER EXERCISE

THE Humberside Police have been chosen by the Police Scientific Development Branch of the Home Office, as the best force in the Country on which to base a computer simulated exercise.

Known in computer language as 'Computer Gaming', this is a decision-making exercise, played by any number of participants, who can make policy decisions, implement new ideas and, by use of the computer, can see the results of their efforts, projected over any length of time. With a

typify a model police force, with all the problems caused by geography, industry and manpower.

The exercise will be played out at the Police College, by members of the Command Course 2. This course is designed to equip senior officers for appointment as Assistant Chief Constables. To do

stands at the present.

By using the computer, the members of the syndicate can see what effect changes on the force would have; and the projected game time will be a ten year period. All the time that the players are using the computer, members of the directing staff of the Police College are assessing them and are

Chapter Twenty

Roger Munn opposes LGORU as contractors

Was Damien a friend or a foe?

I had taken his lending me three Dick Francis novels as a warning. "They are very true to life," he had said. On the other hand I was in no doubt as to what the situation was. All the Humberside Police Force Divisional Commanders and Chief Inspector Brian Nesbit had made it clear to me that plans were afoot for 'C' Division to be disbanded and for the Force Headquarters to be relocated to Beverley, leaving the magnificent modern building in a prime location in the centre of Hull free to become a first class hotel.

There was no doubt that Damien and I had a very good working relationship; and I knew I was both mentally and physically attracted to him. However, he was embarrassing me.

It was also clear to me that Roger Munn intended the Humberside Police Force to be the basis for the Senior Police Management Game for the Police College. The Force would have a clear advantage when answering the questionnaire which was to be circulated to the Chief Constables of the forces chosen as potential candidates. The students would no doubt then be asked to examine the case for changing the Force Divisional Boundaries and be encouraged to amalgamate 'C' Division with 'A' and 'B' Division.

Could I persuade Damien to be a friend?

The afternoon of the Working Party meeting to be held at the Police College arrived. Roger Munn, Superintendent Damien Grant, Superintendent Roland Baxter and I gathered in one of the small committee rooms at the College, and seated ourselves around a small table. Roger passed around a copy of a letter with the attached questionnaire which he had already sent to potential force Chief Constables.

"While we await the replies," he said, "we might as well set out the subject matter of a draft report of the Working Party."

We all agreed, and Roger went through what he wanted to see in the draft report, taking note of the occasional comment from one of us. He closed the meeting with a request to me to produce the draft report for discussion on Thursday morning, just two days ahead, at the Police College.

I wondered how I was going to manage this, especially as I was holding an internal meeting of my Systems III Group and Damien the following day. In normal circumstances I would have written it that evening, but today I hoped to talk to Damien.

Damien and I walked back to the visitors' car park together.

"Damien, may we go somewhere where we can talk?"

"I have to stop at a garage in Camberley to get my car attended to." Damien's tone of voice was discouraging.

"Will it take long?"

"No."

"In that case I can wait for you to get your car fixed, and then we can go to a café."

"Okay," Damien agreed, rather grudgingly.

We set off from the car park, Damien in front. There was a fork in the drive. The left one curved down the hill to the main gate, the right one carried on past the lakes towards the back gate – and home.

Damien took the left fork. I became indecisive. Should I follow him or should I turn right? Left or right? I could not make up my mind. Even as I came to the point of no return I did not know what I was going to do.

At the very last moment I swung the car over to the left. After all it was I who had suggested the talk, I thought, as I followed Damien down the long, winding drive and on to the Camberley road. It felt as though hundreds of police officers' eyes were on us as we drove down the hill.

The car was fixed, and we stopped at a café in the town centre for a cup of tea and a scone. I produced the three Dick Francis paperbacks Damien had lent me, and pushed them across the table towards him. I tried to break the ice by discussing them, but he would not respond. We finished our snack. The café was full; people were waiting for our table. It was no good, we could not talk here. Damien picked up the paperbacks and we left. My mission had not been accomplished.

The following morning I was in my office very early. By 10.30 the manuscript for the draft report had been completed and was in the capable hands of Roger Munn's secretary.

Damien did not arrive for the Systems III Group meeting I had arranged for that morning. I had to send Penny to get him. The meeting over, Elizabeth asked Damien to help her with a problem she was having with her force simulation for the Game. As he followed her out of my office, he turned and gave me an enormous wink. My heart sank. There was trouble afoot, I knew it; and Damien had just told me what to expect.

The next day Roger Munn, Damien, Superintendent Baxter and I were at the Police College once more for the next meeting of the Working Party to select a force for the Game. My draft report was circulated, discussed, and I was asked to revise it in a few places. At the end of the meeting Roger unbent sufficiently to remark, "I would not have been able to have done it."

As I left the visitors' car park by the back road I noticed Damien and Roger getting into Roger's car in the VIPs' car park beside the lake. I had not gone far down the twisting lane when I was aware of a car sitting on my back. I studied it in my mirror. There were two men in it: Roger and Damien. Roger was laughing heartily as he pushed his car closer and closer to mine. I ignored him. I came to a stop at the crossroads and then carried on across it. Roger turned right. As he went, I could hear raucous laughter coming from the other car.

∞

Superintendent Damien Grant's farewell party was held in PRSU's big office. Once again, he succeeded in embarrassing me. Almost throughout his speech he had his eyes fixed firmly on me; and afterwards I was aware of his gaze following me as I circulated amongst the guests.

When it was time for me to leave, I went up to Damien to say 'good-bye'. He was standing very upright, dwarfing Superintendent Jeremy Bright who was standing beside him.

"Goodbye, Damien. I hope all goes well with your future career."

He bent his head and looked deep into my eyes. "I'm coming back. I'm coming back to do preventive policing."

"I'm very glad to hear that," I managed to say as I turned away.

"Be good," he called after me.

"I will be," I replied, rushing off, horrified by that final remark. What must Jeremy Bright have thought!

I got back to my own office on the floor below and made myself a cup of tea. I was sipping it and going through some papers when there was a knock on the door.

"Come in," I called.

Chief Superintendent Ron Davis entered.

"Would you like a cup of tea, Ron?" I asked.

"Yes, please." And he settled his long frame into the easy chair.

"I haven't seen you for a long time Ron," I remarked as I poured his tea.

"Well, you've been rather preoccupied with a certain young man," Ron teased, and he pursued the subject until I sat back and laughed.

"Really, Ron, it's not what you think," I told him.

A little later, after Ron Davis had departed, Superintendent Jeremy Bright opened my office door and remained standing just inside. He had not knocked.

"What did Damien Grant mean when he said he was coming back?" he asked, coming straight to the point.

"I don't know. We'll have to wait and see."

He turned on his heel and departed, leaving the door open.

Roger Munn called me into his office to reiterate his opposition to my single tender action with LGORU. Again, a display of anger on this topic, which I found hard to understand.

I pointed out that the tender had been agreed with F5 Division and with the Police College, and that he himself had initialled the file. LGO-RU's proven ability and experience had convinced me that they would perform well in this instance.

"I'm sorry," Roger rebuffed me, "but I must insist." He handed me a piece of paper. "This is a list of suitable consultants. As you can see it includes LGORU. You are to get out a job specification and circulate these firms with a covering letter."

"Very well." I ran my eyes down the list. "I don't see P A Management Consultants here."

"No, I don't want them included." Roger was firm.

I returned to my office carrying the LGORU contract file and the list of consultants. Superintendent Mike Vickers met me and followed me into the room.

"I am the new PRSU officer assigned to your projects," he announced.

"Welcome on board," I responded. "Would you like a cup of coffee?"

Mike accepted my offer and soon we were chatting and relaxing.

"I have a problem," I told Mike. "As you know, I got the go-ahead from the College and from F5 Division to appoint RMCS and LGORU as contractors for the Senior Police Management Game. Professor Douglas Holden of RMCS has got his contract, but just as LGORU's contract was about to go out to the Unit's Director, Roger Munn vetoed it."

"Hadn't you mentioned LGORU to Roger before?"

"But of course! You don't think I'd have sent the papers to the College and to F5 Division without Roger's agreement do you?"

"I'm sorry."

"You are forgiven. Anyway, Roger is now insisting on multi-tender action for that part of the Game's development which I was assigning to LGORU."

"Will that matter?" asked Mike.

"Well, it's very embarrassing. LGORU have already started work on the understanding that they are getting a contract."

We both sipped our coffee, thinking our separate thoughts.

Eventually I sighed. "There is nothing for it, I'm afraid. "I'll just have to set up an Evaluation Board, with myself as Chairman. The members will be Superintendent Roland Baxter and Mr Barry Hoare from the Police College, you from PRSU, and Professor Holden and Dr Milton Hubbard from RMCS."

"For the purpose, I take it, of interviewing each prospective contractor in turn," commented Mike.

"Yes, but first Roland, you and I will short-list the consultants according to their written proposals.

"Let's hope all this does not hold up the development of the Game too much," said Mike.

"It had better not." I took out my diary. "Let's see, today is Monday 6th June. I can get the specification and letters out to the consultants by Friday. We should give them a month to prepare their proposals. If Roland, you and I do the sifting of the written proposals on Monday 17th July, we can interview the short-listed teams of consultants on Monday 24th July."

"That sounds fine," agreed Mike.

"In the meantime, I'd better write a very apologetic letter to the Director of LGORU." I said.

CHAPTER TWENTY ONE

A MEETING ON PREVENTIVE POLICING

The replies from the Chief Constables, who had been circulated proposing their force as the one on which the Senior Police Management Game might be based, came in. There were parcels of papers in response to the questionnaire to be gone through and assessed according to the pre-arranged marking scheme.

On Monday 17th July, Superintendent Baxter, Mike Vickers and I made a paper sift of the outside consultants' proposals for the Game contract, as arranged. This was in the morning. In the afternoon, the same team joined Roger Munn to discuss the final draft report on which the force was to be chosen.

Unsurprisingly, the vote was for Humberside.

Two days later, I was at work in my office when the door opened and closed. I looked up to see Roger Munn standing in front of my desk.

I rose and pointed Roger to the easy chair.

"Good morning, sir."

Roger ignored the invitation. We both remained standing.

"Arnold Miller Management Services is to be your choice of consultants for the Police Game contract," he told me. "The LGORU personnel do not have the appearance and polish that is required of staff who have to make direct contact with the Police Service."

"Yes, sir."

I was still standing as Roger left my office without a backward glance.

The following day, a meeting to discuss the report of the Working Party on Preventive Policing chaired by the Assistant Secretary from F3 Division of the Police Department was held in the main Home Office building at Queen Anne's Gate. Those present were three from the Home Office Research Unit (HORU), two from the Police Scientific Development Branch (PSDB), two from the Police Research Services Unit (PRSU), a Chief Superintendent from Her Majesty's Inspectorate of Constabulary (HMIC), two from F5 Division and three, including the Chairman, from F3 Division. Superintendent Grant of PRSU, whose name was down on the list of participants, was absent.

"It seems clear," announced the Assistant Secretary, "that, while police forces were keen to support research in preventive policing, they did not have specific proposals and were looking to guidance from the Home Office. The report of the visits contains some provisional proposals for research. The best way to proceed would be for PSDB, PRSU and the Research Unit to elaborate on how those proposals might best be taken further."

He turned to me.

"The aim," I said, "is to determine the minimum level of response policing and the styles and levels of preventive policing which would best be added to this. PSDB," I continued, "would hope to test the effects of community involvement, resident beat or foot patrols, mobile deployment, and all possible combinations of these treatments, including none at all."

I continued with a detailed explanation as to how this might be done and the observations to be made.

Superintendent Mike Vickers was the next to speak. After explaining that the function of PRSU was essentially liaison, he went on, "There are a number of experiments PRSU would like to monitor, with a view to passing on to other forces advice based on the results; but PRSU feel that to go beyond that and undertake the evaluation of experiments is not compatible with our liaison role; it would make relations with forces more difficult. In any case, PRSU's main interest is in what resources are needed to provide the basic minimum level of 'response' policing; that is, resources which are not available for 'preventive' policing."

I could hardly believe what I was hearing. This was not the Mike Vickers who had been working with me on the report.

"PRSU was interested in PSDB's proposal," continued Superintendent Vickers, "which would provide information on the basic minimum level of 'response' policing, although of course, covering a good deal else as well. A more modest experiment would be sufficient to meet PRSU's interest." He ended. He did not meet my eyes across the table.

Dr Ian Jamieson spoke for HORU. "The Research Unit," he said, "were considering a number of more modest projects which might be developed if they were of interest to the police. They included a study of patrol organisation in one or two divisional areas. This would examine the effect of introducing team policing, or split/half policing. A study of the criminal investigation process might also be undertaken, which might give some indication of the deterrent effect of the detection of crime."

The three points of view had been put. Now Roger Munn, the Deputy Director of PSDB, weighed in, and failed to support the PSDB recommendation. "Account has to be taken of the likely willingness of police forces to subject themselves to experimentation on a very large scale," he remarked. "The larger the project the more difficult it would be to ensure that all significant changes were taken into account."

"Mrs Hogg," the Chairman called.

"On the other hand," I said in decided tones, "if a study of this kind is to carry conviction, it has to be done with sufficient thoroughness and vigour for the results not to be questioned. Even if the results were to indicate that the various preventive deployments had no effect in practice, such a finding would, I suggest, be of value as long as the methodology of the experiment cannot be faulted."

"Mr Munn," called the Chairman.

"An experiment in this area can never be conducted so rigorously that the results would be beyond question," Roger retorted. "A more fruitful approach would be to conduct a number of more modest projects on a common theme. The conclusion is more likely to bring general acceptance if it is borne out by the results of several different studies than if it follows from only one experiment, however well conducted."

There was general embarrassment at what was turning out to be a PSDB row. I felt that I was being made to look insubordinate. I was utterly perplexed: why on earth had Roger let the draft report go through if he felt so strongly, I thought, and why had Mike Vickers suddenly changed his tune?

Everyone now seemed to be trying to speak at once.

"As a result of the preventive policing visits, the Home Office is better informed of preventive policing developments," someone put in.

"Yes, and the Home Office is prepared through PRSU to provide information about these to forces generally," came another comment.

"As a result of the visits, the Home Office was developing research proposals to meet the obvious interest of forces in some assessment of preventive police work." This was the Chief Superintendent of HMIC's contribution.

"These proposals would be part of the normal research effort, and funded as such - there was no special, additional programme for which extra resources would be available!"

"The worked-out proposals will be the subject of consultation with the ACPO, probably through the Police Department Research Committee!"

The Chairman banged the table. "It is for PSDB and HORU to develop their proposals further in the light of the discussion," he said, bringing the meeting to a close. "I will make an interim report to the Police Department Research Committee in September. In this paper I will say that the PRSU information desk is the appropriate referral point for all police enquiries about research, including those relating to the Research Unit as well as PSDB."

I was extremely upset. I left the room first and almost ran back to Horseferry House. Up the lift to the fourth floor I went and into Nigel Lomax's secretary's office. The secretary did not need to be asked; she picked up the phone to Nigel.

"Mr Lomax will see you now," she told me after speaking briefly into the instrument.

I went straight in. Nigel was already walking towards the door.

"Have a seat. Will you have a sherry? It will do you good," he insisted, as I raised my hand to refuse.

I capitulated.

"I have just come from the meeting on the report of the Preventive Policing force visits," I told him. "There was a complete *volte face* by PRSU and Roger Munn. In fact, Roger gave everyone present the impression that I was being insubordinate. I would never have put forward the PSDB recommendation for a full scale experiment if he had asked me not to. He knows that. I'm sorry, but I have to tell you that I no longer wish to work for Mr Munn."

Nigel smiled his beautiful smile. "I quite understand." He placed his hand on mine and patted it. "Now, may I suggest that you go home for the rest of the day?"

"You may indeed! I think that is an excellent idea!" And I laughed.

The next day, when I arrived late, at work, the whole team were keen to know what had happened. Rumours were flying about that there had been a dreadful row.

I gave them a brief resume of the discussion at the meeting.

"Why don't we find out what Mike Vickers has to say for himself?" suggested Max.

"That's a good idea," I agreed. "Penny, will you telephone Superintendent Vickers, please, and ask him to come down here?"

Mike Vickers appeared soon afterwards. "I'm sorry, Jane," he said, as he took the proffered chair. "I did the dirty on you yesterday."

"Why did you?"

"I have my job and family to think about."

"You mean, you really think the PSDB proposals are good and viable, but you are hindered in some way from supporting them?" asked Max.

"Yes, that's right."

"Can you tell us why you are hindered from supporting them?" I asked.

"I'm afraid I can't."

"There's something pretty funny going on, if you ask me," said Penny.

"And we'd all like to know what it is," Adam chimed in.

"I'm sorry, team, I just can't tell you," Mike persisted, rising from his seat. "Just take it from me that it's politics." And he left us.

"Politics or not," I said, rising also, "I have some urgent work to see to. The Project Management Committee is due to meet in my office this afternoon to discuss the consultants' written proposals for the Game. After that they hope to see a demonstration of your computer simulation, Elizabeth."

"Penny and I will be waiting for them," responded Elizabeth.

I returned to my office. Not many minutes later there was a knock at the door, and Barry Hoare of the Police College was shown in.

"Forgive me for arriving so early," he apologized, taking a seat. "I know the meeting of the Project Management Committee is this afternoon, but I want to discuss some problems we have at the College with you."

I was listening intently to these when my telephone rang. It was Roger Munn's secretary, telling me that Roger wanted to see me in his office.

"I'm sorry," I spoke as softly as I could, "I saw Mr Lomax yesterday. Mr Munn may wish to have a word with Mr Lomax before seeing me," and I rang off.

Barry continued with his dissertation. Not for long.

Roger threw open the door and stormed into my office. He saw Barry Hoare. "Stay there," he told him. "What I have to say can be said in front of you." Turning round to face me, he virtually screamed at me, "So you no longer wish to work for me! Well, I no longer wish you to work for me! You are sacked! Cancel the meeting for this afternoon and tell the consultants not to come on Monday."

I rose and drew myself up to my full height. With my high heels on I was slightly taller than Roger. I was icily cool. "As I am no longer working for you," I said, "I am not going to do as you ask."

Roger's face turned red with fury. His eyebrows worked up and down. For a moment he stood in front of me beside himself with rage. Then he stormed out of the room slamming the door.

The Project Management Committee meeting and the computer simulation demonstration went ahead, as planned. During the meeting, my telephone rang again. It was Nigel Lomax's secretary. "Mr Lomax would be grateful if you would come and see him when you are free," she said.

I went later that afternoon. Nigel was his usual charming self. "I want you to make it up with Roger Munn," he told me. "After all, I can hardly change the organization of PSDB just to suit you, can I?"

"I wouldn't expect you to. I'll go and apologize to Mr Munn."

"That's a good girl."

I walked down the corridor and knocked on Roger's door.

"Come in."

I went in and stood in front of Roger's desk.

"I apologize for upsetting you," I said.

"Have you been to see Nigel?"

"Yes."

"And he wishes us to continue to work together?"

"Yes, that is so."

"Oh well," said Roger resignedly, "in that case I suppose we must soldier on."

On Monday 24ᵗʰ July the Evaluation Board interviewed the teams of prospective consultants for the Senior Police Management Game and made its choice. I wrote the Board's draft report. On Wednesday I took it to the Police College for the agreement of the other members of the Board, and copies of the final report were circulated on Thursday 27ᵗʰ July.

The Board was of the unanimous opinion that the Local Government Operational Research Unit (LGORU) was the most suitable firm.

Chapter Twenty Two

Humberside & PA Management Consultants

Elizabeth Neve knocked on the door of my office and came in.

"Jane, I'm going to have a baby!"

I came round my desk and took both of Elizabeth's hands in mine.

"How splendid!" I too was delighted. "When is the happy event to be?"

"At the end of February." Elizabeth was all smiles as we both sat down. Then she became serious. "Jane, I'm afraid this means that I will be leaving PSDB at Christmas."

"You mean, that is when you start your maternity leave?" I queried hopefully.

"No. I won't be coming back. My husband and I both feel that a mother should remain at home with her children."

"Well, I can quite understand that," I said. "It's a pity, though, that you are giving up a promising career. I shall certainly miss you. There are few enough career women about. It can make those of us who remain feel quite isolated."

"It was a struggle coming to my decision," admitted Elizabeth.

"Yes," I agreed, "I too had a struggle coming to mine."

An Administrative Note from the Director, dated 24th August 1978, was circulated to all group leaders in PSDB.

TO ALL GROUP LEADERS
INFORMATION EXCHANGE MEETING
The fourth information exchange meeting, a presentation and demonstration by the Electronics Group (E1), will take place at Sandridge on Friday 29 September 1978. All group leaders should attend.

I was delighted. This would be Sally-Ann's fourteenth birthday. Information Exchange meetings always finished in the mid-afternoon, so I would be home early to prepare Sally-Ann's birthday tea.

I had just returned from my annual leave. The development of the Senior Police Management Game was beginning to take off. The Chief Constable of Humberside, Donald Purser, had recruited a new Chief Superintendent, David Lamport.

One of Chief Superintendent Lamport's duties was to be Humberside force's liaison officer on the Game. I had been introduced to him a day or two earlier, when I had travelled up to Hull for a meeting with Donald Purser. The gist of the meeting was that Mr Purser had retained P A Management Consultants to train and direct a team of police officers headed by Chief Superintendent Lamport. This team would be responsible for collecting data for P A Management Consultants, who would analyse these data and publish a report of their findings. The cost would be £100,000. Apparently, P A Management Consultants were expected to start work at the beginning of December. Mr Purser had told me that he did not wish the Senior Police Management Game team to be in the field at the same time as P A Management Consultants, and I had promised that our own data collection would be complete by the end of November.

Poor LGORU, I had thought, I'll have to rope in Mike Vickers and my PSDB team to help, to be sure of meeting that deadline.

Frank Jenner of LGORU, Mike Vickers and I were working out our strategy when my telephone rang.

It was Chief Superintendent David Lamport. "Are you free to meet two Police Federation representatives and a representative of the Superintendents' Association, at 10 am on 6th September in the Federation Office at the Police Headquarters?" he asked.

I checked my diary and confirmed that I was. So was Mike Vickers.

"Both Superintendent Vickers of PRSU and I will be there on the 6th, and possibly Superintendent Baxter of the Police College also," I told him. "Incidentally," I went on, "could we arrange for Superintendent Vickers, Frank Jenner of LGORU, Max Perry and me to spend some time in Humberside? I should like us to visit each Divisional Chief Superintendent in turn to explain the aims of the project, its setting, the data collection requirements; and to introduce the PSDB and LGORU team leaders."

"Leave it with me. I'll set up the visits and be in touch."

"The week beginning Monday 11th September would suit all of us," I told Chief Superintendent Lamport.

The meeting with the representatives of the Superintendents' Association, the Police Federation and the Home Office did not take long. Present were a Chief Superintendent, a Superintendent and a Police Constable from the Humberside force, with Superintendent Roland Baxter of the Police College, Superintendent Mike Vickers and me from the Home Office side.

The police officers were seeking assurances which they at first expressed verbally, and then encapsulated in writing.

To the following, I set my name and the date:

"I, Mrs Jane Hogg, hereby formally give my assurance on behalf of the Home Office, that in the Police Management Game played by the

Senior Command Course students, Humberside will be depicted as it was at the end of 1978/beginning of 1979 and that there will be no use of fictitious names for places."

The following week Frank Jenner, Mike Vickers, Max Perry and I travelled to Humberside, and stayed in the very pleasant family hotel that Inspector Brian Nesbit had previously recommended.

Chief Superintendent David Lamport turned up later that same evening, and took us out to a nearby pub, where he stood a round of drinks. While Mike, Frank and Max found a table to sit at in a corner of the room, I went to the bar with David Lamport. He gave the order to the barmaid. As we waited, he turned to me.

"I'm glad to have had this opportunity to talk to you alone," he said. "The Chief Constable wants you to come to Humberside on Friday 29th September. I can't give you any details, as it's a very 'hush-hush' matter, but the Chief places a great deal of importance on it."

I took my pocket diary out of my handbag and checked it, although I already knew what it contained.

"I can't make it, I am afraid," I said. "My Director has arranged for an Information Exchange Meeting on that day. He is adamant that all group leaders should attend."

The barmaid had our glasses lined up, and was waiting for the money. Chief Superintendent Lamport paid, and we joined the others at their table.

The next three days were spent very profitably visiting, first the Headquarters Commander in charge of finance and personnel, and then each Divisional Chief Superintendent in turn. They were all extremely charming and anxious to help the team in every possible way. The Divisions were visited in alphabetic order: 'A' Division Headquarters at Beverley; 'B' Division HQ at Priory Road; 'C' Division HQ at Queen's Gardens, Hull; ''D' Division HQ at Tower Grange; 'E' Division HQ at Scunthorpe; and 'F' Division HQ at Grimsby.

The telephone rang in my office. I sighed, stopped writing and picked the receiver up.

"Mr Lomax would like to see you now," his secretary told me.

"I'm on my way," I replied.

Nigel was waiting for me, seated behind his desk. He rose as I came in.

"The Chief Constable of Humberside has just been speaking to me on the telephone," he began

I became very alert.

"Mr Purser wants you to go to a very important meeting in Humberside on Friday, 29th September. It is to be an up-and-back one-day visit, and you are to go alone."

I thought Nigel looked a trifle uncomfortable.

"Without Superintendent Mike Vickers, my liaison officer?" I asked.

"Without Superintendent Mike Vickers," Nigel confirmed, looking even more uncomfortable.

"The Information Exchange meeting at Sandridge is on that day," I reminded Nigel. "You wanted *all* your group leaders to be there."

Nigel shuffled his papers. "The Chief Constable's wishes take precedence."

I sat back in my chair, my eyes never leaving his face. "What is the meeting about?" I asked.

"I can't tell you that; all I can say is that the Chief Constable considers it very important."

"Very well," I said, rising. "I'll get in touch with David Lamport."

And I wrote accepting the Chief Superintendent's invitation forthwith.

⁂

Sally-Ann's birthday dawned. She and Jim prepared to leave for the swimming pool as usual. Sally-Ann was clutching her presents, which she would open in the car.

"Don't be too late this evening, Mummy. Remember, it *is* my birthday."

I could feel tears welling up in my eyes. I tried to hide them by giving Sally-Ann a kiss. "I'll try not to be," I promised.

My local train left at 6.57 am for Euston, and I was seated in the Hull train at 7.45, with time to spare.

Four hours and more later, at just after mid-day, it drew in at its destination. It was almost half an hour late, on a three and a half hour journey.

I was fuming. At this rate, I thought, I shall be travelling over ten hours in one 24 hour day.

I gave up my ticket at the barrier and looked round for Chief Superintendent David Lamport.

A young man stepped up to me.

"Mrs Hogg? I am Inspector Robin Callaghan. Chief Superintendent Lamport asked me to meet you and take you to lunch."

I became even more displeased. I did not wish to go to lunch with a strange young man, however presentable. I threw caution to the winds. I hated being secretive, anyway.

"I should like to have lunch at Force Headquarters," I told Inspector Callaghan.

"Chief Superintendent Lamport suggested I take you to a nice quiet country pub."

"I am not a frequenter of pubs," I insisted. "The Force Headquarters canteen would suit me much better."

While we were having coffee in the officers' mess, Superintendent Leslie Rainer joined us. He chatted to me about the choice of Humberside for the Senior Police Management Game and the factors we had chosen for the questionnaire. Superintendent Rainer is reminding me it was a put-up job, I thought angrily, and he is letting me know it. I felt my temper begin to fray. I did not know when or where my meeting was, or with whom for that matter. I decided not to remind Inspector Callaghan about it.

Eventually, he shot a look at his watch, and rose guiltily.

"I'm afraid we're going to be late," he said.

We left Force Headquarters in a hurry and got into Inspector Callaghan's car. He drove as fast as he could in the direction of Beverley. Chief Superintendent Lamport had a set of offices in Beverley, I knew.

"What time is the meeting?" I asked.

"Two o'clock."

I looked at my watch. It was seven minutes to two o'clock. No doubt about it, we were going to be late.

We sped along, leaving Hull behind.

It was just after 2.15 pm when we arrived at Sessions House, Beverley. David Lamport did not seem particularly put out. He greeted me affably enough and showed me into his office. Two men were waiting there.

"Mr Gavin Fuller and Mr Terence Ward of P A Management Consultants. Mrs Jane Hogg, Home Office."

The two men rose and shook hands. We all sat down on hard wooden chairs around a small circular table.

"The Chief Constable thought you should meet," began David Lamport, "as you are both conducting a study in the Force area, and will be requiring very similar data. Mr Fuller is in charge of the P A study, while Mrs Hogg heads the teams developing the Senior Police Management Game for the Police College at Bramshill. Now, if you will excuse me, I'll go and see about some tea."

Mr Fuller produced a P A Management Consultants report on the Humberside Police Force, and handed it to me.

"This is the background to the study. PA did it free of charge."

I flicked through it, noting the main headings. The study was to be a comprehensive investigation of the Force. It was to include the allocation of resources; and the number and pattern of Operational and Traffic Divisions. The Traffic Divisions, I remembered, did not conform to the Operational Divisions. There were fewer of them, and there was no counterpart to 'C' Division.

Mr Fuller and Mr Ward had been watching me in silence. Now Mr Fuller spoke with emphasis. *"You are independently to produce the same findings as PA."*

"Really!" I was cool but furious. So that was why I had been dragged up to Humberside on my daughter's birthday! "My brief is to provide you with all the data on Humberside my teams collect. My conclusions will be my own!"

David Lamport returned just as I finished speaking. Seeing three angry faces, his expression changed.

"You are to return to London. Now!" he commanded me. "And you must hurry. Inspector Callaghan will drive you to Brough to catch the train." And without further ado, he hustled me out of his office, past the steaming cups of tea sitting on a tray with a plate of biscuits. There were four cups, I noted.

Once again, I took my place in the car beside Inspector Callaghan, as he drove madly across the countryside.

"What went wrong?" he asked.

"I'm not sure."

We reached Brough station just as the train from Hull was pulling in. I got on and found that I had to change at Doncaster. That train to London was full. Even with my first class ticket, I could not find a seat. Not in the First Class compartments; not in the Second Class compartments; not in the buffet cars.

I was standing outside a buffet car when a drunk jointed me and tried to be matey. The Head Waiter passed, saw my predicament, and took me into his compartment. There I spent the rest of the journey to King's Cross reading a book and wondering about the abrupt exit from Sessions House, Beverley.

I reached home around 8.30 pm, absolutely shattered, having started out at 6.30 am. Neither Sally-Ann nor Jim were in the least sympathetic.

"Mummy," said Sally-Ann plaintively, "why did you have to go away on my birthday?"

CHAPTER TWENTY THREE

SUPT JEREMY
BRIGHT'S DISGUSTING STORY

A letter from Humberside Police Force was dropped into my in-tray. I picked it up wearily and opened the envelope. It was from David Lamport. A small piece of paper which had been attached fluttered onto my desk.

The official letter, full of details about future arrangements, finished on a charming note. "I am pleased to hear that all your contacts so far have proved friendly and hospitable. Without detracting from your personal charm, I know that this was due in no small measure to the hard work which you put in the P. R. aspects of initial visits."

The message on the smaller piece of paper was handwritten:

"Extra note slipped in to thank you for making journey to Beverley last Friday. Although a long trek for short visit it was, I hope, worthwhile in that you met the P.A. people. Let me reiterate that I don't see P. A. taking precedence over your project – no question the LGORU team taking 2nd place in any data collection; either qualitatively or timing."

I did not hear from Chief Superintendent Lamport again for a week. Then I had a telephone call. "The Chief Constable wishes to see you," he announced in his most official tone. "You are to be in his office at 10 am on Tuesday 17ᵗʰ October."

"What's it about?"

"Your CID programme," and David Lamport rang off.

I looked at the letter from the Chief Superintendent heading the Humberside CID, to which I was just on the point of replying. It set out a detailed programme on CID work, very similar to the Operations programme I had followed in May. This time I was to be on duty from Thursday 19ᵗʰ October to Wednesday 25ᵗʰ October inclusive. At the same time the LGORU and PSDB teams were to be in Humberside data collecting; except these teams were starting on Monday 16ᵗʰ October.

Tuesday morning arrived. I presented myself at the Chief Constable's office on the stroke of 10 o'clock.

Donald Purser was very curt. "I have cancelled the CID programme arranged for you by the Chief Superintendent," he told me severely. "I do not wish you or any member of your team to talk to anyone below Inspector rank. Nor are you to accompany any officer on his operational duties. Interviews only are allowed."

"Yes, sir," I responded and. added, "I do hope that I have not inadvertently caused some trouble."

The Chief Constable seemed to relax slightly at this, but then stiffened again. "These instructions are being promulgated in Force General Orders for all police officers to see and note."

I was dismissed. I was clearly *persona non gratia* with the Chief Constable.

I and my teams concentrated on data collection. Superintendent Mike Vickers was a tower of strength. He worked the LGORU team so hard they were completely worn out by the time they returned to our hotel, hardly able to drag one foot after the other. My PSDB team and I tried to emulate them; even Elizabeth, advanced in pregnancy, came to Humberside.

I did interview after interview; and time and time again the police officers warned me there was something afoot. The proposed hotel to replace the Police Headquarters at Queen's Gardens, I thought, but kept that thought to myself.

By the middle of November our data collection was complete. The field was open to P A Management Consultants.

Elizabeth Neve held her farewell party on Wednesday 13th December.

"Why did you choose this particular date?" I asked her while the party was in full swing.

"Roger Munn suggested it," replied Elizabeth. "He told me Nigel would find the 13th a convenient day."

Adam, who was standing nearby, overheard this. "And I joined Systems III on the 13th of March," he chimed in. "Perhaps there's some significance in the number 13."

"The first time it's chance," explained Max, "the second time it's coincidence, the third time it's deliberate." He laughed. "So the number 13 is just coincidence."

Roger Munn joined us. "What are you talking about?" he asked, having heard the tail end of the conversation.

Elizabeth told him.

It was then I remembered. I had had my first meeting with Roger after joining PSDB on the 13th of October. That was when he had talked about Kafka and only the victim knowing the truth!

Later I said my goodbyes to Elizabeth and wished her well.

"The same to you and the team," responded Elizabeth.

"We may need all the best wishes we can get," I laughed.

Roger Munn gave a sardonic smile.

Jim and Sally-Ann set off by car for Edinburgh. Sally-Ann was entered for the Scottish National Swimming Championships.

I was in my office wondering from time to time how my husband and little daughter were getting on, when the telephone rang. It was Jim, calling from Rugby.

"Come and get us," Jim said. "We've had an accident. The front tyre burst."

My stomach turned over with fear.

"How are you? Where's Sally-Ann? What happened? Oh my God!"

"We're okay." Jim's voice sounded very far away. "Sally-Ann's here with me: she bruised a toe, otherwise she's all right. My neck and back are a bit stiff; no cuts or anything, and no bones broken. We're both a bit shaken up, but we're okay. We were so lucky, Jane! There was nothing I could do."

"Where are you?" And Jim told me.

"Jim, I'm setting out right away. I'll be with you as soon as I can."

How lucky they had really been, only emerged when I heard the story at greater length. The road had been open, and no other vehicle was involved, though the car had veered wildly as soon as the burst occurred. It had hit the central crash barrier to bounce off it and veer to the side of the road to hit the only crash barrier for miles, as the slip road to Rugby was just coming up. The car then turned over onto its roof, sliding for several yards before coming to a standstill.

I saw the car at a local garage when we went round to pick up Jim and Sally-Ann's luggage: it was a total write-off.

⌇

The PSDB and HORU proposals for research into Preventive Policing had been developed further. I had spent several sessions with Nigel and Roger. They were then put forward by the Police Department for consultation with ACPO, through the Police Department Research Committee. They did not get through.

A friendly Home Office Statistician came to tell me the bad news.

"It's a shame about the PSDB proposals," he said. "They looked good, and we would have been very interested in the results."

"Thank you," I replied. "Unfortunately, neither Nigel Lomax nor Roger Munn have any background in statistical methods; and I don't think they were fully committed to them anyway." I spoke without thinking, but from the heart.

"Why didn't you come to the Research Committee meeting and present the proposals yourself?"

"I wasn't asked to. I didn't even know the date of the meeting."

Dr Milton Hubbard of the Royal Military College of Science at Shrivenham was worrying me.

First, he had proposed that a computer at RMCS be used for the Senior Police Management Game. I had vetoed that, as it did not suit the Police College, or the LGORU and PSDB teams; but Dr Hubbard had continued to press for its use.

Then, he had asked that all the place names for the Force on which the Game was based should be fictitious. Remembering my promise to the Superintendents' Association and the Police Federation, I had vetoed that also.

His next proposal was that the Game's main problems should be centred around the growth of a fictitious new town in South Humberside.

I became exasperated. I telephoned Dr Hubbard and invited him to a meeting in my office. He was reluctant, but he came.

"Why are you so keen on this development of a new town as your first scenario?" I asked.

Dr Hubbard had his answer ready.

"It will help to focus the students' attention: they will be concerned with updating the Force establishment; with the identification of a site for a new station and with the planning processes involved in its construction; with the budgeting for new resources; and finally with the planning of new divisional boundaries."

"I have to tell you that I see at least three major problems here," I told Dr Hubbard. "In the first place, siting a new town in South Humber-side does not exacerbate the Force's difficulties, as South Humberside is at present overmanned in comparison to North Humberside. Secondly, this scenario would have to be based on hypothetical data. My understanding is that this would not be appropriate for police officers who are always extremely concerned about the accuracy of their information. They would be inclined to treat the Game as a fun game and not as a serious learning exercise. We have spent a good deal of time and money ensuring that the models being developed by LGORU and PSDB are authentic in every detail. All this would be wasted if the Game were to be based on hypothetical data. And, finally, the Superintendents' Association and the Police Federation have specifically asked for my assurance that the Game would be based on Humberside as it is and would use actual data."

Milton Hubbard cogitated for a while. Then he turned towards me.

"I should like clarification as to who actually is in charge of the development of this Game."

"Why, I am, of course," I replied in surprise.

"That is not my understanding."

"Then who, according to your understanding, is in charge?"

"Roger Munn has been meeting Professor Holden in the company of the Deputy Commandant of the Police College," explained Dr Hubbard, "and that is why I have been having problems with the requirements for the Game."

"Roger Munn, Professor Holden and the Deputy Commandant form the Policy Steering Group," I explained. "Thank you for telling me. It seems that I had better try and sort this problem out within PSDB. Thank you also for coming to see me. You've been most helpful."

The next morning I went to see Nigel Lomax, who listened patiently as I repeated the worries I had expressed to Milton Hubbard.

"Please let me have a written brief," he said, after I had finished. "That was rather a lot for me to digest."

"I'll do it straight away," I promised.

While I was working on my memo to Nigel I found that I needed some information from Frank Jenner of LGORU. He did not know the answer straight away, and promised to call me back.

I put the receiver down just as Sergeant Mary Tierney, Albert Walton's secretary, entered my office. She appeared to be in a state of some excitement.

"Will you come and have coffee with me?"

Something was afoot: that was obvious. I decided I had better find out what that something was. I looked at my watch: the time was 11.15 am.

"Thank you, Mary," I replied, "but I'm waiting for a telephone call. May I come after an early lunch – say, around one o'clock?"

"One o'clock it is," agreed Mary, and made her retreat.

Two hours later, I was having a pleasant chat in the big PRSU office where Mary had her desk, and which she shared with Superintendent Mike Vickers. We were alone.

The door opened and Superintendent Jeremy Bright came in. He settled himself down in a comfortable chair and Mary gave him a cup of coffee. Mary had a soft spot for Jeremy.

Cup in hand, the Superintendent turned to me.

"Heard anything from Damien Grant?" he asked.

"No, nothing."

"He was coming back, wasn't he?"

"So he said."

"When you spent that week on the beat at Humberside last May, Damien was with you, wasn't he?"

"Only for the first day of introductory talks."

"Talking about being on the beat," Jeremy continued, "how squeamish are you? I don't suppose you really experienced the worst horrors."

"No, I don't suppose I did," I agreed

"Would you like to have your education further enlarged?" Jeremy pressed me.

"Why not?"

"In this town in which I once served there was a dame. This dame had a way with dogs. They all loved her. Well, one day we found that we had a use for this dame. There were a lot of stray dogs to be rounded up. So we got a van, went round for this dame and put her in it. Then we circled the town collecting the dogs."

Jeremy stopped and waited for me to say something. I obliged

"How did this lady help you?" I asked.

"Well, the dogs could smell her from miles away, and would home in like bees to honey. They fucked her, you see."

I nearly fainted. I went as white as a sheet and flopped in my chair. The filthy story hit me like a bolt from the blue.

Jeremy Bright rose and looked down at me with satisfaction.

"Take Damien Grant now," he continued. "If you really loved him, you would take his penis in your mouth. What's the matter with you sexually?"

I almost screamed.

"Stop, you're making me feel sick!"

Mary Tierney turned on me. "Shame on you," she said, "a married man with a family!"

Jeremy went to the door, opened it, and paused. "I'll see you again – later," he promised.

I struggled to sit up straight.

"Will you have some more coffee?" asked Mary.

"Yes, please." I really needed some now. I gulped it down gratefully.

In distress, I got to my feet, walked from the room and along the corridor, and down the stairs, clinging to the banister as I went. I was absolutely white and shaking. Dr Alan Hardy, the PSO in charge of the Fingerprints Group saw me, and took me to his office.

"What has happened?" he asked.

I told him, as best I could.

"You'd better tell Roger about this," Alan said.

"No, I don't think so," I replied. "I don't think anyone else should know. But, please, would you do me a favour? Please have a quiet word with Jeremy and advise him to go no further."

"Will do," promised Alan.

Somehow I got through the rest of the day.

CHAPTER TWENTY FOUR

JANE IS ACCUSED
OF 'BEING ON THE GAME'

The next morning I got out a memo pad and wrote a note to Chief Superintendent Albert Walton, requesting a meeting about a private matter.

That afternoon I was summoned to his office. My rage and fear had evaporated. I only hoped I had not stirred up a metaphorical hornets' nest.

Albert Walton went straight into the attack.

"So! You are making a complaint against the police!"

"I am not making a complaint against the police," I replied as calmly as I could. "I just wanted to … ."

"Oh! So you are making a complaint against me!"

He jumped up, and went over to the door which connected with his secretary's room. "Come in, I want you as a witness."

Mary Tierney arrived.

The two police officers sat down and concentrated their attention on me. I wondered how I was going to express my worries now that Mary Tierney was present.

"You are having an affair with Damien Grant," Chief Superintendent Albert Walton stated flatly.

"No, I am not!" I blazed.

"You cannot cope with your job," he went on, in the same monotone. "You are under strain. You're cracking up. You should go and see your doctor."

He paused, but as I struggled for something to say, he continued, "Mark my words, you're a suicide case. I know it. You're going to jump out of the window." He turned to Mary Tierney. "Please will you get us all a cup of tea?"

She left the room.

Almost magically, Albert Walton's mien and manner changed completely.

"I'm a very ill man," he explained to me, in a voice close to a whisper. "I have something fearfully wrong with my stomach. I shall be retiring on medical grounds at the end of April."

I wiped my eyes with my handkerchief.

"I'm so sorry," I sympathised. "I do hope you are not in too much pain."

"It's there all the time," he told me, his hands on his stomach.

Mary Tierney arrived with a full tray. We sat sipping tea and nibbling at biscuits. It was like the calm after a storm.

Albert Walton finished his tea and put down his cup.

"I'll see Nigel about this matter," he promised.

I felt very tired and depressed. "I can't see the point," I said. "It will only make matters worse."

⚜

Matters did indeed get worse. I was summoned to see Roger Munn.

"In future," he barked, like a schoolmaster reproving an erring child, "you are not to travel with any police officer or stay in a hotel with any police officer."

"I should like to point out," I replied, "that it was not me who sent me round the countryside with a police officer or put me up in a hotel with a police officer."

But Roger was not listening. He waved a hand of dismissal at me.

Max Perry was waiting in my office. He laughed as he stood in front of me. "So, police officers need protection from you!"

"Don't be silly," I snapped. "They are grown men."

"Sorry, Jane." Max's expression changed at once. "I hadn't realized it was that bad. You know what a misogynist Roger Munn is. Nobody is taking him seriously."

I sat down, and so did he.

"Thanks, Max. You're quite right. I'm getting things out of proportion. It's just that Roger does rather wear me down sometimes."

Max changed the subject.

"I thought you ought to be the first to know," he said, "that I shall be leaving PSDB at the end of April. I've got a job with Logica. And between you and me, I think Roger Munn had a hand in it. It's worth more than promotion. Sometimes he's not such a bad chap after all."

It was the 2^(nd) of April 1978, and the Institute of Professional Civil Servants had called its members out on a one day strike. I was obliged to stay at home; but I was at my desk in my study, working. I had a presentation to give at the Police College the next day. A copy of the notes of the last meeting of the Project Management Committee lay on the desk. I picked it up, and noted one paragraph:

"Mr Hoare doubted whether anyone at the College could visualize the Game. It was agreed that the workshop would start with short presentations on the purposes and principles of gaming (Mrs Hogg), alternative scenarios and problems (Dr Hubbard), the computerized representation of the relevant environment and interaction with the Directing Staff (Mr Jenner and Mr Perry). These presentations would help familiarize the Senior Command Course staff with the Game's concepts and structure which would enable the maximum benefit to be achieved from the subsequent discussions."

I sighed. I had had no time to prepare my presentation. It would have to be completed today, and I would have to draw my own viewgraphs. I set to work.

Half way through the morning Max Perry, who was not a member of IPCS, telephoned. "Roger Munn is looking for you," he warned.

The next day I led the presentations on the Senior Police Management Game to the Deputy Commandant, the Command Course Director and the Command Course staff. Dr Milton Hubbard of RMCS, Frank Jenner of LGORU and Max Perry of PSDB followed me with their presentations. They were very well received; with the informal discussion continuing after supper. Dr Hubbard's workshop the day after was also a great success.

On Thursday I was back in my office, and was almost immediately called to the Director's office.

Nigel Lomax, seated behind his desk, looked very stern. He left me standing.

"I am giving the Police Management Game to Alex Mason."

I, startled and hardly able to believe what I was hearing, managed to retain a semblance of calm. "I should be grateful for an explanation of this course of action," I said. And when he did not reply, I continued. "The Police College is very pleased with the Game's development, as was evident by the reaction to the presentations and workshop we held there yesterday and the day before."

Nigel softened. "All right. I'll go and see the people concerned at the College."

I breathed a sigh of relief.

"Would you be good enough to let Roger Munn know the outcome of our meeting?" Nigel continued.

"Certainly," I said.

I found Roger alone in his office, and gave him Nigel's message.

"There's nothing to worry about," I added, "as the staff at the Police College, in particular the Command Course Director and the Command Course staff, are very pleased with the progress of the project."

Roger smiled. "The Police College will say what we want it to say," he replied ominously.

The days ticked by. Preparations continued for a presentation of the Senior Police Management Game to the Assistant Under Secretary of State, Her Majesty's Chief Inspector of Constabulary, and other senior Home Office officials; with a rehearsal beforehand on 18th April. On Tuesday 10th April a Project Management Committee was held at the Police College with me in the Chair. Everything seemed normal.

The next day, I was again summoned to the Director's office. This time I was invited to take a seat.

"I have called you in to confirm your 'sack' from the Game project," Nigel told me.

I felt myself fainting. It was as well I had been allowed to sit. I fought to bring myself under control and just succeeded.

"I have seen the staff at the Police College, as promised," he informed me.

"Who did you see?" I asked hoarsely. "You saw only the Deputy Commandant, didn't you? No one else!"

"Yes," agreed Nigel. "I saw only the Deputy Commandant: but I am not changing my mind. Your staff are all leaving you. You have lost the respect of the police. Penny Stevens will transfer to Alex Mason's Group. Adam Tyler remains with you – at his own request. I suggest you take the rest of the day off, and go and see your doctor. Get him to prescribe some Valium. It might soothe your nerves. Your father committed suicide, didn't he?"

Jim learned of this latest twist with every appearance of sympathy; but even on him the strain was beginning to tell.

There was very little work left for me to do. I had passed over all the Game files to Alex Mason and given him a briefing. I had also given him Adam Tyler, despite that young man's protestations.

"It will do you no good to stay with me," I had told him. "Besides, the only work which remains is Preventive Policing and that will not even keep me occupied."

I was left on my own, with Superintendent Mike Vickers watching my every move. I was sent to Lancashire and to Lincolnshire to observe those forces' Preventive Policing experiments, with the Superintendent in close attendance. But on my own initiative I also wrote the PSDB Technical Memorandum *An Introduction to the Senior Police Management Game.* It was given the number 13/79.

I became aware of whisperings in the corridors amongst groups of people as I passed. Some would give me anxious looks. From time to time the words, "suicide … window," seemed to be wafted to my ears.

One morning, unexpectedly, Alan Weston paid me a visit. He looked worried and concerned. He refused a cup of coffee and came straight to the point.

"Jane, are you going to commit suicide? Are you going to jump out of a window?"

I looked at Alan in surprise. "Not likely," I assured him with a mild laugh. "I can't fly. I might hurt my toe."

His whole frame relaxed at that, and he laughed too. "You know, Jane, I think you should come back to SAB."

"Thank you, Alan," I said, genuinely moved. "You're probably right. I'll think about it."

When he had gone, I pondered over my predicament. My office was well equipped with windows: there would certainly be no difficulty in pushing me out of one of them. I began to feel scared. Well, I thought in a slight panic, I'd better give the lie to these rumours. I'll go on some shopping sprees.

A succession of lunchtimes was spent by me at the shops. I bought sets of outfits from Jaeger, shoes from Ferragamo, linen from Harrods.

Then one lunchtime as I was walking through St James' Park, I met Peter Scott who had been a Principal in G1 Division of the Fire Department when I had been in charge of the Fire Section in SAB.

We exchanged friendly greetings.

Peter said, "I hear you are not liking PSDB too much these days."

"That's one way of putting it," I agreed.

"Your AUSS tells me you've been taken off the Game because you are 'on the game'."

I reeled under the metaphorical blow. Barely recovering myself, I replied, "I understand that is the innuendo."

We parted, and I carried on to the shops in a state of complete shock. I did not buy anything.

That afternoon I sat in my office trying to read the American research reports on split-level policing. The words were on the page but they did not convey any meaning to me. At one point, the door opened and Roger Munn's secretary came in to stand before my desk. She was saying something but I could not comprehend what it was. I tried to reply, but found that I was in tears. I could not speak. The secretary went away; and the tears came in a flood.

After five minutes, or perhaps longer, the tears abated. I dabbed at my face with a handkerchief. I got out the Home Office Directory and looked up the telephone number of the Head of Welfare Section at the Establishment Department. He arranged to see me the following morning.

I poured out my story into his friendly ear. He listened in silence. At last I finished and dabbed at my eyes with a handkerchief.

"You have been having such a bad time for so long," the Head of Welfare Section commented, "it would only be fair to you for the Home Office to give you early retirement."

"And I would be only too delighted to accept."

Off he went to see Charles Devereaux, the AUSS, Establishment Department. Ten minutes later he returned. "Mr Devereaux's secretary will arrange an interview; but it will be some weeks as he is going on holiday to Corfu."

I went on sick leave.

When I returned to the office Charles Devereaux's secretary telephoned to confirm a date.

Roger Munn heard about it, and called me into his office. He left me standing while he lolled in his chair.

"What do you hope to achieve?" he asked.

"Early retirement."

"But you will be able to get another job!"

"Yes, I will."

Roger's face darkened. He flapped a hand towards the door. I was dismissed.

Chapter Twenty Five

Jane returns to SAB

There was some kind of conspiracy: that much was obvious. And what I was doing on the Game was somehow interfering with it. If I could only use my training to isolate the common factors .... Then it came to me: I would go through all the files on the Senior Police Management Game.

I did, and some days later I thought that I probably knew the truth – probably, deep down, I had always known it, ever since my days at the Fire Research Station. I remembered telling Jimmy Fry about my decision to go to the Home Office. "Are you sure you are wise?" he had asked me. "You know what is going on there." And what had I replied? "Don't worry, I'll put a stop to it." Brave words! Brave, foolish words!

I picked up my phone and rang my brother at his British American Tobacco office nearby.

"Pascal, Jane here."

"Hullo, Jane! What can I do for you?"

"I should like to see you on a very serious matter."

There was a pause while he examined his diary.

"All right – shall we say 8.15 on Wednesday 23rd May, here in my office?"

Later that same morning, I was summoned to see Roger Munn in his office. He had a completed annual staff report in his hand - it was my own. He handed it over, and I knew at once it must be bad: if good I would never have been shown it.

I sat down at Roger's conference table without being invited and went through it, Roger watching me quietly. The Countersigning Officer's remarks were covered over, I noted, so that I could not see them. That would be Nigel Lomax, I thought. The ASR branded me as inefficient with an overall marking of 5.

I had brought a pad of paper with me, and while Roger continued to sit observing me, and clearly enjoying the scene, I copied the report out. This took some time. When I had finished, I returned the original to him, and left his office without a word. I went straight to Tony Murray, the Administrative Officer, for a blank report form. Back in my own office, I filled it in so that it was identical to the one Roger had shown me except that the space for the Countersigning Officer's remarks remained blank. I then wrote a covering note. "I do not agree with the substance of this report and request that an independent assessor review my performance since September 1977." The original ASR together with my covering note was then sent off to the Establishment Department by Tony Murray. I kept a copy of both.

So that puts paid to my early retirement, I thought. I obviously cannot get another job now; especially not with what Nigel Lomax must have written behind that blanked out Section of my ASR. It would be something about being on the game, I imagined.

At my meeting with Pascal, I briefed him as best I could.

"You've obviously stumbled onto something they don't want you to know about," he said. "If you do nothing to harm them, they will do nothing to harm you. Our first task, therefore, is to contact Damien Grant."

"Why?"

"We have to find out if the stories of your having an affair originated with him. If they did, he'd better stop making them. If they did not, let him come out and deny the allegations."

I was doubtful but I had asked Pascal for his advice and this was it.

"Damien Grant is in Bristol," Pascal continued. "As it happens an ex-Cambridge University friend of mine practises in Bristol. His name is Harry Andrews. I'll arrange for him to come and see you. Then he can contact Superintendent Grant on your behalf."

Harry Andrews telephoned me that same day.

"Your brother Pascal has spoken with me about your case. I suggest that I come up and see you."

"When?"

"Tomorrow morning at your home. What's the address?"

I told him. I was astonished at the speed things were moving.

Harry Andrews arrived promptly at 10.00 am the next day. Once again I recounted the details of my predicament. The solicitor took copious notes and a copy of my ASR with my covering note.

The interview over, Harry Andrews picked up his hat, coat and brief-case.

"By the way," he said, as he was stepping out of the front door, "what's your expertise in?"

"Fire Cover," I told him, with a twinge of pride.

"What's that?"

"The siting and manning of fire stations."

"Ah!... Good day. I'll contact Damien Grant as soon as possible. Don't worry. Everything will be fine."

My meeting with Charles Devereaux, the Assistant Under Secretary of State, Establishment Department, took place. I had to go through my whole story yet again. Charles Devereaux decided to appoint an assessor, "to give opinions as to your technical ability and to the soundness of your technical judgement and proposals at appropriate points," as he put it.

Without warning, some days later, Harry Andrews was ushered into my office.

"This is a surprise," I said, rising and offering him a chair.

"Just a quick visit," Harry replied, settling himself comfortably. "Just to let you know that I've seen Damien Grant. Superintendent Grant had nothing to do with any rumours and is denying the allegations."

"That is good news."

"By the way, is there a police language?"

"Yes, there is."

He became very excited, and immediately asked me to get the secretary of the AUSS, Establishment Department, on the telephone.

I did as he asked, and within minutes he had fixed an appointment to see Charles Devereaux.

"Thank you. Now I must go."

I walked with him to the front door and out into Dean Ryle Street. There Harry Andrews spotted a flower stall. He rushed over to it, bought a large bunch of red roses and thrust it into my hands. Then he tipped his bowler hat at me and strode off.

I was perturbed. I took the bunch of red roses back to my office, prepared a vase of water, and put the roses into it.

Certainly, they look very nice, I thought.

Then I climbed the stairs to my old haunts on the seventh floor. I asked John Clayton's secretary if I could have a word with him.

John Clayton saw me at once. Yes, he assured me, he would be pleased to have me back in SAB.

I was being 'accompanied' wherever I went; on the trains, on the buses, walking in the street, and my telephone at home had developed an 'echo'.

I went to visit my cousin Elizabeth who owned a boutique in Pimlico, called *The Butterfly*. Questions were asked about the boutique. "Elizabeth is my cousin," I replied. I shopped at Janet Reager's in Bond Street. The name 'Janet Reager' was mentioned soon afterwards. I sprinted for a bus. My 'companion' made sure that he boarded that bus too, and scolded me as he sat down beside me. I managed to lose my 'tail' when I changed underground trains at Euston to go to the dentist, instead of going up to the main line station and catching a train to Kings Langley and home. A rather cross ex-military policeman sitting in my usual carriage the next day asked me where I had gone. "To the dentist," I replied serenely.

Some of my 'companions' were at the Home Office; often on short term contracts. Others were people I had been introduced to at a friend's office party, while yet others were complete strangers. I discovered the names of those I could, laughing inwardly at the obvious embarrassment of the Executive Officer with whom I checked the names. These names I listed in my pocket diary.

I also discovered that I had 'friends', some in quite high places. "Keep fighting," one said. "I will," I promised him. "You'll be all right as long as you keep your sense of humour," another told me. "You knew it all the time, didn't you?" said another. I agreed, "Yes, I did. But I didn't have all the links." And then I received the most interesting information of all. "The cause of all your troubles," I was told, "stems from a network of influential people known as 'The System'. The Home Office group was founded sometime after the War by the then Heads of the Police Department, the Establishment Department and the Fire Department." I checked this out with another 'friend'. "Not the Head of the Fire Department," he corrected me, adding, "but since the Head of the Establishment Department was involved, he was able to ensure that the 'right' people are now in the 'right' places."

Others, who were less well disposed, kept insinuating: 'The System' always wins.

Meanwhile, I was transferred back to SAB. I was moved up to the seventh floor suddenly, with no notice, while I was having a cup of coffee; around 10.30 am. I was busy gathering material from the PSDB files for my assessor, Professor Patrick Rivett of Brighton University. The files went with me, and I continued to work on them.

Harry Andrews showed up in my office soon after my return to SAB.

"Hullo Jane" he said. "How are you? I haven't seen you for some time."

"I'm fine, thank you."

I watched him open his briefcase and get out some papers. The moment had arrived, I decided, to face him with a theory I had.

"I know what it's all about," I said. "A hotel in Hull."

Harry Andrews acted very strangely. He jumped! His briefcase and papers went clattering onto the floor.

"Oh, my God! Clients' money involved.... . Don't fight it! Look at your terrible report." He had retrieved the copy of my ASR from the floor. "Look at this dreary office. You wouldn't want to stay here for the rest of your working days. You should take early retirement. It's in your best interests."

I watched the performance with interest. I laughed.

"I think you had better go now," I told him.

Harry Andrews went, with me escorting him out of the building.

Shortly afterwards, he wrote withdrawing his services and enclosing his account. I replied by return of post, thanking him "for putting me in the picture". I enclosed my cheque.

A very cheerful visitor came into my office. He was Alan Weston.

"We are working together again," he announced with a smile as he took a seat.

"What on?"

"You're to develop a casualty model to predict the outcome of a nuclear strike on the UK. You'll be using one of the Zilog micro-computers."

"That's rather a tall order, isn't it? After all, the casualty model developed by Des Perryman is running on a mainframe."

"Oh, but there have been great advances in computer technology recently," Alan assured me. "Anyway, you should find it interesting. As well as the fall-out radiation and blast damage which is in Des's model, John Clayton wants you to include the damage from initial radiation and from fire. You will have to allow for different wind speeds and directions; and also for alternative attack patterns."

"And I suppose we'll be making the usual assumption that the entire population will be holed up in their homes?"

"No, not necessarily. The AS of the Emergency Services Division (that is F6 Division, you know), wants you to allow for alternative policy options on shelter and evacuation," and he described the various options the AS had in mind.

"And you think I can put all this on a micro-computer? What population data am I to use?"

"The 1971 census data for the UK is set up as the number of people to every square kilometre. And there's an associated Local Authority Number file which defines each square kilometre by the district in which that square kilometre falls. Using these, you have to estimate the numbers of dead and seriously injured from blast, burns and radiation, the numbers affected, the numbers unaffected but at risk, the numbers homeless, etc, from any given attack, according to any given policy on evacuation and shelter."

"What about social response? People may take it into their heads to flee regardless of policy, or they may just feel it's a waste of time trying to improve the protection in their own homes. What do I do about that?"

"Nothing as yet."

"Well, that's a comfort anyway."

"Come on, Jane," said Alan, "never say die. I'm sure you will manage – somehow."

I put my face in my hands. "And you are to help me in some way?"

"Well, no," Alan replied apologetically, "but George Carr-Hill will help you with the scientific calculations you require. He's a brilliant scientist and would be a PSO by now except he is poor in communication skills. The two of you together will be an ideal combination."

Sitting up straight, I laughed. "That's great."

He got up, thought of something, and sat down again.

"You must know, Jane, you can't beat 'The System'."

I was not going to let this opportunity slip.

"How is it financed?" I asked.

"Through the use of 'dead votes'," he replied. "For example, there's a particular Immigration and Nationality Department vote on which little or nothing is currently happening, which is being used. There are only three Principals in the Finance Department and they are too overwhelmed to notice it."

※

I was waiting for the train at Euston underground station, quite close to the end of the platform beside the tunnel. Someone was by my side. It was a morning in early December. I had overslept and was late for work. The platform was crowded with a dense mass of commuters.

The person turned out to be a middle aged gentleman, bowler hatted and smartly dressed.

"What a pretty face you have," he said to me.

I smiled bleakly. "I'm afraid it doesn't do me much good."

"Don't I know you?" the gentleman said.

"I don't think so," I replied.

The train came in with a roar, and slowed to a halt. The doors of a very crowded carriage opened in front of me. I started to get in, and the man followed. I changed my mind and stepped back onto the platform, letting the other commuters push their way on. The man changed his mind too, and rejoined me. The doors began to close. At the very last moment I squeezed through them into the carriage. Somehow the man managed to squeeze in too.

During the journey to the Embankment the man introduced himself. "My name is Timothy Devlin. I am an Operational Research Scientist, a SPSO working at the Ministry of Defence Headquarters. I should like to make an appointment for lunch."

I prevaricated.

On reaching the Embankment station, we left the train together and made our way up the stairs towards the exit. Then, breaking swiftly from the man's side, I dashed for the Circle/District line platform. A train had just arrived. I threw myself into the nearest carriage and was carried away to Westminster. From there I walked the rest of the way to Horseferry House.

A couple of days later, Timothy Devlin rang me at my office. "I want you to come to lunch with me."

I thought back. I had not given Timothy Devlin either my name or my telephone number, and neither was, at that time, listed in the Home Office Directory.

"There's a nice Italian restaurant I know," he pursued, giving me its name.

"That restaurant is too far away," I informed him, "but I will be pleased to accept your invitation on condition that we go to the restaurant below my office in Horseferry House."

"I'll meet you there," he promised.

"No," I said. "I'd prefer it if you presented yourself at the entrance desk in Horseferry House and asked the security guard to telephone me."

Lunch was pleasant enough. I quite enjoyed dodging all Timothy Devlin's leading questions about the Home Office.

I allowed myself to be taken out once more by Timothy Devlin, this time to the Marquis of Granby pub for a lunchtime drink. In the meantime I had checked his claim to be a SPSO working at the Ministry of Defence Headquarters. There was no trace of him in the Civil Service directories. I had also telephoned a fellow OR Scientist I knew at the Defence Operational Analysis Establishment at West Byfleet. He had never heard of Timothy Devlin.

"You are not who you say you are," I told him, as I finished my drink in the Marquis of Granby.

Timothy Devlin merely smiled. He made no reply.

CHAPTER TWENTY SIX

AN ASSASSIN AND
A JOURNEY TO BRISTOL

Day in and day out I worked in the computer room on the Zilog. Fortunately I was not alone: whenever I had trouble understanding how my machine worked, one or other of SAB's junior scientists rallied to my aid. Without them I would never have succeeded in writing the enormous nuclear attack casualty program on the tiny Zilog. As the early part of 1980 wore on the program was beginning to take shape, and parts of it were running.

By this date, my assessor, Professor Patrick Rivett of Brighton University, had reported on my technical merit: in my favour.

One day in mid-March, I was at my desk poring over the latest print-out, when Sid Butler arrived with a form in his hand, which he passed over to me. It was my Annual Staff Report for the current year.

"I brought it in for you to complete Section 2a, describing the various tasks on which you have been employed since your last ASR," he told me.

I gave a wry smile; that would not take up much of my time.

Sid Butler spoke again. "Nigel Lomax will be reporting on your period in PSDB, and John Clayton will be the Countersigning Officer."

I looked up at Sid in alarm. "You mean, you won't be my Reporting Officer?"

"That's right," he agreed. "And what is more, the form needs to be completed urgently. Nigel Lomax is retiring at the end of the week."

Sid departed and I was left to mull over the likely sequel. It was not hard to imagine what kind of annual report I would get from Nigel and John Clayton. Slowly I leafed through the report form: and then I cheered up. My service history was faulty! That would give me the time I needed. With a smile I appended a memo to the Establishment Department, pointing out the error and requesting an accurate report form. I slipped the faulty form and my covering memo into an envelope and put it in my out-tray. Then I took my annual leave chit from my drawer; wrote "17 March" in the column headed 'from' and "28 March" in the column headed 'to'. I tidied my office; put on my hat and coat, and set off for home immediately, remembering to leave my annual leave chit with Sid Butler's secretary on my way out.

Back home I went through my diaries. Sitting at my desk in the study, I wrote out the story of my time in PSDB, carefully and with infinite detail. It was to take me the whole fortnight I had taken on leave.

❧

As I went into my study on my second week on leave, I noted for the nth time the hole in the glass of our front door where a bullet had passed through recently. That will go when the extension at the front of the house is built, I thought.

I was writing at my desk when a ring on the bell brought me to the front door. A tall military-looking man with a moustache, wearing a brown trilby, and with a furled umbrella on his arm, stood outside.

I opened the door, slightly.

"I am from the District Surveyor's office. I have come to look at the site for your proposed extension: at the back."

I slammed the door shut. There was the sound of hasty footsteps retreating down our drive, an engine revved, and a car accelerated away, its tyres screeching as it went.

Trembling, I went into the kitchen and made myself a strong cup of coffee. I returned to my desk with it and sat looking out of my study window onto the front garden, and to the grass and trees beyond the road of the private estate on which we lived. It was true we had submitted plans to the Council, but they were for an extension at the *front* of the house, not the back. The proposed extension would be on the spot the man had been standing! And he did not know!

Was that man an assassin? I wondered, terrified.

I returned to my office on Monday 31st March. An ASR form with an accurate service history was in my in-tray. Sid Butler had attached a short note. "I am to be your Reporting Officer," it said. "John Clayton is the Countersigning Officer." I filled in Section 2a of the form and sent it off at once.

The Commander of 'Y' Division, Metropolitan Police, came to call on me unexpectedly. He was a big handsome man with silky white hair, and looked very splendid in his uniform, bedecked with gold braid. He settled himself in my easy chair.

"I'm sorry you decided not to continue with your Preventive Policing studies," he began. "My old Force would have welcomed a report by you." The Commander had only recently moved south, on promotion to the 'Met'.

"Thank you for those kind words," I responded, remaining suspicious and cool. "Now, what may I do for you?"

"Nothing, dear lady. I have come to offer *my* services."

"In what way?" I managed to keep my voice soft.

"All the world loves a lover – the Police Service especially," the Commander told me, adding conspiratorially, "Damien Grant sends a message."

At last I allowed the coldness in my soul to show in my eyes. "If Damien has anything to say to me," I informed him, "he can come and tell me himself."

The Commander seemed unflappable. He changed tack.

"I understand you have a second income."

"What second income?" I was unimpressed.

"Well now, how shall we describe it? One which you might not wish to declare for tax purposes, shall we say?"

"I have no second income."

Imperturbable, he changed tack again.

"The Chief Superintendent in charge of PRSU is very worried about what you may do," he said.

"Why? I have made no complaint against any police officer."

He leaned forward confidentially. "I should very much like to know what all the trouble is about," he said. "I may be able to help."

I gave him a brief resume of the events which had occurred while I was in PSDB. "I've just been on leave compiling a written statement, as a matter of fact," I concluded.

"My dear lady," he said, heaving his huge bulk out of the chair. "I advise you to take your written statement to the Inspector of Constabulary responsible for research."

He held out his hand. I rose too and shook it.

"Good luck," he said, and turning, he seemed to waft from the room without a sound; as is often the way with big men.

The upshot, after a long delay, was an interview with the Inspector of Constabulary, followed by another with Her Majesty's Chief Inspector of Constabulary at Queen Anne's Gate. There I was confronted with a type-written statement which I was asked to sign.

"I voluntarily sign this statement that I have no complaint against any police officer," I read. I did so. My written statement was returned, and I was escorted from the office.

John Clayton arrived in my office, bearing a memo. "The Lord Chancellor's Department has just taken over the criminal legal aid and costs work from the Home Office," he told me as he took a seat. "They require some statistical and Operational Research assistance from us; and the Chief Scientist has suggested you should do the work."

"I should be pleased to."

"Good." He looked at the paper in his hand. "A meeting has been arranged for Friday 30th May at the Lord Chancellor's Department with the Chief Finance and Establishments Officer."

John Clayton rose from his seat and stood looking down at me, stroking his bushy grey beard. "Beware of pointed umbrellas," he almost whispered. "Remember the fate of Georgi Markov." And John Clayton smiled his sly smile as he left my office. I was shaken but nothing about John Clayton surprised me now.

When I arrived at the meeting with the Chief Finance and Establishment Officer at the Lord Chancellor's Department I was told the project on which I was to have been engaged had been changed. I would now be working on the forecasting of manning and costs in the County Courts; and on the prediction of changing fees charged to litigants. The data I would require to undertake the study was held at Bristol - which would necessitate me making a trip to that city.

I made no comment. Superintendent Damien Grant is a member of the Avon and Somerset Police Force and is based at Bristol I remembered, instantly wary.

Further meetings, with lesser functionaries, followed as the study was fleshed out.

Finally, in late June, I received a phone call from the Lord Chancellor Department's Bristol office.

"I am to tell you," the officer informed me, "that it has been arranged for you to visit this office on Friday 4th July. You are to travel on the train departing from Paddington at 8.20 am, and you will be returning on the train leaving Bristol at 1.10 pm."

I was intrigued by such precise times. Whom am I supposed to meet on those trains? I wondered. I bet I need only one guess!

Jim agreed with my surmise. He happened to be free on that Friday, so he and I motored down to Bristol together and parked in the car park opposite the Police Headquarters. I went off to LCD's office while Jim did some sightseeing. We had arranged to meet outside a café opposite the Police Headquarters at 1.00 pm.

Bruce Denby, the Senior Executive Officer in charge of LCD's Bristol office, could hardly conceal his surprise when I entered, hung up my rain-coat and slouchy hat on his coat stand, and then advanced to his desk.

He found his voice at last. "Did you have a good train journey?"

I smoothed the folds of the pleated skirt of my pink Jaeger suit as I sat down without being invited to do so. "Yes, thank you," I replied politely.

"How did you travel through London?"

"I went from Euston to Euston Square, and took the Underground to Paddington," I answered serenely.

"Was the train fare £25?"

I was cross with myself. I had forgotten to check this. "About that," I responded vaguely.

"I'll get us some coffee," he volunteered.

He got up and left the room. When he returned he did so without the coffee. He had to go back for it.

I laughed inwardly.

Bruce got out the forms which contained the data I required and handed them to me. I looked them over. "What a pathetic set up," I thought; for they contained nothing that Bruce himself could not have brought up to London on one of his regular visits. Dragging me down here had been an absolute farce.

"Will you be visiting Bristol again?" he asked.

"No, I will not," I replied firmly. "I will telephone if I have any queries." And I arranged that data going back several years would be sent to me within the next fortnight.

The meeting ended, leaving me with plenty of time to make it to the station before 1.10 pm. I started out in that direction then doubled back through the market to meet Jim outside the café. We went in and had a pizza and coffee.

The following morning George Carr-Hill used the office internal telephone to talk to me.

"What happened on your trip to Bristol?" he asked.

"Nothing," I replied, interested that he should want to know.

George hung up.

The next day, I visited the Assistant Secretary in charge of Finance at the Lord Chancellor's Department to discuss the future direction of the project. It was arranged that I write a short report advising him on the action I thought should be taken.

The report was written and sent; and almost two months went by. No word came from the Lord Chancellor's Department, or any data.

Sid Butler fixed a meeting with the AS. He was then told that no money was available for the purchase of the computer facilities required for the project. He assumed LCD would not therefore need my services, and the AS agreed that this was so.

John Clayton made me the Project Manager for another training game. The name of this game was 'REGENERATE'. It was for the Home Defence College.

Invitations to tender were sent to Professor Douglas Holden, RMCS, Professor McDowell of the Royal Holloway College, and to LGORU.

Professor Holden declined to tender and Professor McDowell decided to act as a special adviser to LGORU, with the result that only LGORU submitted a project proposal. It was good enough for them to be awarded the contract.

I visited the LGORU team at Reading for a briefing. Frank Jenner took me to his office for an informal chat prior to the meeting.

"I must say," Frank said, giving me an appreciative look, "that I am amazed to see you looking so well. I'd been told you were a nervous wreck."

"You must not believe all you hear," I replied with a smile. "And how is LGORU getting on?"

"Not too well," admitted Frank. He paused, and decided to confide in me. "In fact, this project 'REGENERATE' has just about saved our bacon. As it is, we have to move to cheaper premises and make a number of our staff redundant."

"I am sorry to hear that," I said sympathetically.

"Well, you know how these things go. The Senior Police Management Game project is virtually complete. We've had an extension to the contract certainly, but it is only for small fine tuning."

"But the Police Game was surely not your only source of income?"

"Just about," he conceded. "Over the last two or three years we've been losing all our Department of Environment work, and the Local Authority contracts have more or less dried up."

"Didn't you get any Fire Cover work from the Local Authorities as a result of the Testing of Fire Cover Models you did for us?"

"No, we did not. We were very surprised by that. All the computer programs and data are carefully stored away; ready for instant use." He looked at his watch. "Come on, we had better go. Our meeting is due to start."

CHAPTER TWENTY SEVEN

JOHN CLAYTON IS
UNMASKED & STUART IS KILLED

Timothy Devlin came back into my life on Friday 5th December. I was at Euston Station when he approached me, shortly before 10.00 am. Once again I was much later than my normal time, as I was on my way to see my oculist in Harley Street.

"Now how did I know you would be here?" Timothy Devlin asked me with a devilish glint in his eyes.

"I've no idea. Tell me."

He ignored this. He almost had to run to keep up with me. I was swinging along, having taken a front door to the main concourse by storm.

"Will you have lunch with me, Jane? How would you like to go to the Italian restaurant this time?"

"Thank you, but no thank you," I replied, maintaining my fast pace past the shops fronting Euston station. A problem with the training game 'REGENERATE' was on my mind.

"Are you still on the game?" he asked.

"Yes," I said simply, thinking of 'REGENERATE'.

"I'll telephone you at the office." He lifted his hat and departed.

I stopped, suddenly shaken. What Timothy Devlin had really meant had just hit me. I really must do something about Timothy Devlin!

I saw my oculist and rushed into my office; straight onto the telephone to the Security Branch. I arranged to see a Mr Malcolm Brown at Whittington House the following afternoon.

When I got home that evening I poured out the whole story concerning Timothy Devlin to Jim. Poor Jim was getting increasingly frustrated by all of my troubles. Consequently, I told him no more than I felt he needed to know. I had not mentioned Timothy Devlin to Jim before.

"I thought I had got rid of him," I ended, "but today he appeared again at Euston Station and asked me if I was still on the game. Oh, Jim, it makes me feel so sick! And he is going to be phoning me at the office!"

"Come on," said Jim getting up from the sofa. "Let's have a drink and work out what we can do."

The next day, Jim brought home a tape recorder with a telephone attachment.

In the meantime I had visited Malcolm Brown at Whittington House. Mr Brown and another officer, who remained silent throughout, listened to my story. Mr Brown wrote it all down.

When I had finished, I turned to Mr Brown. "While I am about it, I might as well tell you that I have been accompanied on trains and buses and asked questions by a series of people. When I have been able to I have got their names. I've listed them here." I produced my diary, and turned to the appropriate page.

Mr Brown noted these names too. "Who is Martin Glover?" he asked.

"He's an ex-military policeman from one of the insurance companies," I replied.

My diary was handed back. Obviously Mr Brown knew all the other names and was telling me so.

"What will you do about Timothy Devlin?" I asked.

"I will look into the matter," Mr Brown assured me.

"You will ensure that all my telephone conversations are recorded won't you?"

Mr Brown was non-committal.

They probably already were, I thought.

The telephone rang in my office at 11.30 am precisely. With bated breath I picked up the receiver.

"Tim Devlin here."

I swallowed, and attached my tape recorder to the receiver.

"How about having lunch with me today?"

"I am sorry, but no."

"And why not?"

"I'm very upset about what you said to me at Euston Station."

"What did I say to you?" asked Timothy Devlin.

"You asked me if I was still on the game," I responded, trying not to shake.

"That was what you told me when I first met you," Timothy Devlin purred.

I almost choked. "I cannot imagine that I said anything of the sort!"

"You certainly did."

I lost my temper. "I don't ever wish to see you or hear from you again," I told him and slammed down the receiver. I sat still for a moment before wiping my forehead with a handkerchief. Then I removed the attachment and, taking the tape recorder with me, went along the corridor to Brian Davenport's office.

He was not surprised to see me, having been briefed by Malcolm Brown. He took the tape recorder from my shaking hand and, while I sat down, he rewound the tape and started it again.

"Who was that on the other end?" he asked, as he reached out to switch off the machine.

"He calls himself Timothy Devlin. I only started to record after he had given his name." My teeth were chattering as I replied. It had been a shock to hear the conversation again.

"Right, I'll go and report this to the Director and come back to you."

I returned to my office and shortly afterwards Brian joined me there. He looked triumphant.

"John Clayton has given himself away," he told me, holding up the tape recorder. "He knew whose voice was on the tape, and *I* did not tell him."

I closed my eyes as I took in the information.

"I'll send this tape recorder over to Mr Brown," Brian continued. "You'll get it back in a week or two."

Malcolm Brown came to see me in my office in the New Year. He had my tape recorder with him. The conversation on the tape had been erased.

"I have followed this matter up," he told me. "You will hear no more from Timothy Devlin."

❦

The Chairman of Hatfield Swimming Club was Ian Maclaurin, Chairman of Tesco. His three children, Fiona, Gillian and Neil had all been good swimmers, with Gillian being the best. Gillian was the same age as Sally-Ann and had been outstanding in the backstroke for years. Gillian was now at Millfield School in the hope of becoming an international swimmer.

For almost two years I had been the 'A' Team Manager and Team Selector. I had been given the job because I collected the times of all our swimmers in all their events and stuck them on a board Jim had made, with the swimmers' names ranked according to their best time. I was adamant the 'A' Team should be self-selecting with the best swimmer having the swim in Club Galas. The only time I intervened was when one swimmer was the best in more than one stroke, in which case the second best swimmer would be selected. Even so, for really important Galas I would normally pick the best swimmer even if it meant that swimmer would be in more than one event.

London League Galas were held in Lewisham. Hatfield Swimming Club had earned its place in the Finals, where the club which won would represent the London League in a Gala which pitted the best clubs in all the Leagues in England and Wales against each other. Reading Swimming Club was the favourite to win the London League, being the current Champion Club. I knew Hatfield Swimming Club had a good chance of beating Reading to become the Champion Club if our swimmers performed above themselves. I also knew that Reading were not aware of how good Hatfield was as I had been wily and swum our 'B' Team under 12 years of age group in the 'A' team when we had taken part in our annual Reading versus Hatfield Club Gala. Hatfield's Under 12 swimmers were in fact so good that the second ranked swimmers were good enough to be selected for the 'A' team of most other clubs.

Hatfield Swimming Club's swimmers in the Open age group were amongst the best in England and Wales, particularly Mark Pickering (freestyle and butterfly) and Ian Akers (backstroke and individual medley) for the boys and Nicola Fibbens (freestyle and butterfly) and Janine Graysmark (backstroke and individual medley) for the girls. They were almost certain to win their events. In addition, our club had great strength in depth because we had a brilliant, enthusiastic and dedicated coach in Kelvin Juba. The swimmers enjoyed their training sessions so much that Kelvin was able to instil in them tremendous stamina; so that, in a race when the other swimmers were beginning to fade, Kelvin's swimmers could always find that extra strength to either win or steal a higher placing.

Sally-Ann was in the relays. She had not grown tall enough or lean enough to keep her place in the individual freestyle and butterfly events. Instead Sally-Ann looked like Gina Lollobrigida. She had a very curvaceous body, and a very beautiful heart shaped face with dark blue eyes under long lashes, and brown wavy hair. She still enjoyed her swimming and the comradeship which came with it. Sally-Ann was as excited as anyone to be participating in the London League Finals.

On the coach taking us to Lewisham, I spoke to each swimmer in turn. I told the swimmer where he/she was expected to come in his/her race, and I asked each swimmer to try to gain just one more place. "Do not try to win," I said to a swimmer, "just try to be third instead of in the fourth place you are expected to be." To John Good, who invariably won his races in his age group, I said, "Remember you are not in your age group. You must not try to win. You are expected to come fifth. I will be very happy if you manage to come fourth." (John, naturally, managed to be third).

I had prepared a graph which showed how many points Hatfield Swimming Club needed to have after each event during the Gala in order to win. And after each event I was at the end of the pool to congratulate our swimmer on how well he/she had done. In almost every race our swimmer had achieved the extra place and sometimes even an extra two places! It was quite amazing; and our swimmers were getting tremendously excited. They would keep coming up to me to ask if we were on track to win and I would check my graph, together with the cumulative results to date, and I would be able to tell them that we were indeed winning.

With the completion of the relays the Gala was over and Hatfield Swimming Club *had won*. Our supporters were beside themselves up in the gallery, cheering wildly. With much haste I joined them in the gallery; otherwise I would have been thrown into the swimming pool, contact lenses and all, by my extremely excited team of swimmers. It had been a great day for Hatfield Swimming Club and our girls' and boys' Team Captains went up to the dais to proudly receive the Trophy.

It was Friday 13th February. Stuart, one of the Clerical Officers in Registry, was killed. He had been on his way to work in the early morning, and was stationary on his motorbike at a pedestrian crossing when a van ran into him.

Soon after Stuart's death was announced, I met Brian Davenport in the corridor.

"Will you come into my office, please?" he asked me.

Mutely I went.

"This is bad news," said Brian, after we had seated ourselves with the door shut.

"Yes, it is," I agreed.

"In more ways than one."

I was slow on the uptake. "Why?" I asked.

"Because Stuart was in charge of recording all SAB's invoices. Incidentally, you had better have the 'REGENERATE' Account Code Number," he continued, opening his desk drawer and taking out a box. He leafed through the cards it contained, found what he wanted, and read out the digits to me. I made a note of them in my pocket diary.

"At the moment," he went on, "there is no way that Accounts Branch can check the movements on any Account. Everything is done manually and there are thousands of entries daily."

"That is bad news," I agreed.

"However, a computerized system is due to come into operation as from 1st April 1981 and all movements for the financial year 1981/82 onwards will be checkable."

"There's not long to go then," I remarked, "and presumably Stuart kept SAB's Accounts up to date."

"Yes, he was very good; he has left everything in first class order. However, as you've probably heard, there is to be reorganization."

"Yes, I gathered that. An ex-AUSS of the Fire Department has been brought out of retirement to undertake a review of the work of PSDB, SAB and HORU, as I understand it."

"And PSDB expect to *swallow up* most of SAB," Brian told me.

"Is that so!" My tone of voice was sharp. "Well, let no one think I'm going back to PSDB to work under Roger Munn!"

"Rumour has it," Brian continued, "that the Criminal Justice System and the IND Sections will be merged with the Research Unit, while the Civil Defence Sections, Police National Computer work and the Technical Fire Sections will merge with PSDB."

"It was good of you to tell me this, Brian," I said, and returned to my office deep in thought.

Later, a young man, who was due to go to University in the autumn, took Stuart's place. I learned from Tony Murray, the Branch's Administrative Officer, after the reorganization had taken place, that missing receipts for the financial year 1980/81 were found behind radiators, under the carpet, on the top of cupboards; all over the place ...

Later that day, a Dr Delphine Somerville came to see me. The AS, F6 Division, had decided that a short term contract should be given to a high-powered social scientist. She was to evaluate social response before, during and after a nuclear attack.

I greeted Delphine warmly. Even as I shook her hand, I was reflecting how I seemed to be making a habit of winning or losing staff on the 13th day of a month.

Chapter Twenty Eight

The MP and Tom Elliott's confession

Once again I was in Reading for a meeting on 'REGENERATE' with the LGORU people. Once again, Frank Jenner took me to his office for an informal chat beforehand.

"You may be interested to know," he began, "that P A Management Consultants' report on Humberside Police is now out."

"Is it indeed?" I responded. "Have you got a copy?"

"Yes, I have." He took one out of his desk drawer and showed it to me. "As you can see, it is classified 'CONFIDENTIAL'."

"Can you give me the gist of its recommendations?"

Frank began turning the pages. "Basically," he said, "it recommends that the Police Force Headquarters be moved from Hull to Beverley, and that the Uniform Divisions be reorganized to conform to the Traffic Divisions."

"And that would split 'C' Division?" I was suddenly excited..

Frank checked it. "Yes, that would split the 'C' Uniform Division," he agreed.

"So there would be no reason why the Police Headquarters building in Queen's Gardens should then not become available for another purpose?"

"No, none at all," replied Frank. He looked mystified.

"One more question," I went on. "I know it is really none of my business, but I should be grateful for an answer."

"Fire away."

"Has the Senior Police Management Game been played for real yet?"

"Yes, it was run for the first time in October."

"And did any of the syndicates of potential ACPO rank officers split 'C' Division?"

"Not one," replied Frank.

It was time to take things a stage further. That afternoon, I went into the Hemel Hempstead Conservative Association building to see the agent. I explained that I was bound under Home Office regulations not to disclose any information I might acquire through my official duties; unless it should be in the interest of the State for me to do so. Something had now cropped up.

The agent promised to consult with the Member of Parliament, and in due course an invitation came for me to meet him the following Saturday morning.

On the Friday, Sid Butler called me into his office. He had my latest Annual Staff Report in his hand.

"I have recommended you for an appointment as a Special Merit SPSO," he told me.

"Thank you," I said. "I appreciate the gesture, but I must tell you that I would refuse the post if it were to be offered to me."

Sid Butler accepted this with good grace. He knew, as I did, that I had not done anything to deserve such a promotion.

Saturday morning came.

My Member of Parliament, Sir Nicholas Lyle, listened keenly as I unfolded the whole story. When I had finished, he promised to convey my worries to the Minister of the Crown at the Home Office, and to let me know the outcome.

I, for my part, had kept faith with the Divisional Commanders of the Humberside Police Force.

❧

It was Wednesday 8th April 1981.

Sid Butler asked me to come and see him.

"The reorganization of SAB, PSDB and HORU has been finalised and agreed," he told me. "They will be merged into a new Scientific Research and Development Branch and a new Planning and Research Unit. SAB staff will be split between SRDB and PRU. You will be going to SRDB."

"Where are you going?" I asked, the alarms bells sounding.

"I shall be going to PRU with the Criminal Justice System and the Immigration and Nationality Department work. SRDB will simply be the old PSDB enlarged to encompass the additional work from SAB."

"I should like to go to PRU with you," I told Sid.

"I'm afraid that won't be possible," he replied.

"What's happening to John Clayton?"

"He's retiring early."

So much for his determination to get to the top, I thought bitterly, as I returned to my office where I immediately wrote to the Chief Scientist. Under no circumstances was I going to work under Roger Munn again!

The Chief Scientist replied the same day. "The points you make will be taken into account at the appropriate time."

Next, I bombarded the AS, then the AUSS, Establishment Department, with memos objecting to my proposed move. No answer came. In desperation on 12th June I wrote to the Deputy Under Secretary of State, Personnel Management and Welfare Group, Civil Service Department. He merely referred me back to the Home Office Establishment Department.

I wrote to the AS again. At last I got a reply. I would not be assigned to SRDB, I was assured.

At about the same time I heard again from my MP. Enclosed with his note was a letter from the Minister of State at the Home Office.

It was very urbane. The final paragraph stated:

"From what I have said on these matters you will, I am sure, accept that there is no cause for concern about the possibility of corruption."

A course for Scientific Advisers was being held at the Home Defence College. John Clayton put my name down for it, saying it would provide me with useful background knowledge.

The participants were to assemble on the Monday evening and be given a welcome and introductory talk by the Principal of the College. A meeting to discuss the College's computer requirements for 'REGENERATE' was arranged for the afternoon of Monday. George Carr-Hill, SAB's scientific expert, was invited to attend.

One of the course tutors telephoned me to tell me the afternoon meeting was fixed to start at 2.00 pm. Would I and Mr Carr-Hill care to come to a briefing meeting in the morning? I replied that we would be glad to, if it would be helpful; and it was agreed that the briefing should be held at 11 o'clock, allowing me plenty of time to motor up to Easingwold.

Monday morning arrived, and I set off at 8 o'clock. It was a lovely sunny day. Once I had got on to the M1, and with time to spare, I relaxed and enjoyed my driving. At 9.30 am, soon after passing the exit for Nottingham and Derby, I was in the middle lane and had just noted some bridges overhead, when suddenly there was a tremendous crash. For a moment I panicked: I could not see a thing in front of me. Then I realised - the windscreen was smashed! Immediately I flicked my left hand signal, and looked into my mirror. There was a car in the inside lane I was going to impede, but that was too bad. Gradually I worked my way inwards. Through a small hole in the fissured glass I could just make out the road ahead. I crawled on, and by great good fortune the slip road to the Trowell Services came into view not long after. I limped the car up the slip road to the parking area and got out, thoroughly shaken. I found a telephone box. First I phoned a windscreen replacement firm, then the College to apologise for my late arrival. I would have to forego the morning meeting, I said, but I would be at the one in the afternoon.

I arrived at the College a little before 12.30 pm. The janitor signed me in and showed me to my room. It was in the old building, the original mansion house, but right at the top, on the attic floor. Nevertheless, it was beautifully furnished and comfortable.

After settling in, I returned down the back stairs, and made my way to the main part of the house.

In the bar, I finally found signs of life. The College staff, were for the most part ex-military officers. They had gathered there to enjoy a pre-lunch drink. There too I came upon George Carr-Hill and one of the tutors perched on bar stools, and I joined their group.

The afternoon meeting with the LGORU team, headed by Frank Jenner, went smoothly. The purchase of two PDP 11/23 processors with six work stations, each consisting of a VDU and a printer, was agreed.

In the evening the College was full of Scientific Advisers. They were housed in purpose-built bedroom blocks in the grounds. The Scientific Advisers were made welcome by the Principal of the College after dinner that evening, and started their course in earnest the next day. They were divided up into syndicates, each under a tutor; so that each lecture was followed by a tutorial session. I fitted into a syndicate easily enough but could not match the Scientific Advisers in expertise.

The course continued until Friday lunchtime, with a course dinner on Thursday night; this being the usual practice at the College.

At the dinner, I was placed on the Principal's left at the high table; John Clayton, the Director of SAB, was on the Principal's right.

The few ladies present were allowed to stay for the circulation and partaking of the port. Then came the toast to the Queen, followed by the after dinner speeches. The Principal, as ever, was very witty; John Clayton was less so. He ended with a joke about an Irishman, a Scotsman and an Englishman and what each did in turn to a woman 'on the game'. When John Clayton sat down the clapping was desultory.

The men left the tables; I headed for the back stair. My syndicate members caught up with me as I reached it.

"I'm sorry, gentlemen," I said. "I have had all I can take for one night."

"But he is your boss!" said one of my syndicate members, aghast.

I mounted the two sets of backstairs to my bedroom. I sat in the easy chair and read a book, preferring a solitary evening to revelry in and around the bar; and possible further embarrassment.

Back at SAB, Sid Butler played down John Clayton's behaviour. I did not bother with a formal complaint; but I wrote again to the Establishment Department enquiring about my future on SAB's disbandment in September; now less than two months away.

At long last, in August 1981, the AS, Establishment Department, provided this reply:

"You say that you would welcome the opportunity of joining the Research and Planning Unit. However, in order that you may complete your current work on the Home Defence College Gaming project, we propose that you should be attached directly to F6 Division for the duration of the project. Under this arrangement you would continue to look to Mr Butler for supervision on professional matters, and could expect to join the RPU on completion of your project."

F6 Division was situated in Queen Anne's Gate. On Monday 21st September 1981 I and all my belongings were transferred there from Horseferry House.   Dr Delphine Somerville, who had arrived unexpectedly, helped with the move.

My new office on the seventh floor was almost palatial. It was normally used by AUSS staff. It faced south, overlooking Petty France. The windows did not open, but warm or cold air flowed through vents according to the thermostat setting.

"What a super room!" exclaimed Delphine.

"Yes, it is very nice," I agreed.

"What more could you want?" continued Delphine.

"Computing facilities," I replied morosely.

"Do you really need them?"

"Why yes, I do! Without them I shall have to ask LGORU to undertake the work on the casualty program which I would have done; and that includes your results on social response."

"Which will mean that LGORU will need more money and therefore *another extension to their contract*." I was sure Delphine meant me to notice the emphasis she placed on the words at the end of her sentence. I did, and I noted them

Delphine had another appointment, and did not stay much longer. She had scarcely left when the phone rang. It was the AS's secretary. Would I come through now, please?

Hugo Munro was a slim medium sized man, slightly older than me. He had light blue eyes, a receding chin and dark short curly hair, which was beginning to be sparse on the top of his head. He dressed very nattily in smart expensive suits and usually wore a bow tie. He had a reputation for being a first class chairman of meetings.

"Welcome to F6 Division, Mrs Hogg," Mr Munro said, shaking my hand warmly. "Or may I call you Jane?"

"You may," I agreed.

We sat down on comfortable chairs and discussed the 'REGENER-ATE' project and Dr Somerville's part in it for a while.

Hugo Munro then dismayed me. "For political reasons, I want the finances for 'REGENERATE' to come from SRDB's budget," he told me.

"But that will take the finances from F6 Division's direct control," I protested, seeing difficulties ahead.

"Never fear, I can handle that. Now, there are two final matters I wish you to adhere to."

Hugh Munro paused, and I waited, not knowing what to expect.

"You are to have no contact with the police; and you are not to go into pubs," Hugo Munro said.

I had hardly returned to my office when there was a knock on the door. My visitor was Tom Elliott, a Principal in F6, whose office was across the corridor from mine.

Tom came in and carefully shut the door behind him. I was seated behind my desk. Tom took a few steps into the room and stood before me.

"I hope you do not judge us too harshly," he began.

I signalled that I was all attention.

"I have four children," Tom continued. "On a Principal's salary I would never have been able to get them properly educated. One is a teacher and a housewife, while the others are professional people; a doctor, a university lecturer, a lawyer. They are all performing a useful service to society. You can see that it was for the best."

"Yes, I understand," I said sympathetically.

"I hoped you would," he said, and let himself out, as quietly and unobtrusively as he had entered.

I raised my eyebrows, and thought of bugging devices. I knew that Tom was due to retire soon, and was hoping to get an extension to his service. I doubted if he would now.

He didn't.

CHAPTER TWENTY NINE

'THE SYSTEM'
AND LGORU

The Regional Scientific Advisers' Conference at Wakefield was the weekend straddling the end of October and the beginning of November. The whole LGORU team and I were involved with a presentation of 'REGENERATE'. A large map of the United Kingdom, which I planned to use, had been produced by the Reproduction Unit at Horseferry House, but it was incomplete.

Professor McDowell of the Royal Holloway College had promised to provide the missing information. "I'll have it ready for you on Thursday evening," he had said when I had phoned him, "if you'll be so good as to pick it up at the Royal Holloway College before my secretary leaves at 5.30 pm." That would give the Reproduction Unit just the Friday to complete the map; the presentation being at Wakefield the next day.

I managed to squeeze in a final rehearsal with LGORU at Reading on the Thursday, and at 4.00 pm set off for Egham and the Royal Holloway College, leaving myself plenty of time, as I thought, to cover the twenty miles.

At Bracknell I was circumventing a roundabout when suddenly I heard a great clattering noise. This continued, at a slightly lower intensity, as I nursed the car to the nearest garage. There, the exhaust system was found to have come adrift with the end trailing on the road. The garage was unable to help. I went on to the next. Nothing doing. I returned to the garage I had seen on the other side of the road. Again, the people could not help. Time was passing and I was getting frantic. The map and Professor McDowell's data were vital to the success of the presentation.

"Where's the nearest police station?" I demanded of the garage proprietor.

He gave me directions, and soon my car was limping into the police station car park, the exhaust system clattering as it went. I rushed into the entrance lobby and waited my turn to see the sergeant behind the counter. He ushered me into the main office and sent a police constable to see to my requirements. The PC telephoned one of his garage friends, who promised to come at once. The PC and I went outside and waited.

The police constable had heard of me through the grapevine. We had a chat about the Police Force Headquarters at Hull.

The mechanic arrived and fixed the exhaust system temporarily, but it still made a booming noise; almost like a jet breaking the sound barrier. I had no choice. I explained to the police constable why I had to use the car. He was most understanding.

I took to the road again, and drove to Egham as silently as I could; but the noise was deafening. Fortunately, Professor McDowell's secretary had waited on beyond 5.30 pm, so I was able to pick up the data as arranged. Then I was on my way again, back to Hemel Hempstead, doing my utmost to keep the decibels down.

No police car came near me. All police drivers were wearing metaphorical ear muffs that evening.

The Regional Scientific Advisers' Conference at Wakefield went smoothly, and the 'REGENERATE' presentation was well received. I mixed with the oldest Regional Scientific Advisers I could see. Delphine laughed as she remarked on it.

❧

Roger Munn was in charge of Civil Defence temporarily until a PSO was promoted up to SPSO and could take over the work. He kept up the pressure on me with a constant spate of memos on financing. He was also threatening to use the breakpoint in the contract to terminate both LGORU's contract and my work on 'REGENERATE'. That breakpoint was set for the end of March 1982.

The new SPSO was appointed, but he continued in the same vein. His name was Victor Smith.

❧

The next trial play of 'REGENERATE' was due to be held at Reading on 24th February and 25th February. It was obviously crucial that the trial play should go well with the SRDB threat hanging over us.

As it happened, I contracted influenza and was too ill to attend. I came back from sick leave on the first Monday in March, and received a phone call from Frank Jenner that same day.

"How did the trial play go?" I asked him.

"Oh, fine. Victor Smith was pleased."

"Does that mean he no longer intends to operate the breakpoint?"

"So he says."

"That is good news." I was relieved for LGORU's sake.

"Jane, Bill Simpson and I would like to come and discuss the Game's messages with you. Would Thursday this week suit you? We have a meeting with one of last week's players in the morning, and could meet you in a pub for lunch afterwards."

I checked my diary. Then I remembered Hugo Munro's stricture about going to pubs. "Yes, a meeting on Thursday afternoon would suit me, but I would rather have lunch in the Home Office canteen."

"Fine," he said. "Bill and I will be at your office around one o'clock."

Frank Jenner and Bill Simpson were shown into my office on the dot of one o'clock. Together we went up to the tenth floor and stood in the queue at the canteen. When we had chosen our dishes, I made to turn right and sit in the bright and sunny side of the room, but Frank was already walking off to the left, where it was dark. I refused to go too far. I reached an empty table and waited for Frank and Bill to join me.

When we had transferred our plates to the table, I collected the trays together and put them on a nearby trolley. As I did so, I looked in the direction of the dark corner towards which Frank had been heading. Good Heavens! There was Chief Superintendent Damien Grant sitting with a group of men, all of whom looked like police officers.

I deliberately shut that distant group out of my mind, all through the meal, and concentrated on conversing with Frank and Bill. They were still there when Frank went to get the coffee at the coffee bar; but after he had returned and while we were still drinking our coffee, the police officers left. I breathed a sigh of relief.

Tom Elliott invited me to his farewell party. There was no one I really knew present. I stood around with a glass of wine in my hand while a throng of people milled about me.

A small bald headed man appeared by my side, and engaged me in conversation. I recognised him as my AUSS. "I understand you are very ambitious," he said at one point.

"Yes," I admitted, as I tried to keep my balance from the constant jostling. "I am very ambitious."

A few days later Frank Jenner telephoned. "You'll be an AUSS," he told me.

"There is no likelihood of that ever happening," I replied firmly.

"Be careful," he warned, "they are like the Mafia. You've heard of the Mafia, haven't you?"

I had.

It was the end of March 1982. LGORU still had not submitted all the invoices due in the financial year. Most of those missing were for computer hardware and computer maintenance. Larger memories had been required for the PDP 11/23 computers so that they could handle the casualty program, I had been told.

I telephoned Frank Jenner, and made enquiries.

"Would you please contact the treasurer of the Royal Institute of Public Affairs? That is our parent body," Frank replied.

On Tuesday 13th April I had another nasty shock. Frank Jenner sent me a parcel containing the messages which Bill Simpson, a member of the LGORU team, had devised so far for the players of 'REGENERATE'. I read them through, one by one, with a sinking heart. They were terrible. I wondered why Victor Smith of SRDB had not operated the breakpoint.

The next trial play was due to take place at the Home Defence College from Wednesday 12th to Friday 14th May, with several syndicates of players. But first the participants would be on a course, on the 10th and 11th May. The 13th May was going to be a disastrous day, I was sure of that. Was not the number 13 occurring with monotonous regularity!

I picked up a sample of the messages, and set off to see Hugo Munro.

He agreed with me that the messages were abysmal.

"The May trial has to go ahead," he said. "You will just have to do your best. You'll need to rewrite as many messages as you can; but you'll need some assistance. Let's see. Ah yes! Squadron Leader Jack Cornwell is the man. I'm afraid this means that you will have to base yourself at the

College. I'll get one of the syndicate rooms turned into an office for you, Jack and the LGORU team. It's a good time for a move in any case, with the trial plays being put on at the College and one of the computers being installed there. I'll arrange it with the Principal. You should get in touch with Squadron Leader Cornwell in a day or two."

Back in my office, I sighed as I thought what this new development entailed. I wondered how Jim and Sally-Ann would react. I was going to have to commute to Easingwold most weeks, coming home just for the weekend. It really was most depressing.

My telephone rang. It was George Carr-Hill. He was now in SRDB.

"Come and join me for a drink this lunchtime," he invited me.

"I'd like that," I said, forgetting all about Hugo Munro's ban on pubs.

George arrived in my office at one o'clock. I had already eaten my sandwiches and was ready to go. It was good to have the company of my own kind once more. My sojourn in F6 Division was proving a lonely experience.

Over drinks, George and I compared notes. We discussed our ex-SAB colleagues and their new lives, laughing at some of the comical events which had occurred. One ex-SAB colleague had gone berserk that Christmas and had thrown all his furniture, chairs, table, etc, out of his office window. They had flattened a car parked in the street beneath. Two passing police motor cyclists had seen the commotion, had rushed into the building and had arrested the PSO. He had spent the night in a police cell and had appeared at Horseferry Court the next day. He was still in SRDB but had been given a less responsible job.

"Have you ever done anything which could have landed you in court?" George asked me out of the blue.

I smelled trouble. I had not, but I thought that I might as well test out a theory I had about George. One summer in my student days I had been fruit picking on a farm near Wisbech, with a gang of other young people. We had had a competition to see who could pick the most baskets of strawberries. I had filled one of my baskets and left it at the end of the row on which I was working, while I filled a second. When I had returned to take both baskets to the collecting point, the first was no longer to be seen. Someone had taken it. I told George this story, pretending to be the thief.

Squadron Leader Jack Cornwell expressed his pleasure when he heard that he and I would be working directly on the Game. "I must confess I was very unhappy with the trial play in February," Jack confided in me.

Frank Jenner was less pleased. "I can only be at Easingwold some of the time," he told me. "Bill and Martin will be there hardly at all. They have their families to consider." He did however agree to attend during the following week.

On Monday morning, I met the Squadron Leader and had my first view of the syndicate room which the team had been allotted. It would make a splendid working environment, I decided. The room was airy and spacious, and was well equipped. Two of the computer VDUs and print-ers were in the room while the computer itself was housed just across the corridor.

I got on well with Jack. He was a tall, big boned man who looked every inch the ex-RAF Squadron Leader he was. He was full of jokes and was a very good story writer. Many of the course scenarios were his work. He asked me about my journey and my accommodation while I poured the coffee. Very quickly he made me feel at home.

Frank arrived soon after. The coffee was getting cold by this time, but he would not hear of Jack sending for some more. I poured him a cup and watched while he relaxed under the influence of Jack's charm. We were going to make a good team, I thought. By the end of the day progress had been so good, that I was feeling very optimistic.

The following morning I came down to breakfast to find the main din-ing room packed out. A course of senior officers had arrived the previous evening and had all come down to breakfast early.

I made my way to the second dining room. It was empty. A maid who was hovering nearby immediately came forward to serve. Soon after a man joined me and sat beside me. The maid attended to him too, and then withdrew.

"I understand that you know about 'The System'," the man said.

"Yes," I agreed. I was getting used to this kind of conversation.

"Where do they meet?"

Suddenly I thought I knew. "Here," I replied, "here, at the Home Defence College."

"Is that why you're here?"

"No, of course not! I've only just realised it".

We finished our breakfast in silence.

Once again the day's work went well, and at the end of it I was glad to go to the bar for a pre-dinner sherry. As I was entering the room I was accosted by one of the senior officers on the course.

"You're a spy!" he said accusingly, looming over me.

"I am not!" I replied, with equal heat. "I am part of a team developing a training exercise for the College."

The man stepped aside. I went to the bar and ordered. I really did need my sherry now!

CHAPTER THIRTY

THE ACCOUNTS BRANCH PRINT-OUTS

It was the 10th May 1982; the fateful week had arrived at the Home Defence College. So had the LGORU 'REGENERATE' development team, Frank Jenner, Martin Wooldridge and Bill Simpson. They would be acting as Directing Staff.

I had my introductory talk ready. After that I would be sitting in as an observer together with Squadron Leader Jack Cornwell and Dr Delphine Somerville.

I noticed there was one member on the course who was not listed as a participant on the course papers. He was Assistant Commissioner Gerald Fenwick of New Scotland Yard, Metropolitan Police. That evening, as I was passing the open door of the bar on my way to telephone Jim, Assistant Commissioner Fenwick, a huge man, suddenly emerged and stopped me in my tracks. "I understand you are concerned about 'The System' and the siting of police stations," he said, handing me his card.

I examined the card as I replied. "Yes. Is anything being done about them?"

"We have our methods. I should like you to come and talk to me at the Yard. What is your Home Office telephone number?"

I rattled off the number to Mr Fenwick and then remembered, too late, Hugo Munro's command to me to have no dealings with the police.

On the morning of Wednesday 12th May, the course participants were introduced to 'REGENERATE' through a series of talks beginning with the Principal of the College and ending with Frank Jenner.

There was a break for coffee after the Principal's talk. I went to the ladies' room. I was to be on next. I was amazed to see a handbag sitting in the middle of the floor. One of the cubicles was engaged and there was no one else about. So I stood there, on guard beside the handbag, waiting for the occupant of the cubicle to emerge. It took some time but eventually she did.

"Is this bag yours?" I asked, pointing to it.

"Oh yes. It is. I must have forgotten it." The woman picked the bag up and took it with her to the mirror.

When I emerged from a cubicle, she was nowhere to be seen. I washed my hands, combed my hair and went to collect a cup of coffee. Frank Jenner was there drinking his.

"An odd thing happened in the 'ladies'," I said, joining him. "A handbag was left on the floor."

"Honest people are always slow to realise the implications of curious events," commented Frank.

A mental picture of George Carr-Hill in the pub rose in front of me. Ah, so my theory appears to be proven!

The introductory talks went well, as did the briefing session given by Jack Cornwell.

As I had feared, Thursday 13th May was a disastrous day. First, the LGORU team had retained their original messages. "It was too late to change them," Frank protested when Hugo Munro questioned him. Then, the computer broke down as Martin Wooldridge was working with it. As Jack Cornwell commented, remembering his flying days: "He failed to do a cockpit check."

The next Policy Steering Committee meeting was held the follow-ing week at Queen Anne's Gate. It was agreed that the July trial play of 'REGENERATE' would be cancelled, and that the next one would take place in November. Sid Butler of RPU, my supervision officer on technical matters, decided to opt out of any further dealings with 'REGENERATE'.

I took advantage of being in Queen Anne's Gate to go to the library. On the shelves a copy of a Home Office Fire Department Report, pub-lished in 1980, caught my eye. I took it down and went over to a read-ing desk with it. Its title was *Review of Fire Policy. An examination of the Deployment of Resources to combat Fire.* I flicked it open and read with growing consternation. "In general … property protection has not been an acknowledged objective of government policy." The report went on to suggest that revised Standards would provide similar cover to all areas regardless of risk, abandoning the concept of 'the higher the risk the greater the cover'.

In effect, I thought, the Home Office is now saying that government is concerned only with life safety, and that matters such as damage to prop-erty and consequential losses to the nation are irrelevant to it. But in fact the saving of property also saves lives; and reducing the consequential losses saves jobs!

I returned the report to its shelf, and left the library very upset, quite forgetting what I had gone there for.

The next week I was at Easingwold again, working with Squadron Leader Jack Cornwell. Frank did not join us on this occasion. We decided to visit RAF Cranwell in Lincolnshire to collect information.

I found the journey to and back from the base very exhausting even though Jack did all the driving. The interviews had been exhausting too. Jack as an ex-RAF officer had had no difficulty, but I had often found it hard to follow the jargon.

On our return to the College, we bumped into Hugo Munro on a sur-prise visit. He stood us drinks at the bar.

The dinner gong went. Jack left for his cottage on the College's estate, and Hugo Munro and I went in to dinner together.

Afterwards, it being a pleasant evening, Hugo Munro proposed a drive in his car, which I was not loath to accept. He wanted to go to Coxwold, and I, following the signposts, directing him there.

"You can see well then," he commented.

"Oh, yes!" I agreed. I wore contact lenses and I did not bother to tell him that I had a lazy eye. As a result I had always been hopeless at tennis and cricket because I did not have 3-D vision.

At Coxwold, Hugo Munro took me to the local pub, where he had a beer and I had a half pint of lager.

"What do you do in the evenings when you are at the College?" he asked.

"I sit in my room reading a book," I replied. This was not, strictly speaking, the truth: I usually carried on with my work in the syndicate room, and got up early to do more of the same before breakfast. There was so much to get through and so little time in which to do it. I was not sure why I did not wish Hugo Munro to know the true facts.

We left Coxwold and drove on to Oswaldkirk. There we visited another pub. Then on to Stillington, at his insistence, and to yet another.

Hugo Munro brought his beer and my half pint of lager over to the table at which I had seated myself. He settled himself into his chair and took a mouthful of beer. Putting down his tankard, he looked at me. "So, you came across some activities of 'The System' in Humberside."

"Yes, the police put me on to it."

"And you told your MP."

"Yes, I did."

"Do you think that was an isolated incident?"

I wondered if I could trust Hugo Munro. I felt I had to trust someone. However, I remained cautious.

"No, I don't. I think it's pretty general."

"Going on throughout the country, would you say?"

"Probably."

"Throughout the Police Service?"

"And the Fire Service." The pain at the thought was like a blow to my solar plexus.

"You think so?"

"I am sure so."

"What makes you so sure?"

"The events over the years - and the Home Office report *Review of Fire Policy.*"

"This is a serious business," stated Hugo Munro.

"It is indeed."

After this he sat silently for a while, apparently deep in thought.

"Shall we go?" I suggested politely.

The night air was cool and dry. Myriads of stars seemed to twinkle at us from above as we crossed the patch of ground to the car.

Hugo Munro drove back to the College and parked, as before, in front of the main door. We entered the house.

"Thank you for a very pleasant evening," I said, by way of an exit.

"Thank you for accompanying me," he responded.

I began to climb the main staircase; Hugo Munro tagging along. When I reached the top, I wished him, "Good night," firmly and fled down the corridor and up the back stairs.

I had undressed, washed and cleaned my teeth when I heard heavy footsteps coming at speed towards my door.

"Jane!" Hugo Munro's voice cried urgently.

I unlocked my door and opened it slightly. A hand reached out to grab me. I ducked and closed the door to a crack.

"Jane, will you come and have a 'good night' drink with me?" he asked in his most persuasive voice. And he could be very persuasive.

"I'm sorry, I'm afraid I'm not dressed for it. Good night." I closed the door and locked it once more. After a moment, he moved off, and his footsteps died away.

When I came down to breakfast the next morning, Hugo Munro was already in the dining room. I went and joined him, sitting opposite him. He nodded to me in salutation and continued talking to the gentleman sitting next to me. No one else was at the table.

The discussion came to an end. The gentleman beside me turned to me.

"You cannot trust him, you know," he said.

"If someone will look after my back," I replied, "I will take care of my front."

Hugo Munro rose to his feet, glared at me, and abruptly left the room. The gentleman and I continued with our breakfast in silence.

After the disastrous May trial, I found myself spending most weeks at the Home Defence College, working with Squadron Leader Jack Cornwell. Frank Jenner would be present about half the time; Martin Wooldridge and Bill Simpson, more rarely. I would set off at 7.00 am on a Monday morning and return late on Fridays. Jim and Sally-Ann just had to fend for themselves.

In time, I was provided with a plastic card which enabled me to operate the front gate. On those evenings when I felt that the day's work had gone well, I used the card to get out and drive to a local pub in Easingwold, where I would meet Jack Cornwell and his wife, Vera, after dinner. The Cornwells were a very relaxing couple and I soon developed a strong friendship with them.

It was Monday 14th June 1982. I was at my desk in Queen Anne's Gate, catching up on financial and administrative matters. A note from the Administrative Officer in SRDB lay among my papers. Something was amiss. Under the officialise, there was a clear hint that I should check the Accounts Branch computer print-outs.

I made my way down several flights of stairs to Finance Division 1, where I handed the 'REGENERATE' contract Account Code to an Executive Officer, and asked him to obtain the necessary information.

The print-out arrived the next day. I began checking it at once, against my own financial records. The figures were accurate; there were no mistakes. However, all the transactions should have been made to LGORU, but three of them had not. They were to three different Payee Codes, none of which ever recurred.

Another computer print-out from Accounts Branch was on my desk on Friday morning. I had been out of my office for a short time and found it there when I returned.

This too, I checked, noting that many payments had been made to LGORU for the Senior Police Management Game and all of them since 1st April 1981. There should have been very little expenditure on the Senior Police Management Game, I thought. I added it up. It came to £165,454.81 in 1981/82. That was more than had been spent on 'REGENERATE'.

I sat back and thought this over. I turned and looked out of the window. I remembered Assistant Commissioner Gerald Fenwick. I would go and see him, I decided; if nothing else, that would pre-empt any phone call he might make. I made my way out of the Home Office and walked across to New Scotland Yard.

Mr Fenwick saw me at once, and summoned another Assistant Commissioner as a witness before I was allowed to explain the reason for my presence.

"I have a computer print-out from the Home Office Accounts Branch which is worrying me," I explained. "There have been some very large payments made on a contract which should have been completed."

"You have to bring us a proven case before we would be interested," Gerald Fenwick told me. "However, I will get in touch with Her Majesty's Chief Inspector of Constabulary at the Home Office and tell him you have been to see me. I suggest you pass the matter of the finances to him."

"Very well." I got up to leave.

"Do you think that your life is in danger?"

The question from Gerald Fenwick came as a surprise.

"No, I don't believe so," I replied.

CHAPTER THIRTY ONE

THE AUSS IS
VERY ANGRY

I was at the Home Defence College working on 'REGENERATE'. Frank Jenner and Bill Simpson were there too.

On the Wednesday after a hard morning's work, we all trooped into the bar for a pre-lunch drink. I noticed that Frank was looking very worried, and I asked him why.

"LGORU's problems of lack of work are getting worse," he admitted. "We are having to make more people redundant. It's a very unpleasant task deciding who should go."

"But the Home Office has several contracts with you! There's the Police Management Game, as well as 'REGENERATE', which must be bringing you in some funds." In my mind's eye I recalled the huge sums shown on the Accounts Branch print-out.

"Very little besides 'REGENERATE'," Frank sighed.

Bill Simpson put down his tankard of beer and wiped his mouth.

"Only up to £20,000 was spent in the last 18 months by the Police side of SRDB with LGORU," Bill informed me. "A further £20,000 at most, was supplied by the Treasury for the Police Model of the Criminal Justice System."

"And that is all the Home Office work you had?"

"That's right."

I took out my pocket diary and noted down what Bill had said. Frank stood beside me. He looked more worried than ever. Bill returned to his tankard of beer.

❧

On Friday afternoon, the long week at the Home Defence College was over. I got into my car and drove home down the A1. I went slower than usual because I was very tired; and also, I had suffered a series of tyre blow outs. At the junction with the A6001 to Biggleswade, I noticed a garage on the right hand side, but no café. I frowned because I would have been glad to stop. Instead, I accelerated away - and the front offside tyre blew, so that suddenly I found myself struggling to maintain control of the car. Somehow I jumped it onto the grass verge on my left and miraculously it stopped almost instantly.

The walk back to the garage seemed to take an age. When I arrived it was just about to shut for the day; but the proprietor was very kind and let me use the telephone. I called the police.

The WPC in the control room was very reassuring. "Don't worry; I'll get a Landrover to you straight away."

The Landrover was standing by my stricken car as I returned from the garage. Two young police constables were waiting for me. They changed my tyre, got me back on the road, and told me to drive slowly.

"Assistant Commissioner Gerald Fenwick asked me if I thought my life was in danger," I told the police constables, my voice trembling a little. "I told him, 'No, I did not'. Now I am not so sure."

When I finally reached home our mechanic was there, servicing Jim's car. "What, not another one!" the mechanic exclaimed as I was explaining to Jim why I was so late. "That's quite a series. How many is it now?"

"I'm not sure," I felt too tired to think about it, "about four or five."

ⓦ

Monday came. I went into Queen Anne's Gate, and wrote to the Internal Auditor.

A meeting was arranged for early August, between Bill Simpson, a member of the Internal Auditor's staff and me.

I had to come in from leave to attend the meeting. Bill Simpson proved very evasive. I showed him the note in my diary of what he had said at the bar at the Home Defence College.

"If I said that, I should not have," Bill muttered.

Under pressure, he did, however, concede that LGORU had no other work for the Home Office but 'REGENERATE', the Senior Police Management Game and the Police Model of the Criminal Justice System. When faced with the huge payments on the Senior Police Management Game, Bill showed considerable surprise.

ⓦ

My spell of leave was over, and I returned to work at Queen Anne's Gate. To my horror there were no sets of messages for the 'REGENERATE' players from Frank Jenner and Bill Simpson to give to Hugo Munro. This was embarrassing, and I was still wondering what to do when the telephone rang. It was Frank's wife, telling me that Frank would be bringing the messages in shortly.

Later that morning a set of messages arrived; but no Frank. The messages were those done by Jack and me, with a few by Bill in the same style as those which had proved so unsatisfactory at the May trial. There was a note attached. It was from Frank, in his own hand. "I am at the Royal Institute of Public Affairs."

I refused to take the hint. An hour passed before Frank telephoned. I insisted that he should come in to my office.

Frank came.

"Why are there no messages by you, and why are the few by Bill still in his old style?" I demanded of Frank crossly.

Frank put a finger to his lips and whispered, "Do not fight it; it's not worth it." Then in his normal voice, Frank said, "I'm following a different story line." In a whisper again, "SRDB hold the purse strings." Aloud, "You would not wish to stop the extension, would you?" He was referring to the extension to the 'REGENERATE' contract which he was in the process of negotiating.

Frank thinks my office is bugged – as do I, was my thought.

"I would not wish to," I replied, "but I may have to. Frank, I'm very worried."

"Try not to be, Jane. I'll let you have my set of messages on Thursday."

With that promise Frank departed, with me seeing him to the front door.

I returned to my office, picked up the messages I had been given by Frank and took them round to Hugo Munro.

"The plan is to use the May trial memos, with some additions, in the November trial," I told Hugo Munro as I laid the messages before him.

"How did you know?" asked Hugo Munro in surprise.

"I sense it," I replied.

Hugo Munro paused, and then offered me a seat.

"Look here," he implored. "The Director of SRDB would be very happy to have you in SRDB as the Project Manager of 'REGENERATE'. He tells me that he invited you to join SRDB in May, and that you refused. He is, however, still anxious to have you, and I for my part think you should go."

"I'm sorry; but I have no desire to go to SRDB," I replied.

It was Monday 6th September 1982. Again I was in Queen Anne's Gate. At two o'clock my telephone rang, and Hugo Munro called me in to his office.

As I sat down, Hugo Munro handed me a note - written by him. 'REGENERATE' was to be handed over to SRDB on Monday 13th September. Ah, that number again, I thought. It was desirable to have the funds and the project management in the same place. The final paragraph said that my position would be reviewed.

"I suggest you go to SRDB as Project Manager," Hugo Munro said gently.

"A suggestion which I regret I must decline." I rose, they shook hands, and I left the room.

That evening I returned to the Home Defence College for the rest of the week, as had been arranged previously.

I worked hard to set up the suite of computer programs to produce the damage and casualty estimates, Jack putting aside other tasks to help me. On Thursday Martin Wooldridge arrived, and he too joined in, with the result that by Friday evening the revision of the entire suite had been completed and the computer was set up for the final run. We were in for a shock. The last program was too large for the core memory!

"What about the memory units which Frank Jenner purchased?" I asked Martin.

"But that was not what they were for!" Martin replied.

On Monday 13th September 1982, I arrived at my office to find a note from Charles Devereaux, the AUSS, Establishment Department, in my in-tray, requiring me to attend a meeting with him at Whittington House that same morning at 10.00 am.

Charles Devereaux had his Principal sit in as the interview commenced.

"Where would you like to be posted?" he asked.

"I should like to do a trial period as a Principal."

"That would block a post." He began to get angry. "You are to go where I send you; otherwise you will be on a disciplinary charge. You're in no position to dictate conditions."

"It would hardly be sensible to send me to SRDB in view of my experiences in PSDB," I pointed out.

"You will join RPU and work to Sid Butler," he asserted. "Now have you anything to tell me?"

"No, I have not. Why are you going for me in this way?"

Charles Devereaux's face flushed as he replied.

"First, for going to the Police; second, for going to the Internal Auditor; third, for arranging the meeting between the Internal Auditor's staff and Mr Simpson of LGORU; fourth, for going to your MP on the Humberside Queen's Gardens Police Station matter. In future, you are to report all matters of this nature to me only. Do you understand me?"

I swallowed hard in the face of this verbal trouncing.

"I should like early retirement," I said.

"Are you serious?"

"Yes."

"You will take no further interest in either the Senior Police Management Game or 'REGENERATE'."

"My interest is in police and fire cover," I replied. "I'm not concerned about the Senior Police Management Game, or 'REGENERATE': or any other game for that matter!" I was getting angry too.

That afternoon Victor Smith and one of his PSOs came to my office to be briefed on 'REGENERATE'. It took some time. Eventually the two SRDB men rose to leave. I shook hands with them.

"Good luck," I wished them.

"Good luck," they echoed.

The phone rang as they let themselves out. It was Jack Cornwell. His voice sounded urgent.

"Jane, there is to be a moratorium on 'REGENERATE'. You are very efficient. Get an assessor."

"Thanks for telling me, Jack."

The phone went dead.

I went home.

"Jim, it looks as though history's repeating itself. I may have to ask for another assessor."

"You really are having a bad time," he said, drawing me to him. "Don't you think you should ask for early retirement?"

"I already have," I responded, grateful for Jim's shoulder on which to lay my weary head.

The phone rang: I was coming to dread the sound. Jim went to answer it.

"For you."

I took over the receiver.

"Hullo."

"Hullo, Jane. It's Vera here."

Vera was Jack Cornwell's wife.

"Hullo Vera! How nice to hear from you."

"Jane, what did you do in the evenings when you were at the College?"

This was quite unexpected. I said slowly. "When I was not with you and Jack at the pub, I was working in our syndicate room."

"Have you ever been to the tennis club?"

"No, never. I can't even play tennis - my eyes, you know."

"That's good, because there was someone calling herself Jean Hogg going there this summer, who has got herself a very bad reputation for being 'on the game'. Goodbye, Jane. The best of luck to you."

"Goodbye, Vera. Thank you for calling," and I put the receiver down with a sinking heart. History did indeed seem to be repeating itself. I could imagine the gossip: "Jane Hogg has been taken off the game because she is 'on the game'."

The following morning there was a friendly note from Sid Butler of the RPU in my in-tray, welcoming me to the Unit and asking me to come and see him.

I went.

"You'll be working on Immigration and Nationality Department problems," Sid Butler told me, "and will have to spend a lot of your time in Croydon."

I groaned inwardly as I thought of the commuting time that would involve.

"Unfortunately, there's no office available for you on this floor," Sid Butler continued. "You may have to stay where you are for a little while."

"That's all right. It's a very pleasant office."

"Have you any work to do while I organize a programme with the Assistant Secretaries at IND?" he enquired.

"Yes, I've some draft reports of Delphine Somerville's to edit."

"Good. Well, I'll get in touch with you in due course."

I left Sid Butler's office and returned to my own.

I reviewed my situation. I was not to be an integral part of RPU. I would have to commute between Hemel Hempstead and Croydon, which was impossible. My reputation was being destroyed; both my professional reputation and my moral reputation.

It is time to quit! Now!

I put on my hat and coat, picked up my briefcase and my handbag. Leaving my office, I shut the door behind me, and walked down the corridor to the hall. The lift arrived and took me down to the ground floor. A long expanse lay between me and the revolving doors leading out to Petty France. Waving cheerily to the security guard I crossed this Rubicon. The guard smiled as he waved back. Reaching the front doors I passed out into the cool September sunshine. Whew!

I tried not to quicken my step as I crossed the road. The entrance of St James' Underground Station was in front of me.

The sirens of two fire appliances and a police car sounded in the distance.

For whom do the sirens sing? Perhaps they will sing for you.

EPILOGUE

During 1983 and 1984 I wrote *Beware the Mandarins*.

In October 1987 Hertfordshire County Council sent me on a Scientific Advisers Course at the Home Defence College, Easingwold.

As usual the Course Dinner was held on the Thursday evening. The Regional Scientific Adviser seated opposite suddenly said to me, "The BBC will give you £100,000 for your book. What do you say?"

This can be done through the Radio Regulatory Department at the Home Office and £100,000 is almost certainly the maximum they can offer me, I thought.

"No thank you. Half a million, please," I replied hoping this was rather more polite than a flat refusal.

"Do you remember Hilda Morell? Well, she was tied naked to a tree and left to die of hypothermia." It was said so matter-of-factly. I shuddered.

Dinner over, we all trouped into the lounge. I was sipping my coffee gratefully when the gentleman, who had been sitting beside me on my right at dinner, joined me.

"Do you think I will get my half million pounds?" I asked him jokingly.

"No. It is far more likely you will be encased in concrete and dropped into the nearest river," he replied quietly.

As I left the College the following morning the Home Office PSO who had been attending the Course was hovering by the door.

He is hoping I will accept the £100,000 offer, I thought.

I wished the PSO a pleasant goodbye.

BIBLIOGRAPHY

Standards of Fire Cover, Home Office Fire Department, 1958

Jane M Hogg, *Fires involving liquefied petroleum gas*, Fire Research Technical Paper No 8, HMSO, 1963.

Jane M Hogg, *Fires associated with electric cooking appliances*, Fire Research Technical Paper No 9, HMSO, 1963.

Fires caused by electric cooking, Symposium on Electrical Fires, Joint Fire Research Organization, Boreham Wood, July 1963.

Jane M Hogg, *The effect of some climatological variations on the incidence and spread of fires in buildings in England and Wales from 1951 to 1961*, Appl. Statist., 1965, 14 (2 & 3), 140-155.

Jane M Hogg and J F Fry, *The relative fire frequency of different industries*, Fire Note No 7, HMSO, 1966.

Jane M Hogg, *The siting of fire stations*, Opl. Res. Q., 1968, 19, 275-287.

Jane M Hogg, *Planning for fire stations in Glasgow in 1980*, Home Office, Scientific Adviser's Branch, Report No 1/68, October 1968.

Jane M Hogg, *The deployment of the Fire Services in Glasgow in 1980*, Symposium on needs of the fire services, National Academy of Sciences, Washington, D.C., U.S.A., 1969.

Jane M Hogg, *A distribution model for an emergency service*, M.Sc. Thesis, Imperial College of Science and Technology, Management Engineering Section, September 1970.

Holroyd Committee's Report, *The Fire Service*, (Hansard, 18 March 1970).

Jane M Hogg, *Station siting in Peterborough and Market Deeping*, Home Office, Scientific Advisory Branch, Report No 7/70, November 1970.

Jane M Hogg, *A model of fire spread*, Home Office Scientific Advisory Branch, Report No 2/71, March 1971.

Consequential Losses from Fire, Economic Intelligence Unit, December 1971.

Jane M Hogg, *Standards of fire cover – is there a need for revision?*, Lecture at the Fire Service College, Dorking, 1971-1972.

Jane M Hogg, *Operational research on fire at the Home Office*, Informal paper read to the Manchester and District Group of the Institute of Fire Engineers, Manchester, May 1972.

Jane M Hogg, *Losses in relation to the fire brigade's attendance time*, Home Office, Scientific Advisory Branch, Report No 5/73, December 1973.

Jane M Hogg and Diana M Morrow, *The siting of fire stations in North-ampton and Northamptonshire*, Home Office, Scientific Advisory Branch, Report No 4/73, December 1973.

Jane M Hogg, *The development of some algorithms for computerized controls in the Fire Service*, Working Party on Operational Research in Government, EURO I, Rome, July 1975, & Symposium on Operational Research in Government, Civil Service College, London, October 1975.

Jane M Hogg, *Planning a game to exercise Fire Service officers in command and control at the scene of potentially disastrous incidents*, TIMS Symposium, Athens, July 1975.

Edward H Blum, *Emergency Services Research in Great Britain*, International Institute for Applied Systems Analysis, August 1975.

Jane M Hogg, *Report on the First Year's Progress by MARC, Chelsea*, CUEP, DOE, May 1976.

Dr Ronald Rutstein, *An Assessment of the Fire Cover Models*, Home Office, Scientific Advisory Branch, Fire Research Report No 2/76.

Jane M Hogg, *A crude general model of the emergency medical services to be applied to Moscow or London*, ORS, DHSS, August 1976.

Jane M Hogg, *An Introduction to the Senior Police Management Game*, Police Scientific Development Branch, Technical Memorandum, No 13/79.

Warren E Walker, Jan M Chaiken, Edward J Ignall, Editors, *Fire Department Deployment Analysis – A Public Policy Analysis Case Study –The Rand Fire Project*, The Rand Corporation, 1979, Elsevier North Holland, Inc.

Jane M Hogg and G A Carr-Hill, *A simplified casualty model,* Home Office, Scientific Advisory Branch, Report 28/80, November 1980. Home Defence Research, Confidential.

Review of Fire Policy. An examination of the Deployment of Resources to combat Fire, Home Office Fire Department Report, 1980.

Jane M Hogg, *Review of fire cover,* Fire Engineers Journal, Volume 43 No.133, June 1984